The Least You Should Know about English

THIRD CANADIAN EDITION

Teresa Ferster Glazier · Paige Wilson · Kathleen A. Wagner

NELSON EDUCATION

NELSON EDUCATION

The Least You Should Know about English, Third Canadian Edition

by Teresa Ferster Glazier, Paige Wilson, and Kathleen A. Wagner

Vice-President, Editorial Director:
Evelyn Veitch

Editor-in-Chief, Higher Education:
Anne Williams

Executive Editor:
Laura Macleod

Senior Marketing Manager:
Amanda Henry

Developmental Editor:
Jacquelyn Busby

Production Service:
MPS Limited, A Macmillan Company

Copy Editor:
Cathy Witlox

Proofreader:
Dianne Fowlie

Indexer:
David Luljak

Senior Production Coordinator:
Ferial Suleman

Design Director:
Ken Phipps

Managing Designer:
Franca Amore

Cover Design:
Jennifer Leung

Compositor:
MPS Limited, A Macmillan Company

Printer:
RR Donnelley

Library and Archives Canada Cataloguing in Publication Data

Glazier, Teresa Ferster

The least you should know about English / Teresa Ferster Glazier, Paige Wilson, Kathleen A. Wagner. — 3rd Canadian ed. First published in 2 separate vols. with subtitles, Form A and Form B.

Includes bibliographical references and index.

ISBN 978-0-17-650190-7

1. English language—Rhetoric—Problems, exercises, etc. 2. English language—Grammar—Problems, exercises, etc. 3. Report writing—Problems, exercises, etc. I. Wilson, Paige II. Wagner, Kathleen A. III. Title.

PE1408.G59 2010 808'.042 C2010-900147-8

ISBN-13: 978-0-17-650190-7
ISBN-10: 0-17-650190-8

Having served two generations of learners, *The Least You Should Know about English* continues to offer assistance to those needing to review basic English skills. The book's simplified approach focuses primarily on the essentials of English grammar and spelling, with five parts of the book demystifying the most common problem areas in spelling, sentence structure, and punctuation. Part 6 offers a generalized overview of paragraph and multi-paragraph writing strategies with an emphasis on breaking composition into its various tasks and stages.

Throughout the book, linguistic jargon and terminology are avoided as much as possible. A conjunction is a *connecting* word; gerunds and present participles become *ing* words; an infinitive is the *to* form of a verb. As a result, learners work with words they know instead of learning a vocabulary they may never again use.

Historically, the strength of this title has been its inclusion of thematically linked exercises to drive home the concept just studied. The abundance of exercises, including practice with sentence writing and proofreading, enables users of *The Least You Should Know about English* to use the rules automatically and to carry them over into their own writing.

In its text examples and exercises, this third Canadian edition continues to increase its emphasis on themes and concepts of interest to Canadians. From the Canadian Home Renovation Tax Credit to the 2010 Olympic Games in Vancouver, the focus is clearly Canadian. Exercises are culled from Canadian sources and represent virtually every province and territory. The thematically related, informative exercises reinforce the need for coherence and supportive details in written work. With answers provided at the back of the book, readers can work independently and identify their own problem areas.

CHANGES IN THIS EDITION

The third Canadian edition incorporates discussions of several new topics. In **Part 1 (Spelling)**, readers will find information about online dictionaries. An entirely new section in **Part 2 (Knowing Sentence Essentials)** tackles the challenges of adjective and adverb usage. Throughout **Parts 1–5**, multifaceted grammar problem areas now boast sets of exercises targeting each sub-section. Examples of these areas include **Fragments, Pronouns, Modifiers,** and **Shifts**. These more fine-tuned exercises spring from the recommendations provided by the reviewers of the previous edition.

In **Part 6 (Writing Well)**, the scope of this limited chapter is more fully clarified as limited to an overview of the most basic writing strategies. The conversation in **Part 6** continues, nonetheless, to provide background information about writing techniques and a step-by-step analysis of the many stages of the compositional process. Since this book was never designed to include a detailed guide to both grammar and composition, the wording of Part 6 has been redrafted to remind users that specialized writing challenges, including research and documentation, will require consulting a far more comprehensive text. Two recent Canadian titles are offered as possibilities.

Other enhancements, such as **Pre-Tests**, **Progress Tests**, **Post-Tests**, and **Checklists**, first introduced in the second Canadian edition, have been retained.

The Least You Should Know about English functions equally well in a structured classroom and at home as a self-tutoring text. The simple explanations, ample exercises, testing opportunities, and answer key at the end of the book provide learners with everything they need to progress on their own. Students who have previously been overwhelmed by the complexities of English should, through their efforts, gain considerable confidence and comfort in their understanding of the material.

A **Test Packet** featuring ready-to-photocopy tests is available to instructors who adopt this textbook.

We all want to have our opinions heard, our thoughts understood, our input respected. Carefully crafting our messages according to universally accepted rules of grammar, spelling, and usage encourages readers to pay attention to what we have to say. In fact, in decoding our messages, members of our reading audience assume that we have followed the rules.

This textbook offers an upbeat yet comprehensive study of how to express your ideas well. If you have unhappy memories of "dangling participles" and "subordinate clauses," you will be delighted that *The Least You Should Know about English* will guide you through the maze of correct grammar and usage without the use of fancy terminology. As a result, you will find that the book's lessons are accessible and user-friendly. If you are willing to make an honest commitment to learning, you will gain a new sense of self-confidence in tackling sentence-writing tasks.

This book also uses refreshing approaches to upgrade language skills that have gotten a bit rusty over the years. If you once felt in control of your sentence-building skills but are now less sure of your abilities, reading this book and completing its exercises will dust out the cobwebs caused by informal language use. You'll discover that recalling basic principles is not as difficult as you may have feared.

Qualified individuals in every career field know how to use the right tools to get a job done. Naturally, you place a high importance on learning the tools of the trade for the career field you have chosen. But, regardless of where you see yourself headed in life, regardless of which occupation attracts you, the ability to communicate correctly and effectively will make a significant contribution to your professional and personal success. For that reason, fine-tuning your language skills is just as important to your future as learning about the tools and procedures specific to your chosen career path.

Because words are the fundamental building blocks of communication, you need to understand how words work—what jobs they do—before you can comfortably and confidently build sentences, paragraphs, and longer written messages.

Think of this book as a language toolbox. It contains the word and communication tools you will need to build effective pieces of communication. Just as a carpenter carefully selects the right techniques to construct fine furniture, you should carefully apply the principles explained in this book to compose fine written messages.

Simple explanations, no complicated rules to memorize, plenty of opportunities for hands-on application of the principles, and even an answer key to check your work—it just doesn't get any better than this!

The Least You Should Know about English makes it easy to learn exactly what you need to know to avoid the most common writing mistakes. Turn the page and allow this book to be your tour guide on the road to effective communication.

Best wishes on your journey!

Kathleen A. Wagner
Sudbury, Ontario

ACKNOWLEDGMENTS

For their thoughtful commentary on the book, we would like to thank the following reviewers: Irene Badaracco, Fordham University; Cheryl Delk, Western Michigan University; Nancy Dessommes, Georgia Southern University; Donna Ross Hooley, Georgia Southern University; Sandra Jensen, Lane Community College; Anastasia Lankford, Eastfield College; Ben Larson, York College; Sue McKee, California State University at Sacramento; Karen McGuire, Pasadena City College; Kevin Nebergall, Kirkwood Community College; Peggy Porter, Houston Community College; and Anne Simmons, Olean Business Institute.

In addition, we would like to thank our publishing team for their expertise and hard work: Steve Dalphin, acquisitions editor; Michell Phifer, developmental editor; Kathryn Stewart, project editor; James McDonald, production manager; and Garry Harman, art director.

We would also like to thank the following people for their specific contributions: Roman Dodson, Roberta Hales, Paul Miller, Pat Rose, Joseph Sierra, and Lillian Woodward.

Finally, we are indebted to Herb and Moss Rabbin, Kenneth Glazier, and the rest of our families and friends for their support and encouragement.

Teresa Ferster Glazier
Paige Wilson

As in previous editions, the thoughtful comments of many *The Least You Should Know about English* users ensure that this edition continues to represent the perspectives and interests of Canadian readers. In particular, Susan Garlick, Conestoga College Institute of Technology and Advanced Learning; Rhonda Sandberg, George Brown College; Heather Larsen, Cambrian College; and Helen Mildon, Algonquin College, have offered well-considered feedback to guide the changes found in this newest edition.

Additionally, a very special group of publishing professionals at Nelson Education have supported this project from its outset: Anne Williams, now editor-in-chief, worked determinedly a decade ago to acquire the Canadian rights to the book; Jacquelyn Busby, developmental editor, provided enthusiastic support and meshed the efforts of many to bring the final product to life; Susan Calvert, director, content and media production, Cathy Witlox, copy editor, and Gunjan Chandola, project manager, worked their magic to make all of us look good.

This edition is dedicated to my many past students who tell me that they are now sharing *The Least You Should Know* with their own children. I'm exceptionally proud to be associated with this classic title.

Kathleen A. Wagner

Thank you for selecting *The Least You Should Know about English,* Third Canadian Edition, by Teresa Ferster Glazier, Paige Wilson, and Kathleen A. Wagner. The authors and publisher have devoted considerable time and care to the development of this book. We appreciate your recognition of this effort and accomplishment.

CONTENTS

PART 4 KEEPING THE MESSAGE CLEAR   143

PART 6 WRITING WELL   258

What Is the Least You Should Know about Writing?   258

What Is the Least You Should Know?

Most English textbooks try to teach you more than you need to know. This one will teach you the least you need to know—and still help you learn to write acceptably. You won't have to bother with grammatical terms like *gerunds* and *modal auxiliary verbs* and *demonstrative pronouns* and all those others you've been hearing about for years. You can get along without knowing these terms if you learn a few basic concepts thoroughly. You *do* have to know how to spell common words; you *do* have to recognize subjects and verbs to avoid writing fragments; you *do* have to know a few rules of sentence structure and punctuation—but rules will be kept to a minimum.

The English you'll learn in this book is sometimes called Standard Written English, and it may differ slightly or greatly from the spoken English you use. Standard Written English is the accepted form of writing in business and the professions. So no matter how you speak, you will communicate better in writing when you use Standard Written English. You might *say* something like "That's a whole nother problem," and everyone will understand, but you would probably want to *write*, "That's a completely different problem." Knowing the difference between spoken English and Standard Written English is essential in college and university, in business, and in life.

Unless you learn the least you should know, you'll have difficulty communicating in writing. Take this sentence for example:

I hope my application will be excepted by the hiring committee.

We assume the writer will not actually be happy to be overlooked by the committee but merely failed to use the right word. If the sentence had read

I hope my application will be *accepted* by the hiring committee.

then the writer would convey the intended meaning. Or take this sentence:

The manager fired Lee and Dave and I received a $100 raise.

The sentence needs a comma.

The manager fired Lee and Dave, and I received a $100 raise.

But perhaps the writer meant

The manager fired Lee, and Dave and I received a $100 raise.

Punctuation makes all the difference, especially if you are Dave. What you'll learn from this text is simply to make your writing so clear that no one will misunderstand it.

As you make your way through the book, it's important to master every rule as you come to it because many rules depend on previous ones. For example, unless you learn to pick out subjects and verbs, you'll have trouble with fragments, with subject–verb agreement, and with punctuation. The rules are brief and clear, and it won't be difficult to master all of them—*if you want to*. But you do have to want to!

How to Master the Least You Should Know

1. Study the explanation of each rule carefully.

2. Do the first exercise. Correct your answers using the answer section at the back of the book. If you miss even one answer, study the explanation again to find out why you missed it.

3. Do the second exercise and correct it. If you miss a single answer, go back once more and study the explanation. You must have missed something. Be tough on yourself. Don't just think, "Maybe I'll get it right next time." Go back and master the rules, and *then* try the next exercise. It's important to correct each group of ten sentences before going on so that you'll discover your mistakes while you still have sentences to practise on.

4. You may be tempted to quit after you do one or two exercises perfectly. Don't! Make yourself finish another exercise. It's not enough to *understand* a rule. You have to *practise* it.

If you're positive, however, after doing several exercises, that you've mastered the rule, take the next exercise as a test. If you miss even one answer, you should do all remaining questions. But if you again make no mistakes, move on to the proofreading and sentence writing exercises so that your understanding of the rule carries over into your writing.

Mastering the essentials of spelling, sentence structure, and punctuation will take time. Generally, community college and university students spend a couple of hours studying outside of class for each hour they spend in class. You may need more. Undoubtedly, the more time you spend, the more your writing will improve.

PART 1

Spelling

Spelling Pre-Test

Each of the sentences below contains just one spelling error. With the help of a good Canadian dictionary, locate the mistake; then circle the error and insert your correction. You'll find the answers in the answer key at the back of the book.

1. When the councillor layed out the plans for the following year's budget, the citizens booed.

2. Al's fiancé Is a tall blonde who lives in Fort Frances.

3. Mark was to proud to accept the suggestions that would have led to his promotion.

4. In the past, a high school diploma aloud a person entry into many good jobs; now, a college diploma is mandatory.

5. It's difficult to tell who's book this is because there's no name in it.

6. Gareth and Louise submitted their college applications on time.

7. The mechanic relyed on a ball-peen hammer to free up the seized bolt.

8. When Environment Canada sent out a squall warning, the fishers were all advised to tie up their dingies.

9. Although the final goal was scored from the face-off, the hockey game had until than been very close.

10. Jim and his sister Mary have an M.A. and a Ph.D., respectfully.

11. Bill did not beleive in doppelgangers until he met his own on the Arrivals level of Toronto's Pearson Airport.

12. With the sound of the vaccum cleaner in the background, I found her voice difficult to hear.

13. She is totally uninterested in world events and is seldom conscience of her surroundings.

14. In the past, when such punishment was accepted in Canada, prisoners were hung.

15. The principal affect of carbon monoxide poisoning is dizziness.

16. The dog lead its puppies to the garage.

17. Your never too old to enjoy a good, clean game of ice hockey.

18. When attending a job interview, you will want to chose your clothes with care.

19. Many Canadians misspell alot of everyday words.

20. The men's room is around the corner, but the ladie's room is down the hall.

Anyone can learn to spell better. You can eliminate most of your spelling errors if you want to. It's just a matter of deciding you're going to do it. If you really intend to learn to spell, study each of the seven parts of this section until you make no more mistakes in the exercises.

Your Own List of Misspelled Words

Words Often Confused (Sets 1 and 2)

Contractions

Possessives

Words That Can Be Broken into Parts

Rule for Doubling a Final Letter

Using Dictionaries

Study these seven parts, and you'll become a better speller.

Your Own List of Misspelled Words

On the inside cover of your English notebook or in some other obvious place, write correctly all the misspelled words in the papers handed back to you. Review them until you're sure of them.

Words Often Confused (Set 1)

Learning the differences between these often-confused words will help you overcome many of your spelling problems. Study the words carefully, with their examples, before trying the exercises.

a, an Use *an* before a word that begins with a vowel *sound* (*a, e, i,* and *o,* plus *u* when it sounds like *uh*) or silent *h*. Note that it's not the letter but the *sound* of the letter that matters.

> an orange, an essay, an inch, an onion

> an umpire, an understanding friend (the *u*'s sound like *uh*)

> an honour, an honest person (silent *h*)

Use *a* before a word that begins with a consonant sound (all the sounds except the vowels, plus *u* or *eu* when they sound like *you*).

> a chart, a zipper, a history book (the *h* is not silent in *history*)

> a union, a uniform, a university degree (the *u*'s sound like *you*)

> a European vacation, a euphemism (*eu* sounds like *you*)

accept, except *Accept* means "to receive willingly."

> I *accept* your apology.

Except means "excluding" or "but."

> Everyone arrived on time *except* him.

advise, advice *Advise* is a verb (pronounce the *s* like a *z*).

> I *advise* my brother to work hard.

Advice is a noun (it rhymes with *rice*).

> My sister usually listens to my *advice*.

affect, effect *Affect* is a verb and means "to alter or influence."

> All quizzes will *affect* the final grade.

> The happy ending *affected* the mood of the audience.

Effect is most commonly used as a noun and means "a result." If *an* or *the* is in front of the word, then you'll know it isn't a verb and will use *effect*.

> The strong coffee had a powerful *effect* on me.

> We studied the *effects* of sleep deprivation in my psychology class.

all ready, already

If you can leave out the *all* and the sentence still makes sense, then *all ready* is the form to use. (In that form, *all* is a separate word and could be left out.)

> We're *all ready* for the trip. (*We're ready for the trip* makes sense.)

> The banquet room is *all ready*. (*The banquet room is ready* makes sense.)

But if you can't leave out the *all* and still have the sentence make sense, then use *already* (the form in which the *al* has to stay in the word).

> They've *already* left. (*They've ready left* doesn't make sense.)

> We have seen that movie *already*.

are, our

Are is a verb.

> We *are* going to Saskatoon.

Our shows we possess something.

> We painted *our* fence to match the house.

brake, break

Brake used as a verb means "to slow or stop motion." It's also the name of the device that slows or stops motion.

> If you *brake* too suddenly, your car may slide.

> Luckily I just had my *brakes* (the device) fixed.

Break used as a verb means "to shatter" or "to split." It's also the name of an interruption, as in "a coffee break."

> She never thought she would *break* a world record.

> Did Mike *break* his leg when he fell?

choose, chose

The difference here is one of time. Use *choose* (rhymes with *news*) for present and future; use *chose* (rhymes with *nose*) for past.

> I will *choose* a new area of study this semester.

> We *chose* the wrong time of year to get married.

clothes, cloths *Clothes* are something you wear; *cloths* are pieces of material you might clean or polish something with.

I love the *clothes* that characters wear in movies.

The car wash workers use special *cloths* to dry the cars.

coarse, course *Coarse* describes a rough texture, or something crude or vulgar.

The *coarse* material irritates my skin.

George's father uses *coarse* language.

Course is used for all other meanings.

Of *course* we saw the golf *course* when we went to Wasaga Beach.

complement, compliment The one spelled with an *e* means to complete something or bring it to perfection.

Use a colour wheel to find a *complement* for lilac.

Juliet's personality *complements* Romeo's; she is practical, and he is a dreamer.

The one spelled with an *i* has to do with praise. Remember "*I* like compliments," and you'll remember to use the *i* spelling when you mean praise.

My evaluation included a really nice *compliment* from my coworkers.

We *complimented* them on their new home.

conscious, conscience *Conscious* means "aware."

They weren't *conscious* of any problems before the accident.

Conscience means "an inner voice of right and wrong." The extra *n* in *conscience* should remind you of *No*, which is what your conscience often says to you.

My *conscience* told me to turn in the expensive watch I found.

dessert, desert *Dessert* is the sweet one, the one you like two helpings of. So give it two helpings of *s*.

The *dessert* menu included fresh fruit.

The other one, *desert*, is used for all other meanings and has two pronunciations.

I promise that I won't *desert* you.

The *desert* landscape was dry and barren.

do, due   *Do* is a verb, an action. You *do* something.

I always *do* my best work at night.

But a payment or an assignment is *due*; it is scheduled for a certain time.

Our first essay is *due* tomorrow.

Due can also be used before *to* in a phrase that means "because of."

The outdoor concert was cancelled *due to* rain.

feel, fill   *Feel* describes *feel*ings.

Whenever I stay up late, I *feel* sleepy in class.

Fill describes what you do to a cup or a gas tank.

Did they *fill* the pitcher to the top?

fourth, forth   The word *fourth* has *four* in it. (But note that *forty* does not. Remember the word *forty-fourth*.)

The *fourth* horse in the race failed to finish.

My grandparents celebrated their *forty-fourth* anniversary last year.

If you don't mean a number, use *forth*.

The speaker paced back and *forth*.

have, of   *Have* is a verb. Sometimes, in a contraction, it sounds like *of*. When you say *could've*, the *have* may sound like *of*, but it is not written that way. Always write *could have, would have, should have, might have*.

We should *have* planned our vacation earlier.

Then we could *have* used our coupon for a free one-way ticket.

Use *of* only in a prepositional phrase (see p. 71).

She sent me a box *of* chocolates for my birthday.

hear, here   The last three letters of *hear* spell *ear*. You *hear* with your ear.

When I put a seashell next to my ear, I *hear* ocean sounds.

The other spelling, *here*, tells "where." Note that the three words indicating a place or pointing out something all have *here* in them: *here*, *there*, *where*.

I'll be *here* for three more weeks.

it's, its   *It's* is a contraction of "it is" or "it has."

It's hot. (*It is* hot.)

It's been hot all week. (*It has* been hot...)

Its is a possessive. (Possessives such as *its*, *yours*, *hers*, *ours*, *theirs*, *whose* are already possessive and never need an apostrophe. See p. 33.)

The car crashed when it lost *its* front wheel.

This dental office sanitizes *its* instruments in an autoclave.

knew, new   *Knew* has to do with knowledge (both start with *k*).

New means "not old."

They *knew* that she wanted a *new* bike.

know, no   *Know* has to do with knowledge (both start with *k*).

By Friday, I must *know* the names of all the past prime ministers.

No means "not any" or "the opposite of *yes*."

My boss has *no* patience.

No, I need to work late.

E X E R C I S E S

Underline the correct word. Don't guess! If you aren't sure, turn back to the explanatory pages. When you've finished ten sentences, compare your answers with those at the back of the book. Correct each group of ten sentences before continuing so you'll catch your mistakes while you still have sentences to practise on.

Exercise 1

1. (Hear, Here) are some tips on how to stay healthy by eating well, based on (a, an) pamphlet entitled *Canada's Food Guide to Healthy Eating*.

2. The *Food Guide* (advices, advises) you to eat several servings each day from the four basic food groups: grains, vegetables and fruit, milk products, and meat and alternatives.

3. (Its, It's) important to remember that eggs, beans, tofu, and peanut butter can be meat substitutes.

4. Be (conscious, conscience) of the fact that different people need different amounts of food, depending on age, body size, activity level, and gender.

5. Male teenagers, for example, (do, due) eat more because their bodies require it.

6. You may (all ready, already) (no, know) this, but (its, it's) hard to (accept, except) that most (desserts, deserts) are not good for you.

7. (Choose, Chose) low-fat dairy products, lean meat, and healthy foods when you go to the grocery store, and don't feel you should (of, have) purchased that box of cookies.

8. What you eat will (affect, effect) how you feel, as well as how well your (clothes, cloths) fit.

9. Eat in moderation; you will (feel, fill) better if you do not (fill, feel) yourself with too many (courses, coarses).

10. Also, (complimenting, complementing) your diet with lots of fresh air and exercise can have (a, an) excellent (affect, effect) on your eating habits.

Source: Adapted from Health Canada, *Canada's Food Guide to Healthy Eating,* 2009.

Exercise 2

1. (It's, Its) finally been proved to be true!

2. People (do, due) weigh more when standing on carpet.

3. (A, An) unique (affect, effect) of most standard scales makes them add as much as ten percent to people's weight when the scales are placed on thick carpet.

4. David MacKay, (a, an) physicist at the University of Calgary, studied the inner workings of scales to prove whether carpet did (affect, effect) them or not.

5. Many weight-loss services (all ready, already) (knew, new) about the carpet (affect, effect).

6. The difference in weight is (do, due) to the way certain parts bend when a person stands on the scale.

7. When (a, an) typical scale leaves the scale factory, (it's, its) designed to be placed on a hard floor.

8. (It's, Its) parts are calibrated to bend when someone stands on it.

9. The (affect, effect) of plush carpet eliminates the bending, and the scale shows the wrong weight.

10. Experts now (advise, advice) people who weigh themselves on carpet to (choose, chose) a digital scale to help avoid the problem.

Source: Adapted from *New Scientist,* June 2, 2002.

Exercise 3

1. The T-shirt had (it's, its) modern beginnings when the U.S. Navy (choose, chose) it as (a, an) official undergarment in the early 1900s.

2. The first printed T-shirt was used during the 1948 U.S. presidential campaign as (a, an) ad for one of the candidates.

3. (It's, Its) message read "Dew it with Dewey," and (it's, its) now on display at the Smithsonian Institution in Washington, D.C.

4. Whether he was (conscious, conscience) of it or not, Marlon Brando started a fashion trend by wearing (a, an) white T-shirt in the movie *A Streetcar Named Desire.*

5. James Dean's T-shirt and blue jeans also had an (affect, effect) on the look of the 1950s (do, due) to the popularity of his film *Rebel Without a Cause.*

6. After that, people began to (accept, except) T-shirts as regular (clothes, cloths).

7. Advertisers started to use the fronts and backs of T-shirts as spaces to (feel, fill) with slogans, brand names, and pictures of products.

8. In the 1960s, the (knew, new) look was colourful tie-dyed T-shirts used to (complement, compliment) bell-bottomed pants and sandals.

9. Of (coarse, course), an old T-shirt can be cut up into (clothes, cloths) that are the perfect texture to wax a car or to polish silver. The material is not too smooth and not too (coarse, course); (it's, its) just right.

10. Over the (coarse, course) of the twentieth century, we have seen the T-shirt (feel, fill) many of (are, our) needs as comfortable and stylish (clothes, cloths) to wear and as useful (clothes, cloths) to clean with.

Exercise 4

1. Before I went to Japan, my friend said, "I (advise, advice) you not to pack your video camera."

2. However, I wanted to make (a, an) Japanese vacation video to (complement, compliment) the one I (all ready, already) had of our trip to China.

3. Consequently, I (choose, chose) not to take my friend's (advise, advice).

4. That decision had (a, an) unfortunate (affect, effect) on my trip.

5. I could (of, have) enjoyed myself everywhere I went, but instead I (choose, chose) to capture the moment on video.

6. At the hotel, when a woman dressed in traditional Japanese (clothes, cloths) greeted us with refreshments, I couldn't even (accept, except) any because I was too busy recording.

7. I filmed a tea ceremony, though I didn't (do, due) any tea drinking myself.

8. Now as I watch my Japanese video back home, I am (conscious, conscience) of the discussions that I (hear, here) going on in the background.

9. At the airport, one friend says, "I've got to (complement, compliment) Jack on his persistence. He's going to have a great memento of this trip after we've (all ready, already) forgotten it."

10. Next time I go to Japan or anywhere else on vacation, I'll pack everything I need—(accept, except) my video camera.

Exercise 5

1. I've been reading that (are, our) individual dreams say (a, an) awful lot about us but that some dreams (are, our) common to us all.

2. (It's, Its) strange, for example, that many people (feel, fill) as though they are falling or flying in a dream.

3. In another common dream experience, we realize suddenly that we are not wearing any (clothes, cloths), and we don't (know, no) how we got that way.

4. Or we dream that we have missed a deadline when a test or a paper was (do, due), but we have forgotten to (do, due) it.

5. Whether we are (conscious, conscience) of it or not, our dream lives can have (a, an) (affect, effect) on (are, our) real lives.

6. If in a dream we (brake, break) the heart of someone we love, we might wake up the next morning with a guilty (conscious, conscience).

7. Of (coarse, course), we may dream of eating (a, an) entire carton of chocolate ice cream for (dessert, desert) and (feel, fill) another kind of guilt.

8. Dream experts give the following (advise, advice) to those who want to call (fourth, forth) the dreams that slip away from the (conscious, conscience) mind once we are awake.

9. They suggest that dreamers put paper and a pencil by the bed before going to sleep in order to write down a dream as soon as (it's, its) over.

10. We all (know, no) that (know, no) amount of coaxing will bring back a dream that our brain (all ready, already) (choose, chose) to forget.

PROOFREADING EXERCISE

Find and correct the ten errors contained in the following student paragraph. All of the errors involve Words Often Confused (Set 1).

I've always wanted to no what makes a person want to set or brake a Guinness world record. For example, if someone all ready has a record for collecting more than 2,500 rubber ducks, does another person really need to beat that record? Also, the objects that people chose to collect our often strange. There are records for collecting the highest number of erasers from all over the world, tags from designer cloths, and labels from water bottles, to name just a few. Of coarse, it's nice to receive complements and recognition for a impressive collection. Maybe I should of kept all those takeout menus I just threw away and tried to set a new record myself.

SENTENCE WRITING

The surest way to learn these Words Often Confused is to use them immediately in your own writing. Choose the five pairs or groups of words that you most often confuse from Set 1. Then use each of them correctly in a new sentence. No answers are provided at the back of the book, but you can see if you are using the words correctly by comparing your sentences to the examples in the explanations.

_____

_____

_____

_____

_____

_____

_____

_____

_____

Words Often Confused (Set 2)

Study this second set of words carefully, with their examples, before attempting the exercises. Knowing all of the word groups in these two sets will take care of many of your spelling problems.

lead, led

Lead is the metal that rhymes with *head*.

Old paint is dangerous because it often contains *lead*.

The past form of the verb "to lead" is *led*.

Louise *led* the students to the gym.

I *led* our school's debating team to victory last year.

If you mean present time, use *lead*, which rhymes with *bead*.

Maria and Bill *lead* the class.

loose, lose

Loose means "not tight." Note how *l o o s e* that word is. It has plenty of room for two *o*'s.

My dog's tooth is *loose*.

Lose is the opposite of win.

If we *lose* this game, we will be out for the season.

passed, past

The past form of the verb "to pass" is *passed*.

She easily *passed* her math class.

The runner *passed* the baton to her teammate.

We *passed* your house twice before we saw the address.

Use *past* when it's not a verb.

We drove *past* your house. (the same as "We drove *by* your house")

I always use my *past* experiences to help me solve problems.

In the *past*, he had to borrow his brother's car.

personal, personnel

Pronounce these two correctly, and you won't confuse them—*pérsonal, personnél*.

She shared her *personal* views as a parent.

Personnel means "a group of employees."

The personnel in the customer service department are very helpful.

piece, peace	Remember "piece of pie." The one meaning "a *piece* of something" always begins with *pie*.

One child asked for an extra *piece* of candy.

The other one, *peace*, is the opposite of war.

The two gangs discussed the possibility of a *peace* treaty.

principal, principle	*Principal* means "main." Both words have *a* in them: princip*a*l, m*a*in.

The *principal* concern is safety. (main concern)

He lost both *principal* and interest. (main amount of money)

Also, think of a school's "princi*pal*" as your "pal."

An elementary school *principal* must be kind. (main administrator)

A *principle* is a rule. Both words end in *le*: princip*le*, ru*le*.

I am proud of my high *principles*. (rules of conduct)

We value the *principle* of truth in advertising. (rule)

quiet, quite	Pronounce these two correctly, and you won't confuse them. *Quiet* means "free from noise" and rhymes with *diet*.

Some people need to study in a *quiet* location.

Quite means "very" and rhymes with *bite*.

Bill was *quite* unhappy with his test results.

right, write	*Right* means "correct" or "proper."

You will find your keys if you look in the *right* place.

It also means in the exact location, position, or moment.

Your keys are *right* where you left them.

Let's go *right* now.

Write means to compose sentences, poems, essays, and so forth.

I asked my teacher to *write* a letter of recommendation for me.

than, then	*Than* compares two things.

My father is shorter *than* any of his children.

Then tells when (*then* and *when* rhyme, and both have *e* in them).

I always write a rough draft of an essay first; *then* I revise it.

their, there, they're

Their is a possessive, meaning "belonging to them."

Their cars have always been red.

There points out something. (Remember that the three words indicating a place or pointing out something all have *here* in them: *here*, *there*, *where*.)

I know that I haven't been *there* before.

There was a rainbow in the sky.

They're is a contraction of "they are."

They're living in Halifax. (*They are* living in Halifax.)

threw, through

Threw is the past form of "to throw."

We *threw* snowballs at each other.

I *threw* away my chance at a scholarship.

If you don't mean "to throw something," use *through*.

We could see our beautiful view *through* the new curtains.

They worked *through* their differences.

two, too, to

Two is a number.

My *two* brothers both live in California.

Too means "extra" or "also," and so it has an extra *o*.

The movie was *too* long and *too* violent. (extra)

They are enrolled in that biology class *too*. (also)

Use *to* for all other meanings.

They like *to* ski. They're going *to* the mountains.

weather, whether

Weather refers to conditions of the atmosphere.

Snowy *weather* is too cold for me.

Whether means "if."

> I don't know *whether* it is snowing there or not.

> *Whether* I travel with you or not depends on the weather.

were, wear, where   These words are pronounced differently but are often confused in writing.

Were is the past form of the verb "to be."

> The crops *were* ready for harvesting.

Wear means "to have on," as in wearing clothes.

> Workers must *wear* protective clothing.

Where refers to a place. (Remember that the three words indicating a place or pointing out something all have *here* in them: *here, there, where*.)

> *Where* is the mailbox? There it is.

> *Where* are the closing papers? Here they are.

who's, whose   *Who's* is a contraction of "who is" or "who has."

> *Who's* responsible for signing the cheques? (*Who is* responsible...?)

> *Who's* been reading my journal? (*Who has* been...?)

Whose is a possessive. (Possessives such as *whose, its, yours, hers, ours, theirs* are already possessive and never take an apostrophe. See p. 33.)

> *Whose* keys are these?

woman, women   The difference here is one of number: wo*man* refers to one female; wo*men* refers to two or more females.

> One *woman* fainted in the heat.

> Many *women* enjoy quilting.

you're, your   *You're* is a contraction of "you are."

> *You're* as smart as I am. (*You are* as smart as I am.)

Your is a possessive meaning "belonging to you."

> I borrowed *your* lab book.

E X E R C I S E S

Underline the correct word. When you've finished ten sentences, compare your answers with those at the back of the book. Do only ten sentences at a time, so you can teach yourself while you still have sentences to practise on.

Exercise 1

1. Some people will go (threw, through) almost anything to look better.

2. Cosmetic surgeries for men and (woman, women) are more popular (than, then) ever.

3. A person (who's, whose) eyelids sag or someone (who's, whose) not happy with a "spare tire" can just get an eyelift or a lunchtime liposuction job.

4. In the (passed, past), we could read people's ages on (their, there, they're) faces.

5. Now we can't tell (weather, whether) (their, there, they're) young or old except by a close look at (their, there, they're) elbows.

6. A man or a (woman, women) who chooses to (were, wear, where) makeup can even have it permanently applied by a tattoo artist.

7. One must be (quiet, quite) sure before getting makeup tattoos because (their, there, they're) irreversible.

8. Cosmetic surgery candidates should consider this (principal, principle): "If (you're, your) not absolutely certain, (than, then) don't do it."

9. Individuals must make a (personal, personnel) decision (weather, whether) to undergo any kind of cosmetic survey.

10. (Their, There, They're) may be more to (loose, lose) (than, then) (their, there, they're) is to gain.

Exercise 2

1. Test (you're, your) knowledge of animal history by answering the following question: which came first—sharks or dinosaurs?

2. (You're, Your) (right, write) if you answered sharks; they have been around for millions of years, and (their, there, they're) really (quiet, quite) amazing creatures.

3. Most sharks travel (through, threw) the water constantly without stopping, but some appear (two, too, to) sleep (right, write) on the bottom of the ocean.

4. (Their, There, They're) teeth never have a chance to (were, wear, where) down because each tooth is designed to come (loose, lose) easily, and (their, there, they're) is always another tooth waiting to take its place.

5. Sharks range in size from the fifteen-centimetre cigar shark (two, too, to) the eighteen-metre whale shark, and most of them are (quiet, quite) harmless (two, too, to) humans if they are left in (piece, peace).

6. More people die each year from being stung by bees (than, then) from being attacked by sharks, so (their, there, they're) reputation as killers is perhaps exaggerated.

7. Sharks can sense the movements of a fish in trouble or a swimmer (who's, whose) bleeding, and that's when (their, there, they're) likely to attack.

8. A shark doesn't chew its food but bites off and swallows one big (piece, peace) at a time.

9. Baby sharks are called pups, and different species of sharks have different numbers of pups at a time—from (two, too, to) to close to a hundred.

10. A few sharks lay (their, there, they're) eggs in pouches with descriptive names like "mermaid's purses" and "devil's wheelbarrows"; these pouches are then laid on the ocean floor, and they stay (their, there, they're) until the shark pups hatch.

Source: Adapted from *1996 Aqua Facts* (Vancouver Aquarium).

Exercise 3

1. You've probably been (threw, through) this experience.

2. (You're, Your) in a theatre, auditorium, or intimate restaurant, and some-one's cell phone rings.

3. The person (who's, whose) phone it is becomes (two, to, too) embar-rassed (two, to, too) answer it.

4. In the (passed, past), (their, there, they're) was no way to keep this unfortunate event from happening.

5. Now scientists in Japan have invented a type of magnetic wood panel-ling that will maintain the (piece, peace) and (quiet, quite) of public places even if people still refuse to turn off (their, there, they're) cell phones.

6. This new wood will block radio signals and therefore keep such calls from going (threw, through) the walls of a theatre, auditorium, restaurant, or anywhere else (their, there, they're) not wanted.

7. Of course, (their, there, they're) are people who do not want to (loose, lose) (their, there, they're) (right, write) to make (personal, personnel) calls wherever they want.

8. One of the best uses of magnetic wood will be to protect areas (were, wear, where) signals interfere with each other.

9. (Than, Then) wooden panels will be used (two, too, to) divide wireless signals rather (than, then) block calls altogether.

10. (Weather, Whether) (you're, your) for it or against it, magnetic wood will probably be used worldwide (quiet, quite) soon.

Source: Adapted from *New Scientist,* June 27, 2002.

Exercise 4

1. If you live (were, wear, where) there are pine trees, you can make (you're, your) own bird feeder very easily.

2. All you need is a pine cone or (two, too, to), a jar of peanut butter, some birdseed, and a long (piece, peace) of string.

3. The first step is (two, too, to) tie the string to the top of the pine cone securely.

4. Use a string that's long enough to allow the feeder to hang (were, wear, where) you will be able to see it later.

5. Try to use a pine cone that has a (loose, lose) rather (than, then) a tight shape.

6. Step (two, too, to) involves spreading the peanut butter in the spaces all around the outside of the pine cone.

7. This process can be (quiet, quite) messy, so you may want to (were, wear, where) rubber gloves and cover (you're, your) work surface with a (piece, peace) of newspaper.

8. Once (you're, your) finished with the second step, roll the peanut butter–covered pine cone in birdseed.

9. Hang the results from a tree branch, and sit back and watch the birds enjoy (their, there, they're) special treat in (piece, peace) and (quiet, quite).

10. And you can take (personal, personnel) pleasure in the fact that (you're, your) not adding more plastic to the environment since the pine cone bird feeder is made of all-natural ingredients.

Exercise 5

1. Years ago, most children made it (threw, through) (their, they're, there) school years without ever even meeting the school (principal, principle).

2. When it comes to school (personal, personnel), children probably are more aware of the housekeeper (then, than) they are of the individual (who's, whose) job includes creating the right atmosphere for learning.

3. Only when a student violates the rules that maintain order and (peace, piece) will he or she likely be (lead, led) away to the (quiet, quite) office.

4. In the (passed, past), however, schools were smaller and everyone knew (were, wear, where) the office was located.

5. (Then, Than) the man in charge—and it was almost always a man—wore a suit and tight tie that he never allowed to become (loose, lose).

6. Students who misbehaved (were, where, wear) commonly required to sit (they're, their, there) for (to, too, two) and sometimes three hours before being allowed to speak.

7. Perhaps the (principal, principle) reason for a student's fear of the office was that only those in trouble ended up (they're, their, there).

8. Now when (you're, your) driving (passed, past) a school, the principal is likely to be out in the yard talking with students and participating in games on activity days.

9. This (peace, piece) of childhood is no longer a source of fear; instead, children feel (quiet, quite) comfortable around school authorities.

10. Has the pendulum swung (to, too, two) far? What's (you're, your) opinion?

PROOFREADING EXERCISE

See if you can correct the ten errors in this student paragraph. All errors involve Words Often Confused (Set 2).

When I was in high school, the principle was always complaining about our homework record. The teachers had told him that about half the students didn't do there homework on time, and some never did any at all. So one September he started the first-day assembly by saying, "This year your all going to do you're homework every night for at least the first month of school. And if there is a school-wide perfect homework record during September, I will where a swimsuit to school on the first of October and dive off the high diving board into the school's outdoor pool in front of everyone no matter what the whether is like that day." We students were not about to loose a bet like that. September past, and on the first of October, the principal lead us to the school pool; then he through off his heavy coat and climbed to the top of the diving board.

SENTENCE WRITING

Write several sentences using any words you missed in doing the exercises for Words Often Confused (Set 2).

Sentence writing is a good idea not only because it will help you remember these words often confused, but also because it will be a storehouse for ideas you can later use in writing papers. Here are some topics you might consider writing your sentences about:

—Your career goals

—Your favourite movie or TV show at the moment

—A lesson you've learned the hard way

—Where you see yourself in ten years

—How your values are changing

_____

_____

_____

_____

_____

_____

_____

_____

_____

_____

Contractions

When two words are condensed into one, the result is called a contraction:

is not ·········➤isn't   you have ·········➤you've

The letter or letters that are left out are replaced with an apostrophe. For example, if the two words *do not* are condensed into one, an apostrophe is put where the *o* is left out.

do not   don't

Note how the apostrophe goes in the exact place where the letter or letters are left out in these contractions:

I am	I'm
I have	I've
I shall, I will	I'll
I would	I'd
you are	you're
you have	you've
you will	you'll
she is, she has	she's
he is, he has	he's
it is, it has	it's
we are	we're
we have	we've
we will, we shall	we'll
they are	they're
they have	they've
are not	aren't
cannot	can't
do not	don't
does not	doesn't
have not	haven't
must not	mustn't
let us	let's
who is, who has	who's
where is	where's
were not	weren't
would not	wouldn't
could not	couldn't
should not	shouldn't

would have	would've
could have	could've
should have	should've
that is	that's
there is	there's
what is	what's

One contraction does not follow this rule: *will not* becomes *won't*.

In all other contractions that you're likely to use, the apostrophe goes exactly where the letter or letters are left out. Note especially *it's, they're, who's,* and *you're.* Use them when you mean two words. (See p. 33 for the possessive forms — *its, their, whose,* and *your—*which don't have an apostrophe.)

E X E R C I S E S

Put an apostrophe in each contraction. Then compare your answers with those at the back of the book. Be sure to correct each group of ten sentences before going on so you'll catch your mistakes while you still have sentences to practise on.

Exercise 1

1. Classrooms are usually similarly shaped; theyre either square or rectangular.

2. Student desks can be moved around unless theyve been bolted to the floor.

3. Some students prefer to sit in the front so that theyre near the teacher and the board.

4. Ive always liked to sit in the back of the classroom.

5. For me, its the best position to take notes and pay attention to everything thats happening.

6. When were asked to pull our chairs together into small groups, Im most comfortable with my back to the wall.

7. A friend of mine has a different theory; hes certain that the side of the room by the door is the only place to sit.

8. Of course, hes often late to class, so its the best place for him to find a seat without disturbing the teacher.

9. Of course, the row near the windows isnt a good place to sit if theyre open.

10. It can be too noisy, too sunny, or too distracting if theres a view of anything interesting.

Exercise 2

1. Grizzly bears dont live in Canada's prairies anymore; theyve disappeared because they were over-hunted.

2. Youll find that once-plentiful species, such as the whooping crane, the burrowing owl, the bowhead whale, and the wolverine, are now hard to locate in Canada.

3. Even sea otters cant be easily found; theyve become vulnerable because of pollution—especially oil spills.

4. Theyre all on a list of species at risk thats put out by the Committee on the Status of Endangered Wildlife in Canada (COSEWIC).

5. COSEWIC members, made up of scientists, cant actually protect these endangered species; they can only state that theyre threatened and suggest a plan of action.

6. At the COSEWIC annual meeting, each species is discussed, and its decided whos on the endangered species list.

7. Sometimes theres a change in an animal's circumstance, and its status is downgraded to a less serious category, or its even removed from the endangered list; thats good news.

8. Youll be happy to know that other jurisdictions and organizations take over the duties of protecting the animals and their habitats.

9. COSEWIC members are telling industry that corporations cant continue to clear land and pollute as they have in the past, and theyre alerting citizens to these issues.

10. Im sure that air and water pollution, as well as pesticides, arent any better for animals than they are for us.

Source: Adapted from the website http://www.cosewic.gc.ca/COSEWIC/Procedures.cfm.

Exercise 3

1. Ive just discovered that for most of the last hundred years, Yellowstone National Park in the United States hasnt had any wolves in it.

2. With the help of an act of U.S. Congress in 1914, theyd been killed off in an effort to get rid of predators in Yellowstone and on other public lands.

3. Now its obvious that the policy was a mistake; people realized that Yellowstone wouldnt be complete without its wolves.

4. The U.S. Endangered Species Act in 1973 helped to start the plan of putting wolves back into Yellowstone, but its taken 20 years to get to the point where theyre actually being released.

5. The first wolves to be moved were from Alberta; thats where the land is similar to Yellowstone's and where theres no disease among the wolf population.

6. Once transplanted to Yellowstone, the Canadian wolves were kept in pens so that they wouldnt just try to go back home once released into the park.

7. But feeding the wolves in their half-hectare-sized pens wasnt easy; its illegal to use motor vehicles in the wild part of Yellowstone, so the wolves' food had to be brought in on sleds pulled by mules.

8. Other animals dont like wolves, so as soon as a mule saw the hungry wolves circling for dinner, the mule wouldnt go any farther; thats a problem that was eventually solved.

9. In March of 1995, the gate was opened on one of the pens to release the first group of wolves back into their natural habitat, but the wolves wouldnt use the gate.

10. Scientists realized that they shouldve known that the wolves wouldnt trust the opening that the humans used, so a hole was made in the fence near the spot where the wolves felt most comfortable, and thats where the wolves made their escape to freedom in Yellowstone.

Source: Adapted from *The Wolves of Yellowstone* (San Diego: Voyageur Press, 1996).

Exercise 4

1. As I was driving home the other day, I saw a fully equipped camper shell for sale on someone's front lawn, and I shouldve stopped to look at it.

2. At first, I didnt think I wanted a camper for my pickup truck, but now I wish Id gone back for it.

3. I remember that it didnt look brand new; it had a door in the back and windows with curtains that I couldve replaced if I didnt like them.

4. And there wasnt any price posted, so I dont know how much it cost.

5. Its just that, for some reason, I feel as though Ive missed an opportunity.

6. Whenever Im driving on a long trip and pass a truck with a camper on it, I always think of how much fun itd be to park on a beach and spend the night.

7. To get all of the comforts of home, I wouldnt have to stop at a hotel; theyd be right in the back of the truck.

8. A friend of mine whos got a motor home said that it was the best purchase hed ever made because it always gives him a reason to take a trip.

9. A camper shell mightve been just what I needed to bring some adventure into my life.

10. Of course, theres nothing stopping me from buying a new one.

Exercise 5

1. Although he isnt the leader of the federal New Democratic Party (NDP) anymore, Ed Broadbent insists hes enjoying as much influence as he ever did.

2. Broadbent, whos an old political warhorse, says theres a fine skill to being an MP after having been a leader for so many years.

3. Jack Layton, the current NDP leader in the House of Commons, wasnt involved in federal politics before seeking the party leadership.

4. Hes certainly a familiar face and name to most Canadians now.

5. The mayors of Canadian towns and cities of all sizes had known Layton a long time; theyd remembered him for his leadership of the Federation of Canadian Municipalities (FCM), a position he held for a number of years.

6. During that period, Layton didnt represent just his own city, Toronto; hed learned to listen to and advocate for cities across the country.

7. To this day, many Canadian city government officials admire his contributions to local government even though its not the most glamorous or powerful level of government.

8. Hes well-known for speaking out strongly in favour of higher support payments from upper levels of government.

9. In 2002, Layton resigned from the FCM leadership so hed be able to run an effective campaign for the NDP leadership.

10. His flamboyant personality and ready smile captured the fancy of many Canadians who werent interested in the old style of political leadership.

PROOFREADING EXERCISE

Can you correct the ten errors in this student paragraph? They could be from any of the areas studied so far.

Iv'e had trouble excepting the fact that I cant learn to speak German. I have taken first- and second-year German, but their was'nt much speaking in either of those too classes. My mouth doesn't make the write sounds when I try to say German words. I think that my teeth get in the way. I have decided to ask my teacher for advise but cant bring myself to go see her because I know that shes going to ask me to tell her about my problem—in German.

SENTENCE WRITING

Doing exercises helps you learn a rule, but even more helpful is using the rule in writing. Write ten sentences using contractions. You might write about your reaction to the week's big news story, or you can choose your own subject.

_____

_____

_____

_____

_____

_____

_____

_____

Possessives

The trick in writing possessives is to ask yourself the question, "Who (or what) does it belong to?" (Modern usage has made _who_ acceptable when it comes first in a sentence, but some people still say, "_Whom_ does it belong to?" or even "_To whom_ does it belong?") If the answer to your question doesn't end in _s,_ then add an apostrophe and _s._ If the answer to your question ends in _s,_ add an apostrophe. Then you must see if you need another sound to make the possessive clear. If you need another _s_ sound, add another _s_ after the apostrophe (as in the last of the following examples).

one girl (uniform)	Who does it belong to?	girl	Add _'s_	girl's uniform
two girls (uniforms)	Who do they belong to?	girls	Add _'_	girls' uniforms
a man (coat)	Who does it belong to?	man	Add _'s_	man's coat
men (hats)	Who do they belong to?	men	Add _'s_	men's hats
children (game)	Who does it belong to?	children	Add _'s_	children's game
a month (pay)	What does it belong to?	month	Add _'s_	month's pay
Brahms (Lullaby)	Who does it belong to?	Brahms	Add _'_	Brahms' Lullaby
my boss (office)	Who does it belong to?	boss	Add _'s_	boss's office

This trick will always work, but you must ask the question every time. Remember that the key word is *belong*. Who (or what) does it belong to? If you ask the question another way, you may get an answer that won't help you. Also, if you just look at a word without asking the question, you may think the name of the owner ends in *s* when it really doesn't.

To Make a Possessive

1. Ask "Who (or what) does it belong to?"
2. If the answer doesn't end in *s*, add an apostrophe and *s*.
3. If the answer ends in *s*, add just an apostrophe *or* an apostrophe and *s* if you need the extra *s* sound to show a possessive (as in *boss's office*).

E X E R C I S E S

Follow the directions carefully for each of the following exercises. Because possessives can be tricky, explanations follow some exercises to help you understand them better.

Exercise 1

Cover the right column and see if you can write the following possessives correctly. Ask the question "Who (or what) does it belong to?" each time. Don't look at the answer before you try!

1. an employee (qualifications) _____ an employee's qualifications

2. the women (gym) _____ the women's gym

3. Janina (degree) _____ Janina's degree

4. Charles (major) _____ Charles' or Charles's major

5. the Johnsons (house) _____ the Johnsons' house

6. Ms. Yamamoto (trees) _____ Ms. Yamamoto's trees

7. the boss (computer) _____ the boss's computer

8. the baby (feet) _____ the baby's feet

9. the babies (feet) _____ the babies' feet

10. a country (laws) _____ a country's laws

(Sometimes you may see a couple of options when the word ends in *s*. *James' major* may be written *James's major*. That is also correct, depending on how you want your reader to say it. Be consistent when given such a choice.)

> **CAUTION:** Don't assume that any word that ends in *s* is a possessive. The *s* may indicate more than one of something, a plural noun. Make sure the word actually possesses something before you add an apostrophe.

A few commonly used words are already possessive and don't need an apostrophe added to them. Memorize this list:

our, ours	its
your, yours	their, theirs
his, her, hers	whose

Note particularly *its*, *their*, *whose*, and *your*. They are already possessive and don't take an apostrophe. (These words sound like *it's*, *they're*, *who's*, and *you're*, which are *contractions* that use an apostrophe in place of their missing letters.)

Exercise 2

Cover the right column below and see if you can write the correct form. The answer might be a *contraction* or a *possessive*. If you miss any, go back and review the explanations.

1. (It) been raining.	It's
2. (You) car needs washing.	Your
3. (Who) keys are these?	Whose
4. The blizzard lost (it) force.	its
5. I don't know (who) been invited.	who's
6. (We) shopping for a new car.	We're
7. (It) time to turn in the quizzes.	It's
8. (They) minivan seats seven.	Their
9. These are my books; are those (you)?	yours
10. (You) a real friend to me.	You're

Exercise 3

Here's another chance to check your progress with possessives. Cover the right column again as you did in Exercises 1 and 2, and add apostrophes to the possessives. Each answer is followed by an explanation.

1. Our neighbours went to their grandparents house.	grandparents' (You didn't add an apostrophe to *neighbours*, did you? The neighbours don't possess anything.)
2. The teams bus broke down during the road trip.	team's (Who does the bus belong to?)
3. I invited Rylen to my friends party.	friend's (if the party belongs to one friend) or friends' (two or more friends)
4. Two of my sisters went to my mothers alma mater.	mother's (The sisters don't possess anything in the sentence.)
5. Sandeeps apartment is similar to yours.	Sandeep's (*Yours* is already possessive and doesn't take an apostrophe.)
6. Last weeks tips were the best yet.	week's (The tips belonged to last week.)
7. The Wilsons farm is just outside of town.	The Wilsons' (Who does the farm belong to?)
8. The womens team played the mens team.	women's, men's (Did you ask who each team belongs to?)
9. The jurors handed the judge their verdict.	No apostrophe. *Their* is already possessive, and the jurors don't possess anything in the sentence.
10. The sign by the gate said, "The Lapointes."	Lapointes (meaning that the Lapointes live there) or Lapointes' (meaning that it's the Lapointes' house)

Exercises 4 and 5

Now you're ready to add the apostrophe to each possessive in the sentences that follow. Check your answers at the back of the book.

Exercise 4

1. Supermodel Jerry Hall has long been famous for being Mick Jaggers wife.

2. Since the couples divorce, she has continued to work as a model and an actress.

3. On February 24, 2004, Halls fame grew when she set a new world record in London.

4. A world record may take days, weeks, or even years to accomplish.

5. Jerry Halls record-breaking activity took just three and a half hours.

6. During one of Londons many organized events to promote theatre and culture, Hall appeared as a character in six different musicals in one night.

7. All of her characters parts were small, and none of them included lines.

8. The six theatres audiences were unaware that the actresss brief appearances were contributing to a world record.

9. Although her shortest roles duration was just thirty seconds, Halls six performances added up to thirty-three minutes on stage.

10. Hall carefully followed the Guinness judges rules by using various means of transportation between theatres and by changing each characters costume before moving on to the next.

Source: Adapted from Visit London (visitlondon.com) press release, February 25, 2004.

Exercise 5

1. The vampire bats habit of sucking an animals blood is aided by a substance that stops the blood from clotting.

2. This same substance might come to a stroke patients aid very soon.

3. Sometimes a persons brain function becomes blocked by a blood clot.

4. This conditions medical label is "ischemic stroke."

5. Obviously, the vampire bats ability to unclot its victims blood would come in handy.

6. Luckily for stroke patients, the substance would be removed from the bat first.

7. Doctors believe that if stroke patients families could get them to the hospital fast enough, the bats enzyme could reduce the clot to avoid brain damage.

8. The enzymes technical name is DSPA.

9. Researchers have tested DSPAs abilities on mice with great success.

10. Perhaps the vampire bats bad reputation will change with the discovery of its healing powers.

Source: Adapted from The American Heart Association's *"Stroke Journal Report,"* January 9, 2003.

PROOFREADING EXERCISE

Find the five errors in this student paragraph. All of the errors involve possessives.

The Labelles are a family that has lived next door to me for twenty years. I have grown up with the Labelle's daughter, Nicole. My family is bigger than her's. When I go to her house, Nicoles favourite pastime is doing jigsaw puzzles. We always start off by separating a puzzles pieces into different categories. She makes piles of edge pieces, sky pieces, flower pieces, and so on. Then I start putting the edge piece's together to form the border. The Labelles' son is named Marc, and he usually shows up just in time to put the last piece in the puzzle.

SENTENCE WRITING

Write ten sentences using the possessive forms of the names of members of your family or the names of your friends. You could write about a recent event where your family or friends got together. Just tell the story of what happened that day.

_____

_____

_____

_____

_____

_____

_____

_____

REVIEW EXERCISES—CONTRACTIONS AND POSSESSIVES

Here are two review exercises. First, add the necessary apostrophes to the following sentences. Try to get all the correct answers. Don't excuse an error by saying, "Oh, that was just a careless mistake." A mistake is a mistake. Be tough on yourself.

1. Ive never looked forward to anything on TV as much as I did *Seinfeld*s last episode.

2. The shows premise wasnt hard to understand—it was about nothing.

3. Im sure that many viewers waited anxiously to see what would become of televisions favourite group of misfits—Jerry, George, Elaine, and Kramer—in the series final moments.

4. Although there wasnt any way to know in advance what would or wouldnt happen, part of the last shows script was leaked to the press.

5. There would be a plane crash, and while the plane was going down, Elaine was supposedly going to confess her love for Jerry.

6. There actually was plane trouble in the last show, but the plane recovered its power just before a crash.

7. Most of the final shows scenes took place in court, where the four friends were on trial for not trying to stop a mugging that theyd all witnessed.

8. The four main characters earlier despicable actions were shown in the form of flashbacks while the witnesses testimonies were being given.

9. The jurys verdict of guilty for all four characters surprised me because theyre really no worse than many of the rest of us.

10. Jerry, George, Elaine, and Kramer are off to prison in the end, yet theres no doubt that its a show that will be seen in reruns for a long time to come.

Second, add the necessary apostrophes to the following short student essay.

A Journal of My Own

Ive been keeping a journal ever since I was in high school. I dont write it for my teachers sake. I wouldnt turn it in even if they asked me to. Its mine, and it helps me remember all of the changes Ive gone through so far in my life. The way I see it, a diarys purpose isnt just to record the facts; its to capture my true feelings.

When I record the days events in my journal, they arent written in minute-by-minute details. Instead, if Ive been staying at a friends house for the weekend, Ill write something like this: "Sharons the only friend I have who listens to my whole sentence before starting hers. Shes never in a hurry to end a good conversation. Today we talked for an hour or so about the pets wed had when we were kids. We agreed that were both 'dog people.' We cant imagine our lives without dogs. Her favourites are Pomeranians, and mine are golden retrievers." Thats the kind of an entry Id make in my journal. It doesnt mean much to anyone but me, and thats the way it should be.

I know that another persons diary would be different from mine and that most people dont even keep one. Im glad that writing comes easily to me. I dont think Ill ever stop writing in my journal because it helps me believe in myself and value others beliefs as well.

Words That Can Be Broken into Parts

Breaking words into their parts will often help you spell them correctly. Each of the following words is made up of two shorter words. Note that the word then contains all the letters of the two shorter words.

chalk board	...	chalkboard	room mate	...	roommate
over due	...	overdue	home work	...	homework
super market	...	supermarket	under line	...	underline

Becoming aware of prefixes such as *dis*, *inter*, *mis*, and *un* is also helpful. When you add a prefix to a word, note that no letters are dropped, either from the prefix or from the word.

dis appear	...	disappear	mis represent	...	misrepresent
dis appoint	...	disappoint	mis spell	...	misspell
dis approve	...	disapprove	mis understood	...	misunderstood
dis satisfy	...	dissatisfy	un aware	...	unaware
inter act	...	interact	un involved	...	uninvolved

inter active	...	interactive	un necessary	...	unnecessary
inter related	...	interrelated	un sure	...	unsure

Have someone dictate the above list for you to write, and then mark any words you miss. Memorize the correct spellings by noting how each word is made up of a prefix and a word.

Rule for Doubling a Final Letter

Most spelling rules have so many exceptions that they aren't much help. But here's one worth learning because it has only a few exceptions.

Double a final letter (consonants only) when adding an ending that begins with a vowel (such as *ing*, *ed*, *er*) if all three of the following are true:

1. the word ends in a single consonant,

2. which is preceded by a single vowel (the vowels are *a, e, i, o, u*),

3. and the accent is on the last syllable (or the word has only one syllable).

This is not, however, always the Canadian preference. Sometimes the final letters *l, p, s, t* are doubled when the accent in a word with more than one syllable is *not* on the last syllable (travelled, counselled). When in doubt, look up the first choice in a Canadian dictionary. The main rule here is to be consistent, whichever choice you make.

We'll try the rule on a few words to which we'll add *ing*, *ed*, or *er*.

begin   **1.** It ends in a single consonant (*n*).
       2. That single consonant is preceded by a single vowel (*i*).
       3. And the accent is on the last syllable (*be gin ´*).
       Therefore we double the final consonant and write *beginning, beginner.*

stop   **1.** It ends in a single consonant (*p*).
       2. That single consonant is preceded by a single vowel (*o*).
       3. And the accent is on the last syllable (there is only one).
       Therefore we double the final consonant and write *stopping, stopped, stopper.*

filter   **1.** It ends in a single consonant (*r*).
       2. That single consonant is preceded by a single vowel (*e*).
       3. But the accent isn't on the last syllable. It's on the first (*fil ´ter*).
       Therefore we don't double the final consonant. We write *filtering, filtered.*

keep   **1.** It ends in a single consonant (*p*).
       2. But it isn't preceded by a single vowel. There are two *e*'s.
       Therefore we don't double the final consonant. We write *keeping, keeper.*

NOTE 1: Be aware that *qu* is treated as a consonant because *q* is almost never written without *u*. Think of it as *kw*. In words like *equip* and *quit*, the *qu* acts as a consonant. Therefore *equip* and *quit* both end in a single consonant preceded by a single vowel, and the final consonant is doubled in *equipped* and *quitting*.

NOTE 2: The final consonants *w*, *x*, and *y* do not follow this rule and are not doubled when adding *ing*, *ed*, or *er* to a word (as in *bowing*, *fixing*, and *enjoying*).

E X E R C I S E S

Add *ing* to these words. Correct each group of ten before continuing so you'll catch any errors while you still have words to practise on.

Exercise 1

1. scan		**6.** miss
2. trust		**7.** read
3. trip		**8.** occur
4. plan		**9.** skim
5. benefit		**10.** scream

Exercise 2

1. shop		**6.** omit
2. rap		**7.** honour
3. wrap		**8.** brag
4. nail		**9.** mark
5. knit		**10.** hop

Exercise 3

1. steam	**6.** set
2. expel	**7.** stress
3. sip	**8.** flop
4. suffer	**9.** spin
5. war	**10.** differ

Exercise 4

1. creep	**6.** weed
2. subtract	**7.** fog
3. abandon	**8.** occur
4. droop	**9.** refer
5. drop	**10.** submit

Exercise 5

1. interpret	**6.** infer
2. prefer	**7.** guess
3. bet	**8.** bug
4. stoop	**9.** jog
5. stop	**10.** build

Spelling Progress Test

This test covers everything you've studied so far. One sentence in each pair is correct. The other is incorrect. Read both sentences carefully before you decide which is which. Then write the letter of the *incorrect* sentence in the blank. Try to isolate and correct the error if you can.

1. ___ **A.** The tutor complemented me on my well-organized essay.

    B. She said that my examples complemented my ideas perfectly.

2. ___ **A.** I took two coffee breaks at work today.

    B. Do you know wear I put my keys?

3. ___ **A.** Students could of registered two days earlier if there hadn't been an error in the computer program.

    B. That would have made the first day of classes much easier.

4. ___ **A.** Pat and Jill have tutorred in England many times.

    B. Their trips have never been cancelled.

5. ___ **A.** When people lie, they are usually bothered by their conscious.

    B. We could tell that the first pianist at the recital was feeling self-conscious.

6. ___ **A.** The childrens' bicycles were lined up in front of the adults' bikes.

    B. One of a child's first major accomplishments is learning to ride a bicycle.

7. ___ **A.** We've always taken her advice about movies.

    B. We have all ready seen that movie.

8. ___ **A.** My mother is trying to quit smoking, and it's affecting the whole family.

    B. The harmful affects of smoking are well-known.

9. ___ **A.** Many people still believe in the principal "Money can't buy everything."

    B. We shouldn't invite Jenny and Joe; they're always late.

10. ___ **A.** Your the happiest person I know.

    B. When I see your face, it's always got a smile on it.

Using a Dictionary

When asked why dictionaries are helpful, you might answer that dictionaries show correct spelling and clear definitions. However, a good dictionary gives you access to far more information than this. Here's some of the information you might find in a high-quality Canadian dictionary:

- spelling, including Canadian preferences

- definitions, in order of popular usage and including specialized usages

- idioms

- pronunciation

- parts of speech

- syllables and hyphenation

- irregular forms of verbs and plural nouns (such as *go, went, gone* and *child, children*)

- sentence examples

- history of words

- acronyms ("words" formed from the first letters or syllables of other words, like *Canadarm*)

- abbreviations (such as *COD, AL, km*)

- homonyms (words that are pronounced the same)

- synonyms (words that mean the same)

- antonyms (words that mean the opposite)

- usage notes (to explain commonly confused usages, like *uninterested/disinterested*)

- illustrations

- capitalized names of people, places, and things

Some dictionaries are more general than others. For example, specialized dictionaries are published for specific subject areas (like law, science, health, and engineering) and focus on the words and phrases used in those fields. At the other extreme, a tiny pocket-sized dictionary or one that fits on a single sheet in your notebook may help you find the spelling of very common words. Neither extreme is a good choice to get you through the general writing tasks you are sure to face.

For Canadian preferences in usage and spelling, choose an up-to-date Canadian dictionary, such as the *Gage Canadian Dictionary*, the *Canadian Oxford Dictionary*, or the *Nelson Canadian Dictionary*. A good Canadian dictionary contains entries that reliably reflect Canada's own political, cultural, historical, and geographic realities, including words borrowed from the French and other settlers. A Canadian dictionary will not label the spelling of *cheque* as British, although it might indicate that the same meaning is expressed by the spelling *check* in the United States. Look for entries for *résumé, catalogue, all-candidates meeting, CPP* (Canada Pension Plan), *BQ* (Bloc Québécois), or *Francophone*. Their presence will assure you that you have found a dictionary that reflects your society and culture.

USING ONLINE DICTIONARIES

As the world becomes increasingly reliant on word processing, web searching, and other computer-based technology, many writers find that using an online dictionary is a more "user-friendly" approach to accessing information previously available only in a heavy book.

However, since the world of online dictionaries is still developing, many of the currently available ones fail to provide the depth of information that their print-book cousins offer. Some of the best-known dictionaries, including the *Canadian Oxford Dictionary*, 2nd edition (available via Oxford University Press at http://www .oupcanada.com), require users to pay a subscription fee. Others, like *Merriam-Webster OnLine* (at http://www.merriam-webster.com), flood your monitor with links to external, often U.S., commercial sites. Finally, as with any other online material, you as the user will need to spend significant time evaluating the site's value, ease of use, and reliability. For example, virtually all online dictionaries will require you to know exactly what you are looking for and how to navigate through the site to get to the information you need. In short, although using an online dictionary initially seems to offer a cost-free source of word information, it may not address all your needs.

Exercise

For the following sections, choose two online dictionaries from the results of an online search for "online dictionaries." If possible, choose Canadian sites. Then find or borrow a desk-sized Canadian dictionary, such as the *Gage Canadian Dictionary*, the *Canadian Oxford Dictionary*, or the *Nelson Canadian Dictionary*. As a writer, you will want to know where you can go to obtain critical information about the vocabulary you plan to use. To get a good overview, compare the results of your searches by referring to all of these sources. While completing the exercises, you will learn the advantages and limitations of both types of dictionaries. Then, when you need a word reference tool, you will be in a better position to select which one to use.

1. Pronunciation

Look up the word *hyperbole* and copy the pronunciation here.

_____

_____

_____

_____

Now under each letter with a pronunciation mark over it, write the keyword having the same mark. You'll find the keywords at the bottom or top of one of the two dictionary pages open before you. Note especially that the upside-down e (ə) always has the sound of _uh_ like the _a_ in _ago_ or _about_. Remember that sound because it's found in many words.

Next, pronounce the keywords you have written, and then slowly pronounce _hyperbole_, giving each syllable the same sound as its keyword.

Finally, note which syllable has the heavy accent mark. (In most dictionaries the accent mark points to the stressed syllable, but in some it is in front of the stressed syllable.) The stressed syllable is _per_. Now say the word, letting the full force of your voice fall on that syllable.

When more than one pronunciation is given, the first is more common. If the complete pronunciation of a word isn't given, look at the word above it to find the pronunciation.

Look up the pronunciation of these words, using the keywords at the bottom of the dictionary page to help you pronounce each syllable. Then note which syllable has the heavy accent mark, and say the word aloud.

facsimile   malign   longitude   piquant

2. Definitions

The dictionary may give more than one meaning for a word. Read all the meanings for each italicized word, and then write a definition appropriate to the sentence.

1. Parsa and Isabella have an M.A. and a Ph.D., _respectively._ _____

_____

2. She was one of several _eminent_ speakers at the conference. _____

_____

3. They took their _biennial_ trip to Banff. _____

_____

4. As a lifeguard, he suffered from a _sporadic_ fear of water. _____

_____

3. Spelling

By making yourself look up each word you aren't sure how to spell, you'll soon become a better speller. When two spellings are given in the dictionary, the first one (or the one with the definition) is preferred. In a Canadian dictionary, the first one is the Canadian preference.

Use a dictionary to find the preferred spelling for each of these words. Canadian and American dictionaries may differ in their preference.

cancelled, canceled   dialog, dialogue

judgment, judgement   gray, grey

4. Compound Words

If you want to find out whether two words are written separately, written with a hyphen between them, or written as one word, consult your dictionary. For example:

second cousin   is written as two words

sister-in-law   is hyphenated

stepchild   is written as one word

Write each of the following correctly:

mix up   _____   left handed _____

on going _____   week day   _____

5. Capitalization

If a word is capitalized in the dictionary, that means it should always be capitalized. If it is not capitalized in the dictionary, then it may or may not be capitalized, depending on how it is used (see p. 246). For example, *Asian* is always capitalized, but *school* is capitalized or not, according to how it is used.

Last year, I graduated from high school.

Last year, I graduated from Laura Secord Secondary School.

Write the following words as they're given in the dictionary (with or without a capital) to show whether they must always be capitalized or not. Take a guess before looking them up.

democracy   _____   maple leaf _____

thanksgiving _____   french   _____

6. Usage

A word's entry in the dictionary doesn't mean that the word is appropriate for standard use. The following labels indicate whether a word is used today and, if so, where and by whom.

obsolete	no longer used
archaic	not now used in ordinary language but still found in some biblical, literary, and legal expressions
colloquial, informal	used in informal conversation but not in formal writing
dialectal, regional	used in some localities but not everywhere
slang	popular but nonstandard expression
nonstandard, substandard	not used in Standard Written English

Look up each italicized word and write the label indicating its usage for the meaning intended in the sentence. Dictionaries differ. One may list a word as slang whereas another will call it colloquial. Still another may give no designation, thus indicating that that particular dictionary considers the word in standard use.

1. The hula hoop was a *fad* that began in the 1950s. _____

2. You *guys* don't know how to have fun anymore. _____

3. That *tidbit* of gossip made my day. _____

4. I got a *cool* new pair of boots. _____

5. We would like to *bum* around with you all summer. _____

7. Derivations

The derivations or stories behind words will often help you remember the current meanings. For example, if you read that someone is *narcissistic* and you consult your dictionary, you'll find that *narcissism* is a condition named after Narcissus, who was a handsome young man in Greek mythology. One day Narcissus fell in love with his own reflection in a pool, but when he tried to get closer to it, he fell in the water and drowned. A flower that grew nearby is now named for Narcissus. And *narcissistic* has come to mean "in love with oneself."

Look up the derivation of each of these words. You'll find it in square brackets either just before or just after the definition.

Procrustean _____

rigmarole (or rigamarole) _____

malapropism _____

Gordian knot _____

8. Synonyms

At the end of a definition, a group of synonyms is sometimes given. For example, at the end of the definition of *injure*, you'll find several synonyms, such as *damage* or *harm*. And if you look up *damage* or *harm*, you'll be referred to the same synonyms listed under *injure*.

List the synonyms given for the following words.

native _____

plan _____

summit _____

9. Abbreviations

Find the meaning of the following abbreviations.

R.S.V.P. _____   e.g. _____

N.B. _____   i.e. _____

10. Names of People

The names of famous people will sometimes be found either in the main part of your dictionary or in a separate biographical names section at the back.

Identify the following famous people.

Muhammad   _____

M. Montessori   _____

A. Kurosawa   _____

N. Mandela   _____

11. Names of Places

The names of places will sometimes be found either in the main part of your dictionary or in a separate geographical names section at the back.

Identify the following places.

Liverpool _____

Somalia _____

Mount Ossa _____

The Hague _____

12. Foreign Words and Phrases

Find the language and the meaning of the italicized expressions.

1. A child's mind seems like much more than a *tabula rasa*. _____

2. We were given *carte blanche* to gamble at the casino. _____

3. I met my *doppelgänger* in a Montreal airport. _____

13. Miscellaneous Information

See if you can find these miscellaneous bits of information in a dictionary.

1. What part of its body does a *gastropod* walk on? _____

2. How many zeroes does a *googol* have? _____

3. What duty is a *devil's advocate* supposed to perform? _____

4. In what year did *virtual reality* become an expression? _____

5. What sound does *tintinnabulation* refer to? _____

Spelling Post-Test

Each of the sentences below contains just one spelling error. Use a good Canadian dictionary to locate the mistake; then circle the error and insert your correction.

1. Linda easily past the courses in her cooperative education program.

2. Her councillors in high school always advised her to go to university.

3. Bill suddenly panicked when his kayak fliped over in the swirling rapids near the falls.

4. The room went quite when the TV showed graphic photos of the accident.

5. My parents through a party to celebrate the arrival of their first grandchild.

6. The disintegrating fibre on my snowboard means that it is to dangerous to ride.

7. My roomate often waits too long to submit her assignments and then wails about losing marks because her work is overdue.

8. Warm weather just dosen't come quickly enough for most Canadians.

9. Our neighbour's yard always looks much neater than our's.

10. When Bill heard he might lose his job, he spoke with a representative from the personal department.

11. Some people think that choosing coloured stationary will create a poor effect in a job application.

12. As soon as she arrived at the accident scene, the police constable began filling out an occurence report.

13. The seven witness's statements were already completed before the ambulance arrived.

14. There was no obvious reason for the accident; it's possible that it was caused by faulty breaks on one vehicle.

15. Likely, a mechanic will be asked to determine if its mechanically fit.

16. Drivers need to remember that their responsabilities include regular car servicing.

17. Some individuals beleive that driving a car is their right, but it's really a privilege.

18. Ignoring a solid yellow line on a highway will led to problems if a driver decides to pass another car.

19. Even a broken line doesn't necessarily mean it's alright to pass.

20. Experienced individuals no that many factors affect safe highway driving.

Knowing Sentence Essentials

Sentence Essentials Pre-Test: Finding Subjects and Verbs

Each of the following word groups qualifies as a sentence. Study the groups and locate their *subjects* and *verbs,* two elements every sentence contains. Underline each sentence's subject word (or words) <u>once</u>. Underline each sentence's verb word (or words) <u>twice</u>. Check your answers in the answer key before beginning Part 2.

1. The arrival of warmer weather encourages Canadians to make plans.

2. Some of my friends are planning to purchase new bicycles this spring.

3. Unfortunately, the most popular model of bike often sells out before May.

4. Hiking through a remote forest and canoeing on a peaceful northern lake remind many people of the importance of nature in their lives.

5. Families take advantage of warmer weather and visit other parts of the country together.

6. For many in the cold north, the lengthening days bring new hope.

7. As early as February, northern Canadian gardeners start designing flower beds and making lists of seeds to order.

8. Others turn their attention to outdoor sporting activities.

9. Does your golf game need improvement this summer?

10. One of my friends prefers swimming to playing golf.

Like stocking a toolbox for a job, building an accurate and correct vocabulary is only the first step. Effective communicators construct sentences that convey complete, clear messages. The next three sections of this book are focused on understanding the sentence basics, using various sentence structure patterns, and applying strategies to keep your message clear.

Identifying Sentence Parts

Choosing the right word is an important aspect of writing. Some words sound alike but are spelled differently and have different meanings (*past* and *passed*, for instance), and some words are spelled the same but sound different and mean different things (*lead*, for the action of "leading," and *lead*, for the stuff inside pencils).

One way to choose words more carefully is to understand the roles that words play in sentences. Just as one actor can play many different parts in movies (a hero, a villain, a humorous sidekick), single words can play different parts in sentences (a noun, a verb, an adjective). These are called the *eight parts of speech*, briefly defined with examples below.

1. **Nouns** name some*one*, *thing*, *place*, or *idea* and are used as subjects and objects in sentences.

   The **technician** fixed the **computers** in the **lab**.

2. **Pronouns** are special words that replace nouns to avoid repeating them.

   She (the technician) fixed **them** (the computers) in **it** (the lab).

3. **Adjectives** add description to nouns and pronouns—telling *which one*, *how many*, or *what kind*, *colour*, or *shape* they are.

   The **new** technician fixed **30 old** computers in the **writing** lab.

4. **Verbs** show action or state of being.

   The new technician **fixed** the old computers in the writing lab; Terri **is** the technician's name.

5. **Adverbs** add information—such as *when*, *where*, *why*, or *how*— to verbs, adjectives, and other adverbs, or to whole sentences.

   Yesterday the new technician **quickly** fixed the **very** old computers in the writing lab.

6. **Prepositions** show position in *space* and *time* and are followed by nouns to form prepositional phrases.

    The technician fixed the computers **in** the writing lab **at** noon.

7. **Conjunctions** are connecting words—such as *and, but,* and *or*—and words that begin dependent clauses—such as *because, since, when, while,* and *although*.

    Students still visited the lab **and** the media centre **while** the computers were broken.

8. **Interjections** interrupt a sentence to show surprise or other emotions and are rarely used in Standard Written English.

    Wow, Terri is a valuable new employee!

To find out what parts of speech an individual word can play, look it up in a good dictionary (see p. 43). A list of definitions beginning with an abbreviated part of speech (*n, adj, prep,* and so on) will catalogue its uses. However, seeing how a word is used in a particular sentence is the best way to identify its part of speech. Look at these examples:

The **train** of a wedding gown flows elegantly behind it.

(*Train* is a noun in this sentence, naming the part of a gown we call a "train.")

Sammy and Helen **train** beluga whales at the Vancouver Acquarium.

(*Train* is a verb in this example, expressing the action of teaching skills we call "training.")

Doug's parents drove him to the **train** station.

(*Train* is an adjective here, adding description to the noun "station," telling what *kind* of station it is.)

All of the words in a sentence work together to create meaning, but each one serves its own purpose by playing a part of speech. Think about how each of the words in the following sentence plays the particular part of speech labelled:

ADJ	ADJ	N	V	PREP	N	CONJ	PRO	ADV	V	N

Cash-strapped college students work during the day, so they usually take classes

PREP	N

at night.

Below, you will find an explanation for each label in the above sentence.

Cash-strapped	**ADJ**	identifies what kind of the noun *students*
college	**ADJ**	describes the noun *students*
students	**N**	names the people who are the subject of the sentence
work	**V**	tells their action
during	**PREP**	shows position in time
day	**N**	acts as the noun concluding a prepositional phrase
so	**CONJ**	connects two parts of the sentence
they	**PRON**	replaces the noun *students* to avoid its repetition
usually	**ADV**	adds information—in this case, when
take	**V**	tells action
classes	**N**	names things, acts as object of verb *take*
at	**PREP**	shows the action's position in time
night	**N**	acts as the noun concluding a prepositional phrase

Familiarizing yourself with the parts of speech will help you spell better now and understand phrases and clauses better later. Each of the eight parts of speech has characteristics that distinguish it from the other seven, but it takes practice to learn them.

EXERCISES

Label the parts of speech above all of the words in the following sentences using the abbreviations *N, PRO, ADJ, V, ADV, PREP, CONJ*, and *INTERJ*. For clarity's sake, the sentences here are very brief, and you may ignore the words *a, an,* and *the.* Those three words are actually special forms of adjectives (called articles), but they are so numerous that there's no need to mark them.

Refer to the definitions and examples of the parts of speech whenever necessary. When in doubt, leave a word unmarked until you check the answers at the back of the book after each set of ten sentences. You'll find that many of the ones you found difficult to label will be adverbs, the most versatile of the parts of speech.

Exercise 1

1. In the past, nearly everyone carried a handkerchief.

2. Those were the days before disposable tissues became so popular.

3. People gave decorative hankies as gifts and bought them as souvenirs.

4. My aunt and uncle have two separate vintage handkerchief collections.

5. Her collection includes ones with provincial and territorial flags or maps of famous cities on them.

6. Others have flower designs, geometric patterns, and clever sayings as decorations.

7. Men's vintage handkerchiefs are usually white or grey with coloured lines or monograms.

8. My uncle still owns a few hankies from his childhood.

9. They depict characters and animals from nursery rhymes and fairy tales.

10. These two collections are very valuable to my family and to me.

Exercise 2

1. I really love cookies.

2. They are my favourite snack.

3. I prefer the ones with chocolate chips or nuts.

4. Cookies taste best when they are fresh.

5. Sometimes, I have cookies and milk for breakfast.

6. Now some fast-food restaurants offer fresh-baked cookies.

7. Oatmeal cookies are delicious when they are still warm.

8. Companies release new versions of traditional cookies.

9. One variety of Oreos now has chocolate centres.

10. Wow, are they yummy!

Exercise 3

1. Tall office buildings are dangerous for migrating birds at night.

2. The buildings' lighted windows confuse the birds.

3. They fly toward the glowing windows and lose their way.

4. Bird experts studied this phenomenon.

5. McCormick Place is a tall building in Chicago.

6. Scientists counted the number of bird deaths there for two years.

7. Hundreds of birds flew into the lighted windows.

8. Only one-fifth of that number hit the dark windows.

9. Scientists suggest a lights-out policy for tall buildings from midnight to dawn during migration periods.

10. Birds migrate from March to May and from August to November.

Source: Adapted from *Discover*, August 2002.

Exercise 4

1. Jan Demczur recently donated several objects to the Smithsonian Institution.

2. Demczur was a window washer at One World Trade Center.

3. He was in an elevator of the building when terrorists attacked the tower.

4. With the help of his squeegee handle, Demczur saved several people's lives.

5. Demczur and the others in the elevator used the handle as an axe.

6. They cut an opening from the elevator shaft into the building.

7. Demczur and his five elevator-mates escaped just before the tower fell.

8. Such survival stories give people hope.

9. The Smithsonian is the U.S.'s place for rare artifacts.

10. Demczur's squeegee handle and his dusty clothes are now on display at the Smithsonian.

Source: Adapted from *Smithsonian*, July 2002.

Exercise 5

1. Plants need water and sunlight.

2. Sometimes houseplants wither unexpectedly.

3. People often give them too much water or not enough water.

4. I saw an experiment on a television show once.

5. It involved two plants.

6. The same woman raised both plants with water and sunlight.

7. The plants grew in two different rooms.

8. She yelled at one plant but said sweet things to the other.

9. The verbally praised plant grew beautifully, but the other one died.

10. Plants have feelings too.

PROOFREADING EXERCISE

Here is a brief excerpt from a book called *The Question and Answer Book of Every-day Science*, by Ruth A. Sonneborn. This excerpt answers the question, "Why do our eyes blink?" We have modified some of the phrasing in the excerpt for this exercise. Label the parts of speech above as many of the words as you can before checking your answers at the back of the book.

Your eyelids blink regularly all day long. They stop only when you sleep.

Blinking protects your delicate eyes from injury. When something flies toward you,

usually your lids shut quickly and protect your eyes.

Blinking also does a kind of washing job. It keeps your eyelids moist. If a

speck of dirt gets past your lids, your moist eyeball traps it. Then your eyes fill with

water, your lids blink, and the speck washes out of your eye.

Understanding Adjectives and Adverbs

Two of the eight parts of speech, adjectives and adverbs, are used to *add* information to other words. "To modify" means to change or improve something, usually by adding to it. English has only two kinds of modifiers: adjectives and adverbs. Try to remember that both *ad*jectives and *ad*verbs *add* information.

ADJECTIVES

- Adjectives *add to nouns and pronouns* by answering these questions: *Which one? What kind? How much or how many? What size, what colour, or what shape?*

         ADJ   N   ADJ   N   ADJ ADJ ADJ

She bought a *new* backpack with *multicoloured* pockets. It has *one large blue*

  N   ADJ   ADJ   ADJ   N   ADJ   ADJ   ADJ PRO

pocket, *two medium yellow* pockets, and *three small red* ones.

- Adjectives usually come *before the nouns they modify*.

     ADJ N   **ADJ N**   **ADJ ADJ ADJ**   **N**
  An *oak* tree stands in the *front* yard of *that big green* house.

- However, adjectives can also come *after the nouns they modify*.

       N   **ADJ**   **ADJ**
  The cake, *plain* and *undecorated*, sat in the middle of the table.

- Adjectives may also come *after linking verbs* (*is, am, are, was, were, feel, seem, appear, taste . . .*) to add description to the subject. For further discussion of these special verbs, see page 155.

        N   **V**   **ADJ**   **ADJ**
  The branches are *sturdy* and *plentiful*.

       N   **V**   **ADJ**   **ADJ**   **N**   **V** **ADJ**   **ADJ**
  The cake tasted *sweet* and *delicious*.   (or)   The cake was *sweet* and *delicious*.

- Adjectives can be *forms of nouns and pronouns* that are used to add information to other nouns.

     ADJ   **N**   **ADJ**   **N**   **ADJ** **ADJ**   **N**
  The *tree's* owner always trims *its* branches during *his summer* vacation.

       ADJ   **N**   **ADJ** **N**
  I love *chocolate* cake for *my* birthday.

ADVERBS

- Adverbs *add to verbs, adjectives, and other adverbs* by answering these questions: *How? In what way? When? Where? Why?*

      ADV   **V**   **ADV**   **V**
  I *quickly* called my sister, who *sleepily* answered her cell phone.

       V **ADV**   **V**
  She did *not* recognize my voice at first.

         ADV **ADJ**   **N**
  He wore his *light* blue shirt to the party.

         ADV   **ADJ** **N**
  It was an *extremely* tall tree.

            ADV **ADJ**   **ADV**   **ADJ**
  Its branches were *very* sturdy and *quite* plentiful.

         ADV   **V**   **ADV** **ADV**
  People *often* drive *really fast* in the rain.

- Unlike adjectives, some adverbs can move around in sentences without changing the meaning.

  ADV
  Now I have enough money for a vacation.

  ADV
  I *now* have enough money for a vacation.

  ADV
  I have enough money *now* for a vacation.

  ADV
  I have enough money for a vacation *now*.

Notice that many—but not all—adverbs end in *ly*. Be aware, however, that adjectives can also end in *ly*. Remember that a word's part of speech is determined by how the word is used in a particular sentence. For instance, in the old saying "The early bird catches the worm," *early* adds to the noun, telling which bird. *Early* is acting as an adjective. However, in the sentence "The teacher arrived early," *early* adds to the verb, telling when the teacher arrived. *Early* is acting as an adverb.

Now that you've read about adjectives and adverbs, try to identify the question that each modifier (adj or adv) answers in the example below. Refer back to the questions listed under Understanding Adjectives and Adverbs.

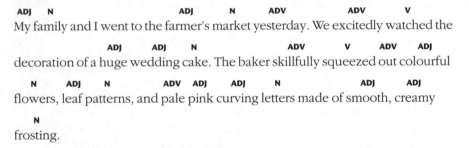

ADJ N   ADJ   N   ADV   ADV   V
My family and I went to the farmer's market yesterday. We excitedly watched the

        ADJ   ADJ   N   ADV   V   ADV   ADJ
decoration of a huge wedding cake. The baker skillfully squeezed out colourful

  N   ADJ   N   ADV ADJ ADJ   N   ADJ   ADJ
flowers, leaf patterns, and pale pink curving letters made of smooth, creamy

  N
frosting.

NOTE: Although we discuss only single-word adjectives and adverbs here, phrases and clauses can also function as adjectives and adverbs following the same patterns.

Choosing between Adjectives and Adverbs

Knowing how to choose between adjectives and adverbs is important, especially in certain kinds of sentences. See if you can make the correct choices in these three sentences:

We did (good, well) on that test.

I feel (bad, badly) about quitting my job.

She speaks (really clear/really clearly).

Did you choose *well*, *bad*, and *really clearly*? If you missed *bad*, you're not alone. You might have reasoned that *badly* adds to the verb *feel*, but *feel* is acting in a

special way here—not naming the action of feeling with your fingertips (as in "I *feel*

V

ADV   **N**   **ADJ**

the fabric *carefully*") but describing the feeling of it (as in "The *fabric* feels *smooth*"). To test your understanding of this concept, try substituting "I feel (happy, happily)" instead of "I feel (bad, badly)" and note how easy it is to choose.

Another way that adjectives and adverbs work is to compare two or more things by describing them in relation to one another. The *er* ending is added to both adjectives and adverbs when comparing two items, and the *est* ending is added when comparing three or more items.

ADJ   N   ADJ   ADJ   N   ADJ   ADJ   N

The red pockets are *big*. The yellow pockets are *bigger*. The blue pocket is

ADJ   PRO

the *biggest* one of all.

V   ADV   V   ADV   V   ADV

She works *hard*. He works *harder*. I work *hardest*.

In some cases, such comparisons require the addition of a word (*more* or *most*, *less* or *least*) instead of a change in the ending from *er* to *est*. Longer adjectives and adverbs usually require these extra adverbs to help with comparisons.

ADJ   ADV   ADJ   ADV   ADJ

Food is *expensive*. Gas is *more expensive*. Rent is *most expensive*.

ADV   ADV   ADV   ADV   ADV

You danced *gracefully*. They danced *less gracefully*. We danced *least gracefully*.

E X E R C I S E S

Remember that adjectives add to nouns and pronouns, while adverbs add to verbs, adjectives, and other adverbs. Check your answers frequently.

Exercise 1

Identify whether each *italicized* word is used as an adjective or an adverb in the sentence.

1. The "New Books" display at the library *always* attracts me. (adjective, adverb)

2. This set of bookshelves stands right next to the *circulation* desk. (adjective, adverb)

3. It holds everything from *tiny* paperbacks to huge reference works. (adjective, adverb)

4. These books are brand new and cover *various* topics. (adjective, adverb)

5. *Yesterday*, I discovered a whole book about flowers. (adjective, adverb)

6. The book had a *very* simple title: <u>Flowers</u>. (adjective, adverb)

7. However, its *interesting* subtitle caught my eye: <u>How They Changed the World</u>. (adjective, adverb)

8. The *bright* pink flower on its cover also appealed to me. (adjective, adverb)

9. I *never* considered the effects of flowers on the world. (adjective, adverb)

10. Therefore, I checked out the book and took it *home* to read. (adjective, adverb)

Exercise 2

Identify whether the word *only* is used as an adjective or an adverb in the following sentences. In each sentence, try to link the word *only* with another word to figure out if *only* is an adjective (adding to a noun or pronoun) or an adverb (adding to a verb, adjective, or other adverb). Have fun with this exercise!

1. I reached into my wallet and pulled out my *only* dollar. (adjective, adverb)

2. I had *only* one dollar. (adjective, adverb)

3. *Only* I had a dollar. (adjective, adverb)

4. One company *only* paints buildings. (adjective, adverb)

5. That company paints *only* buildings, not houses. (adjective, adverb)

6. Another company replaces *only* shingles, not clapboards. (adjective, adverb)

7. In my French class, we speak in French *only*. (adjective, adverb)

8. In my French class, we *only* speak in French. (adjective, adverb)

9. I was happy as an *only* child. (adjective, adverb)

10. She was the *only* one with a car. (adjective, adverb)

Exercise 3

Choose the correct adjective or adverb form required to complete each sentence.

1. I have a (close, closely) relative in show business.

2. I am (close, closely) related to someone in show business.

3. I feel (close, closely) to my family at the holidays.

4. My boss suffered (bad, badly) with a cold for several weeks.

5. He felt really (bad, badly) because of his fever.

6. Then he had a (bad, badly) reaction to a prescription drug and felt even worse.

7. The students jogged (very happy, very happily) in the cool morning mist.

8. They were (very happy, very happily) with their choice of P.E. class.

9. The whole class received (good, well) grades on the test.

10. The whole class performed (good, well) on the test.

Exercise 4

Choose the correct adjective or adverb form required to complete each sentence.

1. Kyle rents the (large, larger, largest) apartment in the whole building.

2. Jane's apartment is (large, larger, largest) than her parents' house.

3. Everyone needs a space that is (large, larger, largest) enough for the essentials.

4. We looked at many apartments with (ugly, uglier, ugliest) carpeting.

5. The thick orange plush carpeting in one of them was very (ugly, uglier, ugliest).

6. But the (ugly, uglier, ugliest) of them all had medallion shapes in bright pink and green all over it.

7. I've never seen a carpet pattern (ugly, uglier, ugliest) than that.

8. Unfortunately, the (friendly, friendlier, friendliest) people lived in the ugly-carpet building.

9. The tenants of the other buildings were (friendly, friendlier, friendliest), too.

10. They were all (friendly, friendlier, friendliest) than my current neighbours.

Exercise 5

Label all of the adjectives (adj) and adverbs (adv) in the following sentences. Mark the ones you are sure of; then check your answers at the back of the book and find the ones you missed.

1. I took an optional but helpful class in the spring.

2. A reference librarian taught us research skills.

3. We discovered very useful tools for Web research.

4. Then the librarian carefully explained the library's resources.

5. She often presented our research assignments in the form of scavenger hunts.

6. The topics were always interesting and fun.

7. I see the benefits of these self-help classes now.

8. I am more motivated in my studies as a result.

9. And I am definitely less afraid of the library's computer.

10. Since that class, I write term papers easily and enjoy them completely.

PROOFREADING EXERCISE

Correct the five errors in the use of adjectives and adverbs in the following student paragraph. Then try to label all of the adjectives (adj) and adverbs (adv) in the paragraph for practice.

My favourite movie of all time is *The Matrix*. This movie is intenser than any other. The main character of Neo is smart and more creative. He feels badly in the beginning of the story. His job is dull, and he wants excitement. Eventual, he meets the team of real people from outside the Matrix. Neo joins their team and fights real hard against the agents in the Matrix. *The Matrix* is the first of a three-movie series. In my opinion, it is the best of the three.

SENTENCE WRITING

Write a short paragraph (five to seven sentences) describing your favourite former teacher. Then go back through the paragraph and label your single-word adjectives and adverbs.

_____

_____

_____

_____

_____

_____

_____

Finding Subjects and Verbs

The most important words in any sentence are those that tell your reader *who* or *what* you are writing about (the subject) and what that subject *does* or *is* (the verb). In fact, the subject and verb make up the core of every sentence.

For the examples in this book, we will underline the subject word (or words) once and the verb word (or words) twice, like this:

Lightning strikes.

The word *Lightning* is *what* is being written about in this sentence, so it's the subject. Because *strikes* tells what the subject *does*, we know it is the verb.

But few sentences have just two words. When sentences contain many words, subjects and verbs can be harder to find.

Lightning strikes very quickly from the clouds to the ground.

Often lightning strikes people on golf courses or in boats.

Because the verb often shows action, look for it first. Can you find the subject and verb in the following sentence?

The neighbourhood cat folded its paws under its chest.

The word *folded* shows the action, so it's the verb. Underline *folded* twice. Now ask who or what *folded*? The answer, *cat*, is the subject. Underline *cat* once.

Study the following sentences and explanations until you feel comfortable with picking out subjects and verbs.

Tomorrow our school celebrates its 50th anniversary. (Which word shows the action? Celebrates. It's the verb. Underline it twice. Who or what celebrates? School. It's the subject. Underline it once.)

The team members ate several boxes of chocolate. (Which word shows the action? Ate. Who or what ate? Members ate.)

Internet users crowd the popular web cafés downtown. (Which word shows the action? Crowd. Who or what crowd? Users crowd.)

SPECIAL SUBJECT AND VERB IDENTIFICATION CHALLENGES

Non-Action Verbs

Often the verb doesn't show action but only tells what the subject *is* or *was*. Learn to spot non-action verbs like *am, is, are, was, were, seems, feels, appears, becomes, looks*.

At the first sound of thunder, Lou feels afraid.

Serena Williams is one of the world's finest tennis players.

Inverted Order Sentences

In all the examples so far, the subject is located before the verb in the sentence. Be careful! Sometimes this natural order is reversed, and the subject appears after the verb. Here are two situations where such inverted order always occurs:

1. "Here" sentences (sentences beginning with *here, there*)
    When a sentence begins with one of these words, the subject follows its verb.

    There was a fortune teller at the carnival.

    Here comes my favourite chemistry lab partner.

> **NOTE:** Remember that *there* and *here* are not subjects. They simply point to something later in the sentence.

2. Direct questions

   When a sentence ends in a question mark, the verb often appears before its subject.

   Why <u>are</u> the <u>topics</u> of this lesson so difficult?

   <u>Wa</u>sn't last night's <u>sunset</u> spectacular? (The contraction of *not*, *n't*, is an adverb because it changes the meaning of the verb.)

Commands

In commands, usually the subject is not expressed. It is *you* (understood).

   Sit down. (<u>You</u> <u>sit</u> down.)

   Place flap A into slot B. (<u>You</u> <u>place</u> flap A into slot B.)

   Meet me at 7:00. (<u>You</u> <u>meet</u> me at 7:00.)

Compounds

If two or more separate subjects share the *same* verb, the sentence has a *compound subject*.

   <u>Drill bits</u>, <u>wrenches</u>, and <u>micrometers</u> <u>are</u> tools of a millwright's trade.

When two or more separate verbs share the *same* subject, the sentence has a *compound verb*.

   The <u>carpenter</u> carefully <u>measured</u> the material, <u>made</u> the necessary cuts, and <u>assembled</u> the decking.

E X E R C I S E S

Underline the main subject words once and the verbs twice. When you've finished ten sentences, compare your answers carefully with those at the back of the book.

Exercise 1

1. Right after Thanksgiving, the malls begin to fill with Halloween shoppers.

2. There are many reasons for this.

3. Many consumers spend hundreds of dollars on this popular holiday.

4. Halloween costumes are the most popular items.

5. Yards and homes fill with exhibits of witches, ghosts, and black cats.

6. Parents and their children often go to Halloween house parties and then cruise their neighbourhoods for treats.

7. From the first knock on the door, residents feel the excitement.

8. There's nothing as alarming to most dogs as the sound of running feet pounding down the driveway.

9. In some neighbourhoods, the ages of trick-or-treaters range from newborns to teenagers.

10. Many seem to be in a contest to fill the most pillowcases with candies.

Exercise 2

1. Weather forecasts affect many people.

2. But they are not always correct.

3. Sometimes rain and wind arrive instead of sunny skies.

4. Travellers need accurate weather predictions.

5. There are many possible dangers in travelling.

6. A hurricane is never a welcome event on a vacation.

7. At times, the weather seems more enemy than friend.

8. Often the skies cooperate with people's travel plans.

9. At times like this, the sun shines as if by special request.

10. Then the weather is perfect and feels like a friend again.

Exercise 3

1. There is a long-standing tradition in aviation.

2. Passengers get peanuts and a drink as a mid-flight snack.

3. Any drink tastes better with peanuts.

4. And the tiny foil packages please people.

5. But peanuts are dangerous to passengers with peanut allergies.

6. Most people eat peanuts and feel fine.

7. A mildly allergic person gets watery eyes and hives.

8. In extreme cases, people with peanut allergies die.

9. So, many airlines propose peanut-free zones on airplanes.

10. Needless to say, peanut companies are not happy about the proposal.

Exercise 4

1. Plastic snow globes are popular souvenir items.

2. They are clear globes usually on white oval bases.

3. People display these water-filled objects or use them as paperweights.

4. Inside are tiny replicas of famous tourist attractions like the Eiffel Tower or Big Ben.

5. Snow or glitter mixes with the water for a snowstorm effect.

6. These souvenirs often hold startling combinations.

7. In a snow globe, even the Bahamas has blizzards.

8. There is also a globe with smog instead of snow.

9. Some people consider snow globes valuable collectables.

10. Others just buy them as inexpensive mementos.

PROOFREADING EXERCISE

Underline the subjects once and the verbs twice in the following student paragraph.

My friend Maria spends every weekday afternoon in the school library. She does her homework, finishes her reading assignments, and organizes her notes and handouts. I envy her good study skills. She is always ready for the next day of class. I, however, go back to my apartment in the afternoon. There are so many distractions at home. The television blares, and my roommates invite their friends over. I am usually too tired to do schoolwork. Maybe the library is a better place for me too.

SENTENCE WRITING

Write ten sentences about any subject—your favourite colour, for instance. Keeping your subject matter simple in these sentence writing exercises will make it easier to find your sentence structures later. After you have written your sentences, go back and underline your subjects once and your verbs twice.

_____

_____

_____

_____

_____

_____

_____

_____

_____

Locating Prepositional Phrases

Prepositional phrases are among the easiest structures in English to learn. A phrase is just a group of words (at least two) without a subject and a verb. And don't let a term like *prepositional* scare you. If you look in the middle of that long word, you'll find a familiar one—*position*. In English, we tell the *positions* of people and things in sentences using prepositional phrases. Look at the following sentence with its prepositional phrases in parentheses:

Our field trip (to the mountain) begins (at 6:00) (in the morning) (on Friday).

One phrase tells where the field trip is going (*to the mountain*), and three phrases tell when the trip begins (*at 6:00*, *in the morning*, and *on Friday*). As you can see, prepositional phrases show the position of someone or something in space or in time.

Here is a list of prepositions that can show positions in space:

above	behind	in	past
across	below	inside	through
against	between	near	to
among	beyond	on	under
around	by	outside	without
at	from	over	

Here are prepositions that can show positions in time:

after	by	in	throughout
at	during	past	until
before	for	since	within

These lists include only individual words, *not phrases*. Remember, a preposition must be followed by an object—someone or something—to create a prepositional phrase. Notice that in the added prepositional phrases that follow, the position of the plane in relation to the object, *the clouds*, changes completely.

The passenger plane flew *above the clouds.*
below the clouds.
within the clouds.
between the clouds.
past the clouds.
around the clouds.

Now notice the different positions in time:

The plane landed *at 3:30.*
around 3:30.
past 3:30.
before the thunderstorm.
during the thunderstorm.
after the thunderstorm.

NOTE: A few words—such as *of, as, like,* and *except*—are prepositions that do not fit neatly into either the space or time category, yet they are very common prepositions (box *of candy*, note *of apology*, type *of bicycle*; act *as a substitute*, use *as an example*, as happy *as my little brother*; vitamins *like A, C, and E*, shaped *like a watermelon*, moved *like a snake*; everyone *except Gilbert*, the whole house *except the upstairs washroom*, all knobs *except the red one*).

By locating prepositional phrases, you will be able to find subjects and verbs more easily. For example, you might have difficulty finding the subject and verb in a long sentence like this:

> After the rainy season, one of the windows in the attic leaked at the corners of its moulding.

But if you put parentheses around all the prepositional phrases like this

> (After the rainy season), <u>one</u> (of the windows) (in the attic) <u><u>leaked</u></u> (at the corners) (of its moulding).

then you have only two words left—the subject and the verb. Even in short sentences like the following, you might pick the wrong word as the subject if you don't put parentheses around the prepositional phrases first.

> <u>Many</u> (of the characters) <u><u>survived</u></u> (in that movie).

> The <u>waves</u> (around the ship) <u><u>looked</u></u> real.

NOTE: Don't mistake *to* plus a verb for a prepositional phrase. For example, *to quit* is not a prepositional phrase because *quit* is not the name of something. It's a form of verb.

Remember: Subjects and verbs are never inside prepositional phrases.

E X E R C I S E S

Locate and put parentheses around the prepositional phrases in the following sentences. Be sure to start with the preposition itself (*in, on, to, at, of ...*) and include the word or words that go with it (*in the morning, on our sidewalk, to Halifax ...*). Then underline the subjects once and the verbs twice. Review the answers given at the back for each group of ten sentences before continuing.

Exercise 1

1. One (of Canada's) best-known virtues is its health care system.
2. (Throughout the world,) governments (of every type) strive to keep the costs (of health care) down (without sacrificing services.)

3. Nurses from Canada find employment at hospitals in almost any part of the world.

4. Their training in Canadian postsecondary institutions places them at the top of the class.

5. Physicians from Canada often move to the United States to earn more money.

6. Several years ago, one of Canada's former governors general, Roy Romanow, chaired a task force to study Canada's health care system.

7. Members of the general public, health care professionals, and other interested parties made written submissions before the Romanow Commission.

8. In several Canadian communities, the Commission listened to individual oral submissions as well.

9. Unlike reports from other commissions, the Romanow task force's final document appeared online at a federal government website and drew considerable attention.

10. Now, after nearly ten years, some of the Commission's recommendations, including the concern about wait times, are the focus of action at both the provincial and federal levels.

Exercise 2

1. Most of us remember playing with Frisbees in our front yards in the early evenings and at parks or beaches on weekend afternoons.

2. Fred Morrison invented the original flat Frisbee for the Wham-O toy company in the 1950s.

3. Ed Headrick, designer of the professional Frisbee, passed away at his home in California in August of 2002.

4. Working at Wham-O in the 1960s, Headrick improved the performance of the existing Frisbee with the addition of ridges in the surface of the disc.

5. Headrick's improvements led to increased sales of his "professional model" Frisbee and to the popularity of Frisbee tournaments.

6. After Headrick's redesign, Wham-O sold 100 million of the flying discs.

7. Headrick also invented the game of disc golf.

8. Like regular golf but with discs, the game requires specially designed courses like the first one at Oak Grove Park in California.

9. Before his death, Headrick asked for his ashes to be formed into memorial flying discs for select family and friends.

10. Donations from sales of the remaining memorial discs went toward the establishment of a museum on the history of the Frisbee and disc golf.

Source: Adapted from *Los Angeles Times,* August 14, 2002.

Exercise 3

1. *Romeo and Juliet* is my favourite play by William Shakespeare.

2. It is one of the most famous love stories in the world.

3. Many movies use this story as part of their plots.

4. One thing about the story surprised me.

5. Both Romeo and Juliet have other love interests at some point in the play.

6. Romeo has his eyes on another woman before Juliet.

7. And after Tybalt's death, Juliet promises against her will to marry Paris.

8. But before that, Juliet marries Romeo in secret.

9. Friar Lawrence helps the newlyweds with a plan for them to escape without anyone's notice.

10. However, the complicated timing of the plan has tragic results in the lives of Romeo and Juliet.

Exercise 4

1. For a change of pace, I shopped for my Mother's Day gift at an antique show.

2. I found old jewellery in every shade of yellow, red, blue, and green.

3. There were even linens from all the way back to pre-Confederation.

4. One booth sold only drinking glasses with advertising slogans and cartoon characters on them.

5. Another stocked old metal banks with elaborate mechanisms for children's pennies.

6. In the back corner of the show area, I found a light blue pitcher with a dark blue design.

7. My mother used to have one like it in the early days of my childhood.

8. My sisters and I drank punch from it on hot days in the summer.

9. I checked the price on the tag underneath the pitcher's handle.

10. But at a moment like that, money was the least of my concerns.

Exercise 5

1. Over the weekend, I watched a hilarious old movie, *Genevieve,* on late-night television.

2. The whole story takes place in the countryside of England.

3. It is a black-and-white movie from the 1930s or 1940s.

4. The clothes and manners of the characters in *Genevieve* are very proper and old-fashioned.

5. Two young couples enter their cars in a road rally for fun.

6. They participate in the race strictly for adventure.

7. Genevieve is the name of the main couple's car.

8. During the road rally, the two couples' polite manners disappear in the rush for the finish line.

9. Predictably, they begin to fight with each other and try to sabotage each other's cars.

10. But like all good comedies, *Genevieve* and its ending hold a surprise for everyone.

PARAGRAPH EXERCISE

Put parentheses around the prepositional phrases in the following excerpt from the book *Joey Green's Amazing Kitchen Cures: 1,150 Ways to Prevent and Cure Common Ailments with Brand-Name Products*. In this fun but challenging exercise, you'll find prepositional phrases ranging in length from two to eight words. Don't forget to look for one in the title!

HEARSAY ON Q-TIPS

In 1922, Leo Gerstenrang, an immigrant from Warsaw, Poland, who had served in the United States Army during World War I and worked with the fledgling Red Cross Organization, founded the Leo Gerstenrang Infant Novelty Co. with his wife, selling accessories used for baby care. After the birth of the couple's daughter, Gerstenrang noticed that his wife would wrap a wad of cotton around a toothpick for use during their baby's bath and decided to manufacture a ready-to-use cotton swab.

After several years, Gerstenrang developed a machine that would wrap cotton uniformly around each blunt end of a small stick of carefully selected and cured nonsplintering birch wood, package the swabs in a sliding tray-type box, sterilize the box, and seal it with an outer wrapping of glassine—later changed to cellophane. The phrase "untouched by human hands" became widely known in the production of cotton swabs. The Q in the name Q-Tips stands for *quality*, and the word *tips* describes the cotton swab on the end of the stick.

SENTENCE WRITING

Write ten sentences on the topic of your favourite snack—or choose any topic you like. When you go back over your sentences, put parentheses around your prepositional phrases and underline your subjects once and your verbs twice.

_____

_____

_____

_____

_____

_____

_____

_____

Identifying Verb Phrases

Sometimes a verb is one word, but often the whole verb includes more than one word. These are called verb phrases. Look at several of the many forms of the verb _speak_, for example. Most of them are verb phrases, made up of the main verb (_speak_) and one or more helping verbs.

speak	is speaking	had been speaking
speaks	am speaking	will have been speaking
spoke	are speaking	is spoken
will speak	was speaking	was spoken
has spoken	were speaking	will be spoken
have spoken	will be speaking	can speak
had spoken	has been speaking	must speak
will have spoken	have been speaking	should have spoken

Note that words like the following are never verbs even though they may be near a verb or in the middle of a verb phrase:

already	finally	now	probably
also	just	often	really
always	never	only	sometimes
ever	not	possibly	usually

Jason has _never_ spoken to his instructor before. She _always_ talks with other students.

Two verb forms—*speaking* and *to speak*—look like verbs, but neither can ever be the verb of a sentence. No *ing* word by itself can ever be the verb of a sentence; it must be helped by another verb in a verb phrase. (See the discussion of verbal phrases on pp. 81–82.)

Natalie speaking French. (not a sentence because there is no complete verb phrase)

Natalie is speaking French. (a sentence with a verb phrase)

And no verb with *to* in front of it can ever be the verb of a sentence.

Ted to speak in front of groups. (not a sentence because there is no real verb)

Ted hates to speak in front of groups. (a sentence with *hates* as the verb)

These two forms, *speaking* and *to speak*, may be used as subjects, or they may have other uses in the sentence.

Speaking on stage is scary. To speak on stage is scary. Ted had a *speaking* part in that play.

But neither of them alone can ever be the verb of a sentence.

E X E R C I S E S

Underline the subjects once and the verbs or verb phrases twice. It's a good idea to put parentheses around prepositional phrases first. (See pp. 70–72 if you need help in locating prepositional phrases.)

Exercise 1

1. Felix Hoffman, a chemist trying to ease his own father's pain, discovered Aspirin in 1897.

2. Each year, people around the world give themselves 50 billion doses of the popular painkiller.

3. But people in different countries take this medication in different ways.

4. The British like to dissolve Aspirin powder in water.

5. The French have insisted on the benefits of slow-release methods.

6. Italians prefer Aspirin drinks with a little fizz.

7. And North Americans have always chosen to take their Aspirin in pill form.

8. Aspirin continues to surprise researchers with benefits to human health.

9. It has been found to benefit people susceptible to heart attack, colon cancer, and Alzheimer's disease.

10. Where would we be without Aspirin?

Source: Adapted from *Newsweek*, August 18, 1997.

Exercise 2

1. I like to walk around the park with my two little poodles in the early evening.

2. The three of us have enjoyed this ritual for several years now.

3. On Friday evening, a big dog with no owner ran over to us near the duck pond.

4. It was obviously looking for other dogs to play with.

5. Yip and Yap have never barked so loudly before.

6. I had originally named them for their distinct barking noises.

7. But lately I had not heard these short, ear-splitting sounds very often.

8. The big dog was shocked by the fierceness of my little dogs' reply and quickly ran to find other friends.

9. Even I could not believe it.

10. I will never worry about their safety around big dogs again.

Exercise 3

1. Scientists of all kinds have been learning a lot about traffic safety lately.

2. In their studies, they have recently discovered a puzzling truth.

3. Fewer traffic signs and traffic lights affect drivers in a counter-intuitive way.

4. The reason behind the "shared space" theory is relatively easy to explain.

5. Without signs and lights, drivers will regulate their speed and pay closer attention to other vehicles.

6. Those traffic lights and signals apparently give drivers a false sense of security.

7. In locations without signs or signals to provide guidance, drivers must think more about their own safety and drive more cautiously.

8. Many towns in Europe and North America have already taken steps to test the truth of this theory through so-called "passive" road engineering.

9. For example, in some cases, all lights, signs, and barriers have been removed from the roadway.

10. In such situations, all drivers and pedestrians must negotiate with one another to proceed through the town.

Exercise 4

1. I have just discovered "the Farnsworth Chronicles," an Internet site about Philo T. Farnsworth.

2. You may not have heard of Farnsworth.

3. In 1922, at the age of 13, he visualized the concept of transmitting television waves.

4. Others were already working on the idea of sending images through the air.

5. But young Farnsworth solved the problem by looking at rows of ploughed land.

6. In his imaginative mind, images could be broken down into rows.

7. Then each row could be sent through the air and onto a screen.

8. Farnsworth's idea made television a reality.

9. Unfortunately, he has never been fully recognized for this and several other achievements.

10. In 1957, he was featured as a guest on *I've Got a Secret*, a television show with mystery contestants.

Exercise 5

1. Most people do not connect bar codes and cockroaches in their minds.

2. We do expect to see bar codes on almost every product in shopping malls.

3. And we might not be surprised to see a cockroach by a trash can outside one of those malls.

4. But we would definitely look twice at a cockroach with a bar code on its back.

5. In 1999, exterminator Bruce Tennenbaum wanted everyone to watch for his roaches.

6. He had attached bar codes to one hundred cockroaches and released them in Tucson, Arizona, as a public-awareness campaign.

7. People capturing a bar-coded bug could return it for a hundred-dollar prize.

8. One of the roaches was even tagged with a unique bar code and was worth fifty thousand dollars.

9. Many of the tagged roaches were found.

10. But the fifty-thousand-dollar bug was never seen again.

Source: Adapted from *Today's Homeowner,* May 1999.

Recognizing Verbal Phrases

We know (from the discussion on p. 77) that a verb phrase is made up of a main verb and at least one helping verb. But sometimes certain forms of verbs are used not as real verbs but as some other part of a sentence. Verbs put to other uses are called *verbals*.

A verbal can be a subject:

Skiing <u>is</u> my favourite Olympic sport. (*Skiing* is the subject, not the verb. The verb is *is*.)

A verbal can be a descriptive word:

His *bruised* <u>ankle</u> <u>healed</u> very quickly. (*Bruised* describes the subject, ankle. *Healed* is the verb.)

A verbal can be an object:

I <u>like</u> *to read* during the summer. (*To read* is the object. *Like* is the verb.)

Verbals link up with other words to form *verbal phrases*. To see the difference between a real verb phrase and a verbal phrase, look at these two sentences:

I <u>was bowling</u> with my best friends. (*Bowling* is the main verb in a verb phrase. Along with the helping verb *was*, it shows the action of the sentence.)

I <u>enjoyed</u> bowling with my best friends. (Here the real verb is *enjoyed. Bowling* is not the verb; it is part of a verbal phrase—*bowling with my best friends*—which is what I enjoyed.)

THREE KINDS OF VERBALS

1. *ing* verbs used without helping verbs (*running, thinking, baking* ...)

2. verb forms that often end in *ed, en,* or *t* (*tossed, spoken, burnt* ...)

3. verbs that follow *to* ____ (*to walk, to eat, to cause* ...)

Real verbs will never be inside verbal phrases.

Look at the following sentences using the previous examples in verbal phrases:

Running five kilometres a day <u>is</u> great exercise. (real verb = is)

She <u>spent</u> two hours *thinking of a title for her essay.* (real verb = spent)

We <u>had</u> such fun *baking those cherry vanilla cupcakes.* (real verb = had)

Tossed in a salad, artichoke hearts <u>add</u> zesty flavour. (real verb = add)

Sung in Italian, the opera <u>sounds</u> even more beautiful. (real verb = sounds)

The gourmet pizza, *burnt by a careless chef*, <u>shrunk</u> to half its normal size. (real verb = shrunk)

I <u>like</u> *to walk around the zoo by myself.* (real verb = like)

To eat exotic foods <u>takes</u> courage. (real verb = takes)

They actually <u>wanted</u> *to cause an argument.* (real verb = wanted)

EXERCISES

Each of the following sentences contains at least one verbal or verbal phrase. Double underline the real verbs or verb phrases and put brackets around the verbals and verbal phrases. Remember to locate the verbal first (*running, wounded, to sleep ...*) and include any word(s) that go with it (*running a race, wounded in the fight, to sleep all night*). Check the first set before going on to the rest.

Exercise 1

1. Parents who like to go clubbing can now take their children along—well, sort of.

2. On weekend afternoons, nightclubs around the United States childproof their facilities to allow children to dance the day away.

3. An organization called Baby Loves Disco orchestrates these events, offering real drinks for the parents and juice boxes and healthy snacks for the kids.

4. The nightclubs try to keep the club atmosphere realistic for the families while making sure that the volume of the music is not too loud for the children's ears.

5. They keep the music real, too, playing songs by the best-known bands of the 1970s and '80s.

6. Kids up to eight years old have fun dancing, dressing in disco styles, wearing fake tattoos, jumping around, and yelling with other kids and parents.

7. Baby Loves Disco provides special areas for parents to change their children's diapers or to treat themselves to a massage.

8. Baby Loves Disco has its own website, posting videos, news stories, and future events taking place in various cities.

9. To attract parents who don't like disco music, the BLD home page includes links to a kids' version of hip hop—called "Skip Hop"—and jazz for kids.

10. Videos and testimonials on the site show that kids love dancing at night-clubs as much as adults do.

Exercise 2

1. I have learned how to manage my leisure time.

2. I like to go to the movies on Friday nights.

3. Watching a good film takes me away from the stress of my job.

4. I especially enjoy eating buttery popcorn and drinking a cold pop.

5. It is the perfect way for me to begin the weekend.

6. I get to escape from deadlines and the pressure to succeed.

7. I indulge myself and try to give myself a break.

8. All day Saturday I enjoy lounging around the house in my weekend clothes.

9. I do a little gardening and try to relax my mind.

10. By Sunday evening, after resting for two days, I am ready to start my busy week all over again.

Exercise 3

1. Many people dislike speaking in front of strangers.

2. In fact, there is an almost universal fear of giving speeches.

3. Feeling insecure and exposed, people get dry mouths and sweaty hands.

4. Note cards become useless, rearranging themselves in the worst possible order.

5. To combat this problem, people try to memorize a speech, only to forget the whole thing.

6. Or the microphone decides to quit at the punch line of their best joke.

7. Embarrassed and humiliated, they struggle to regain their composure.

8. Then the audience usually begins to sympathize with and encourage the speaker.

9. Finally used to the spotlight, the speaker relaxes and finds the courage to finish.

10. No one expects giving a speech to get any easier.

Exercise 4

1. Canadian astronaut Roberta Bondar blasted off into space to gather data on how living things function in space.

2. Bondar was aboard the space shuttle *Discovery* in January 1992, setting a milestone as Canada's first woman in space.

3. After graduating from high school, Bondar assertively pursued her career, obtaining five university degrees in science and medicine.

4. She applied to the new Canadian Space Agency to become a candidate for astronaut.

5. Bondar's wait to go into space lasted nine years.

6. Leaving the launch pad on the *Discovery*, Bondar thrust her fists in the air, shouting "Yes, yes, yes!"

7. Bondar and her six colleagues spent eight days in space, investigating the effects of weightlessness on the human body.

8. Today, Bondar does research at the University of Western Ontario, travelling around the country to encourage young people in the sciences.

9. Bondar was appointed chair of the Science Advisory Board, a board set up to advise the federal health minister.

10. She believes that protecting the environment is one of the most important responsibilities we have today.

Source: Adapted from Gale Infobase, August 1997.

Exercise 5

1. E-mail has begun to be the most popular form of written communication.

2. In the beginning, people searched for a way to show emotion.

3. It was time to invent a new type of punctuation, now known as "emoticons."

4. Scott Fahlman proposed two of the first emoticons in the early 1980s to show when something was meant to be funny or not.

5. Called the "smiley" and the "frown," these combinations of colon, hyphen, and parentheses look like :-) and :-(

6. In an effort to document computer history, Mike Jones, Jeff Baird, and others worked hard to retrace the steps of the first uses of the smiley and the frown.

7. They found them used by Scott Fahlman in a posting to a computer bulletin board in 1982.

8. These and other emoticons have continued to help people express themselves online.

9. So when you finish typing your next joke in an e-mail, don't forget to add a :-)

10. Frowning :-(is seen by some as questionable net etiquette and is consequently not as common.

Source: Adapted from http://www.cs.cmu.edu/~sef/sefSmiley.htm.

PROOFREADING EXERCISE

Double underline the real verbs or verb phrases and put brackets around the verbals and verbal phrases in the following paragraph from the book *Saloons of the Old West* by Richard Erdoes.

In the opinion of most westerners "barkeeps were ... the hardest worked folks in camp.... " One of these burdens was to act as a human fire alarm. Western saloons never closed. Therefore, to sound the alarm, the saloon owner would dash into the street, running up and down hollering and emptying his six-shooter at the moon. The commotion would send the volunteer firemen pouring into the street in their long johns to put out the fire. Having done so, all and sundry naturally assembled in the saloon to mull over the event while imbibing a tumbler of gut-warming red-eye.

SENTENCE WRITING

Write ten sentences that contain verbal phrases. Use the ten verbals listed here to begin your verbal phrases: *speaking, typing, driving, reading, to eat, to go, to chat, to cook, impressed, taken*. There are sample sentences listed in the answers at the back of the book. But first, try to write your own so that you can compare.

_____

_____

_____

_____

_____

_____

_____

_____

_____

_____

Using Standard English Verbs

The next two discussions are for those who need practice in using Standard English verbs. Many of us grew up doing more speaking than writing. But in college and university, and in the business and professional world, the use of Standard Written English is essential.

The following charts show the forms of four verbs as they are used in Standard Written English. These forms might differ from the way you use these verbs when you speak. Most verbs in English are called regular verbs because they end according to a predictable pattern. The first text box on the next page shows the endings of the regular verb *talk*. The other three verbs charted here (*have, be*, and *do*) are irregular and are important because they are used not only as main verbs but also as helping verbs in verb phrases.

Don't go on to the exercises until you have memorized the forms of these Standard English verbs.

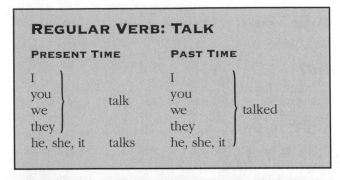

REGULAR VERB: TALK

PRESENT TIME		**PAST TIME**	
I		I	
you	talk	you	
we		we	talked
they		they	
he, she, it	talks	he, she, it	

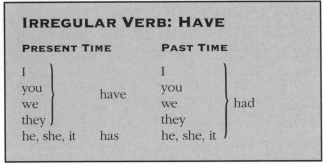

IRREGULAR VERB: HAVE

PRESENT TIME		**PAST TIME**	
I		I	
you	have	you	
we		we	had
they		they	
he, she, it	has	he, she, it	

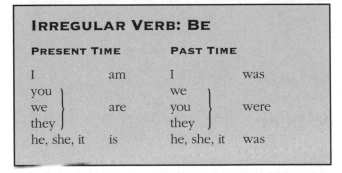

IRREGULAR VERB: BE

PRESENT TIME		**PAST TIME**	
I	am	I	was
you		we	
we	are	you	were
they		they	
he, she, it	is	he, she, it	was

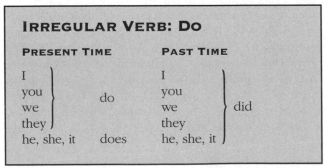

IRREGULAR VERB: DO

PRESENT TIME		**PAST TIME**	
I		I	
you	do	you	
we		we	did
they		they	
he, she, it	does	he, she, it	

Sometimes you may have difficulty with the correct endings of verbs because you don't hear the words correctly. Note carefully the *s* sound and the *ed* sound at the end of words. Occasionally the *ed* is not clearly pronounced, as in *They tried to help*, but most of the time you can hear it if you listen.

Read the following sentences aloud, making sure that you say every sound.

1. He seems satisfied with his new job.

2. She likes saving money for the future.

3. It takes strength of character to control spending.

4. Todd makes salad for every potluck he attends.

5. I used to know all their names.

6. They supposed that they were right.

7. He recognized the suspect and excused himself from the jury.

8. Susan sponsored Reina in the school's charity event.

Now read some other sentences aloud from this text, making sure that you pronounce all the *s*'s and *ed*'s. Reading aloud and listening to others will help you use the correct verb endings automatically.

E X E R C I S E S

In these pairs of sentences, use the present form of the verb in the first sentence and the past form in the second. All the verbs follow the pattern of the regular verb *talk* except the irregular verbs *have*, *be*, and *do*. Refer to the tables if you're not sure which form to use. Correct your answers for each exercise before going to the next.

Exercise 1

 1. (walk) I often _____ my dog to the store. I _____ him to the store yesterday.

 2. (be) She _____ glad to be graduating. She _____ unsure about her future just two years ago.

 3. (have) They _____ a minivan now. They _____ a station wagon before.

4. (do)   I _____ my homework in the afternoons. I _____ my homework in the evenings in high school.

5. (need)   He _____ a new pair of skis. He _____ new boots last season.

6. (be)   Now I _____ a part-time employee. I _____ a full-time employee last year.

7. (have)   I bought an antique ring; it _____ a large green stone in its setting. It _____ another stone in it before, but it was chipped.

8. (be)   They _____ the hosts of the family reunion this year. They _____ not the hosts of last year's reunion.

9. (do)   He _____ the dishes when I cook. He _____ the dishes yesterday.

10. (work)   She _____ several hours of overtime a week. She _____ twelve hours of overtime last week.

Exercise 2

1. (be)   She _____ an employee now. She _____ an intern last year.

2. (do)   They _____ their best work at home. They _____ an especially good job on their homework last night.

3. (have)   I _____ two weeks left to prepare for my trip. I originally _____ six weeks, but I procrastinated.

4. (ask)   He never _____ his friends for help anymore. He _____ them for help before without results.

5. (have)   I always _____ a cold at this time of year. I _____ one last year right on schedule.

6. (learn)   We _____ a new technique each day in my ceramics class. Yesterday we _____ how to throw pots on a wheel.

7. (be)   Most of us _____ beginners. We _____ not particularly interested in art before we took this class, but now we love it.

8. (do)   He _____ well on all of his tests. He _____ very well on the final exam.

9. (play)   She _____ the guitar now. She _____ the piano as her first instrument.

10. (be)   I _____ a collector by nature. However, last month I _____ too busy to go shopping.

Exercise 3

Circle the correct Standard English verb forms.

1. I (start, started) a new volunteer job last month, and so far I really (like, likes) it.

2. The organization (offer, offers) relief boxes to victims of crime or natural disasters around the world.

3. The other volunteers (is, are) all really nice, so we (has, have) a good work environment.

4. Yesterday, we (finish, finished) a project that (need, needed) lots of boxes.

5. The supervisors who (run, runs) the organization always (do, does) their best to explain the victims' situations to us.

6. And they (advise, advises) us to make sure that the boxes (comfort, comforts) the victims as much as possible.

7. I can tell that the supervisors (enjoy, enjoys) their work; they (is, are) always happy to see the relief on the victims' faces.

8. My fellow volunteers and I (complete, completed) our latest project in just one week even though the supervisor (expect, expected) it to take us two weeks.

9. We (has, have) our supervisors to thank for a smooth-running organization.

10. And I (thank, thanks) my coworkers for being my friends.

Exercise 4

1. My sister and I (do, does) our homework together every night so that we (don't, doesn't) fall behind.

2. I (is, am) better in math, and my sister Aileen (is, am) better in English.

3. When I (need, needs) help with grammar, Aileen (explain, explains) the rule to me.

4. And if she gets stuck on a math problem, I (help, helps) her understand it; then she (do, does) it herself.

5. This system (work, works) very well for us, and I (hope, hopes) we will always use it.

6. Before we (do, did) it this way, I (drop, dropped) an English class.

7. It (was, were) too hard for me, but now I (do, does) as well as the other students.

8. Aileen and I both (work, works) hard, and we (check, checks) each other's progress.

9. When I (learn, learns) more English skills and Aileen (learn, learns) more math skills, we will be equal.

10. Our parents (expect, expects) a lot from both of us, and we (don't, doesn't) want to let them down.

Exercise 5

Correct any of following sentences that do not use Standard English verb forms.

1. Last year all the students in our high school drama class travels to London, England.

2. Twenty of us and one teacher boarded the plane.

3. We was all very excited about the trip.

4. Before the trip, we learn to read the London subway map.

5. We discover that the people in London call the subway "the tube."

6. Once we was there, we understood why.

7. The underground walls is round just like a tube.

8. We liked the Tower of London and Big Ben and the boats on the Thames.

9. We even walk right past the crown jewels.

10. They were close enough to touch.

PROOFREADING EXERCISE

Correct any sentences in the following paragraph that do not use Standard English verb forms.

Every day as we drive through our neighbourhoods on the way to school or to work, we see things that needs to be fixed. Many of them cause us only a little bit of trouble, so we forget them until we face them again. Every morning, I has to deal with a truck that someone park right at the corner of my street. It block my view as I try to turn onto the main avenue. I need to move out past the truck into the oncoming lane of traffic just to make my left turn. One day last week, I turn too soon, and a car almost hit me. This truck don't need to be parked in such a dangerous place.

SENTENCE WRITING

Write ten sentences about a problem in your neighbourhood. Check your sentences to be sure that they use Standard English verb forms. Exchange papers with another student if possible.

_____

_____

_____

_____

_____

_____

_____

_____

_____

Using Regular and Irregular Verbs

All regular verbs end the same way in the past form and when used with helping verbs. Here is a table showing all the forms of some regular verbs and the various helping verbs they are used with.

REGULAR VERBS				
BASE FORM	**PRESENT**	**PAST**	**PAST PARTICIPLE**	***ING* FORM**
(Use after can, may, shall, will, could, might, should, would, must, do, does, did.*)*			*(Use after* have, has, had. *Some can be used after forms of* be.*)*	*(Use after forms of* be.*)*
ask	ask*(s)*	asked	asked	asking
bake	bake*(s)*	baked	baked	baking
count	count*(s)*	counted	counted	counting
dance	dance*(s)*	danced	danced	dancing
decide	decide*(s)*	decided	decided	deciding
enjoy	enjoy*(s)*	enjoyed	enjoyed	enjoying
finish	finish*(es)*	finished	finished	finishing
happen	happen*(s)*	happened	happened	happening
learn	learn*(s)*	learned	learned	learning
like	like*(s)*	liked	liked	liking
look	look*(s)*	looked	looked	looking
mend	mend*(s)*	mended	mended	mending
need	need*(s)*	needed	needed	needing
open	open*(s)*	opened	opened	opening
start	start*(s)*	started	started	starting
suppose	suppose*(s)*	supposed	supposed	supposing
tap	tap*(s)*	tapped	tapped	tapping
walk	walk*(s)*	walked	walked	walking
want	want*(s)*	wanted	wanted	wanting

NOTE: When there are several helping verbs, the last one determines which form of the main verb should be used: they *should* finish soon; they should *have* finished an hour ago.

When do you write *ask*, *finish*, *suppose*, *use*? And when do you write *asked*, *finished*, *supposed*, *used*? Here are some rules that will help you decide.

Write *ask*, *finish*, *suppose*, *use* (or their *s* forms) when writing about the present time, repeated actions, or facts:

He *asks* questions whenever he is confused.

They always *finish* their projects on time.

I *suppose* you want me to help you move.

Birds *use* leaves, twigs, and feathers to build their nests.

Write *asked*, *finished*, *supposed*, *used*

1. When writing about the past:

He *asked* the teacher for another explanation.

She *finished* her internship last year.

They *supposed* that there were others bidding on that house.

I *used* to study piano.

2. When some form of *have* comes before the word:

The teacher has *asked* us that question before.

She will have *finished* all of her exams by the end of May.

I had *supposed* too much without any proof.

We have *used* many models in my drawing class this year.

All the verbs in the chart on page 84 are regular. That is, they're all formed in the same way—with an *ed* ending on the past form and on the past participle. But many verbs are irregular. Their past and past participle forms change spelling instead of just having an *ed* added. Here's a chart of some irregular verbs. Notice that the base, present, and *ing* forms end the same as regular verbs. Refer to this list when you aren't sure which verb form to use. Memorize all the forms you don't know.

IRREGULAR VERBS

BASE FORM	PRESENT	PAST	PAST PARTICIPLE	*ING* FORM
(Use after can, may, shall, will, could, might, should, would, must, do, does, did.*)*			*(Use after* have, has, had. *Some can be used after forms of* be.*)*	*(Use after forms of* be.*)*
be	am, is, are	was, were	been	being
become	become*(s)*	became	become	becoming
begin	begin*(s)*	began	begun	beginning
break	break*(s)*	broke	broken	breaking
bring	bring*(s)*	brought	brought	bringing
build	build*(s)*	built	built	building
buy	buy*(s)*	bought	bought	buying
catch	catch*(es)*	caught	caught	catching
choose	choose*(s)*	chose	chosen	choosing
come	come*(s)*	came	come	coming
do	do*(es)*	did	done	doing
draw	draw*(s)*	drew	drawn	drawing
drink	drink*(s)*	drank	drunk	drinking
drive	drive*(s)*	drove	driven	driving
eat	eat*(s)*	ate	eaten	eating
fall	fall*(s)*	fell	fallen	falling
feel	feel*(s)*	felt	felt	feeling
fight	fight*(s)*	fought	fought	fighting
find	find*(s)*	found	found	finding
forget	forget*(s)*	forgot	forgotten	forgetting
forgive	forgive*(s)*	forgave	forgiven	forgiving
freeze	freeze*(s)*	froze	frozen	freezing
get	get*(s)*	got	got *or* gotten	getting
give	give*(s)*	gave	given	giving
go	go*(es)*	went	gone	going
grow	grow*(s)*	grew	grown	growing
hang	hang*(s)*	hung	hung	hanging
hang (put to death)	hang*(s)*	hanged	hanged	hanging
have	have *or* has	had	had	having
hear	hear*(s)*	heard	heard	hearing
hold	hold*(s)*	held	held	holding
keep	keep*(s)*	kept	kept	keeping

BASE FORM	PRESENT	PAST	PAST PARTICIPLE	*ING* FORM
know	know*(s)*	knew	known	knowing
lay (to put)	lay*(s)*	laid	laid	laying
lead ("bead")	lead*(s)*	led	led	leading
leave	leave*(s)*	left	left	leaving
lie (to rest)	lie*(s)*	lay	lain	lying
lose	lose*(s)*	lost	lost	losing
make	make*(s)*	made	made	making
meet	meet*(s)*	met	met	meeting
pay	pay*(s)*	paid	paid	paying
read ("reed")	read*(s)*	read ("red")	read ("red")	reading
ride	ride*(s)*	rode	ridden	riding
ring	ring*(s)*	rang	rung	ringing
rise	rise*(s)*	rose	risen	rising
run	run*(s)*	ran	run	running
say	say*(s)*	said	said	saying
see	see*(s)*	saw	seen	seeing
sell	sell*(s)*	sold	sold	selling
shake	shake*(s)*	shook	shaken	shaking
shine (give light)	shine*(s)*	shone	shone	shining
shine (polish)	shine*(s)*	shined	shined	shining
sing	sing*(s)*	sang	sung	singing
sleep	sleep*(s)*	slept	slept	sleeping
speak	speak*(s)*	spoke	spoken	speaking
spend	spend*(s)*	spent	spent	spending
stand	stand*(s)*	stood	stood	standing
steal	steal*(s)*	stole	stolen	stealing
strike	strike*(s)*	struck	struck	striking
swim	swim*(s)*	swam	swum	swimming
swing	swing*(s)*	swung	swung	swinging
take	take*(s)*	took	taken	taking
teach	teach*(es)*	taught	taught	teaching
tear ("air")	tear*(s)*	tore	torn	tearing
tell	tell*(s)*	told	told	telling
think	think*(s)*	thought	thought	thinking
throw	throw*(s)*	threw	thrown	throwing
wear	wear*(s)*	wore	worn	wearing
win	win*(s)*	won	won	winning
write	write*(s)*	wrote	written	writing

Sometimes verbs from the past participle column are used after a form of the verb *be* (or verbs that take the place of *be* like *appear, seem, look, feel, get, act, become*) to describe the subject or to say something in a passive, rather than active, way.

She is contented.

You appear pleased. (You are pleased.)

He seems delighted. (He is delighted.)

She looked surprised. (She was surprised.)

I feel shaken. (I am shaken.)

They get bored easily. (They are bored easily.)

You acted concerned. (You were concerned.)

He was thrown out of the game. (Active: *The referee threw him out of the game.*)

They were disappointed by the news. (Active: *The news disappointed them.*)

Often these verb forms become words that describe the subject; other times they still act as part of the verb of the sentence. What you call them doesn't matter. The only important thing is to be sure you use the correct form from the past participle column.

E X E R C I S E S

Write the correct form of the verb. Refer to the tables and explanations on the preceding pages if you aren't sure which form to use after a certain helping verb. Check your answers after each exercise.

Exercise 1

1. (look)   Once again, I have _____ everywhere for my keys.

2. (look)   I could _____ in a few more places, but I'm late.

3. (look)   I feel so foolish while I am _____ for them.

4. (look)   I know that if I _____ too hard I won't find them.

5. (look)   Once I _____ for them for over two hours.

6. (look)   I can _____ right past them if I am too frantic.

7. (look)   I have _____ in places where they would never be.

8. (look)   My daughter once caught me while I was _____ for them in the refrigerator.

9. (look)   In fact, my family now _____ at me with scorn whenever I ask, "Has anybody seen my keys?"

10. (look) From now on I will _____ in the obvious places first and keep my problem to myself.

Exercise 2

1. (drive) I always _____ my sister to school; in fact, I have _____ her to school for a whole year now.

2. (think) The other day, I was _____ of new ways to get her there in the morning, but she _____ that they were all bad ideas.

3. (take) She could _____ a school bus that stops nearby; instead she _____ me for granted.

4. (tell) It all started when she _____ our mother that some of the other children were _____ her to stay out of their seats.

5. (write) I _____ a note to the bus driver to see if she could help ease my sister's mind, but so far she hasn't _____ back.

6. (know) When I was my sister's age, I _____ some tough kids at school, so I _____ how she must feel.

7. (teach) But experiences like that _____ us how to get along with everyone; they sure _____ me.

8. (tear) Now I am _____ between wanting to help her avoid the tough kids and _____ my hair out from having to take her to school every day.

9. (ride) We have _____ together for so long that I might miss her if I _____ alone.

10. (make) I have _____ up my mind. I will _____ the best of it while she still needs me. What else are big sisters for?

Exercise 3

1. (be, hear)   We _____ surprised when we _____ Uncle Wolf's message on our answering machine yesterday.

2. (see, begin)   We hadn't _____ him in over a year, and we had _____ to wonder if he would ever visit us again.

3. (fly, eat)   He had _____ in from Vancouver earlier in the day but hadn't _____ dinner yet.

4. (get, do)   We _____ back to him at his hotel and _____ our best to convince him to join us for dinner.

5. (take, eat)   It did not _____ much to convince him, and soon we were _____ roast beef sandwiches at our favourite deli.

6. (write, come, lose)   He said that he had _____ to tell us that he was _____ , and he asked if we had _____ the letter.

7. (swear, feel)   We _____ that we never received it, and he _____ better.

8. (buy, pay)   Just to make sure there were no hard feelings, we _____ his sandwich, and he _____ the tip.

9. (get, think)   It was _____ late, so we _____ that he should go back to his hotel to get some sleep.

10. (see, tell, lie)   When we _____ Wolf the next day, he _____ us that he was so tired the night before that as soon as he _____ down on the hotel pillow, he fell asleep.

Exercise 4

1. (use, put)   Many people _____ a direct deposit system that _____ their salary money directly into their bank accounts.

2. (do, do)   With such a system, the employer _____ not have to issue paycheques, and employees _____ not have to cash or deposit them.

3. (transfer, spend)   The employer's computer just _____ the money to the bank's computer, and the employee can _____ it as usual after that.

4. (be, like, choose)   Direct deposit _____ almost always optional, but so many people _____ the system that most people _____ it.

5. (do, want)   My roommate _____ not trust such systems; he _____ to have complete control over his cash.

6. (trust, be)   He barely even _____ banks to keep his money safe for him, so he _____ definitely suspicious of direct deposit.

7. (imagine, make)   I can _____ him as a pioneer in an old Western movie sleeping on a mattress stuffed with all of the money he has ever _____ .

8. (talk, ask, worry)   I was _____ to my roommate about money the other day, and I _____ him why he always _____ about it so much.

9. (look, say, live, understand)   He just _____ at me and _____ , "If you had ever _____ without money, you would _____ ."

10. (wonder, be)   I _____ about my roommate's past experiences and hope that he _____ never without money again.

Exercise 5

1. (lay, lie, feel)   I _____ my towel down on the hot cement next to the pool and was _____ facedown on the towel when I _____ a bee land on the back of my ankle.

2. (know, be)   I _____ that special sensation of a bee's legs on my skin because I have _____ stung before.

3. (break, have)   Last time, I _____ out in hives and _____ to go to the doctor to get an injection of antihistamine.

4. (become, think)   My eyes _____ swollen, and I _____ that I was going to die.

5. (be)   I _____ not going to let that happen again.

6. (read, frighten)   I had _____ that bees sting only when they're _____ .

7. (keep, shake)   So this time I _____ calm and gently _____ my ankle to shoo away the bee without angering it.

8. (work, rise)   My plan _____ , and the bee _____ in the air to find a new spot to land.

9. (leave, find)   I _____ my towel by the pool, and I didn't _____ it in the lost-and-found the next day.

10. (lose, sting)   Of course, I would rather _____ a towel than be _____ by a bee again.

Sentence Essentials
Progress Test

Test yourself on how much you have learned about subjects and verbs in sentences. Study the following sentences and locate their subjects and verbs. Identify the subject word (or words) with a single underline. Identify the verb word (or words) with a double underline. Check your answers in the answer key before taking the Post-Test.

1. There are several personality types in my family.

2. My sister Linda and one of her roommates simply agree to disagree.

3. My brother Homer studies every night, works on the weekend, and plays on the school's varsity hockey team.

4. My uncle George and his wife spend every evening silently watching TV.

5. My mother and her favourite niece go shopping together every Friday and often invite me.

6. Herman, my brother's son, has never shared his feelings.

7. On the other hand, his sister Lydia is always finding problems in her life and sharing them with the rest of us.

8. Father laughs with my mom but takes us children far too seriously.

9. He once told the three of us never to get married or join the military.

10. Years later we learned about his brother's death in WWII and his first wife's death in a serious auto accident.

Sentence Essentials
Post-Test

Study the following sentences and locate their subjects and verbs. Identify the subject word (or words) with a single underline. Identify the verb word (or words) with a double underline. Check your answers in the answer key.

1. There have been five children born in our family in the past year.

2. My brother George's wife Martha just welcomed their third girl.

3. George, in particular, would have enjoyed having a son to keep him company in this all-woman home.

4. Little Kaitlyn Lori arrived last Thursday, went home the following day, and already sleeps several hours at a time.

5. Kaitlyn's sisters Marianne and Susanne greeted their little sister with gentle hugs and kisses and made Welcome Home posters for her.

6. The rest of the family's new babies this year have been boys.

7. Martin, my sister's newest child, was born in May.

8. To everyone's surprise, my twin sister successfully carried triplets to full term.

9. Her sons' names, in order of their birth two months ago, are William, Benjamin, and Jason.

10. The three of them already sleep through the night, play with soft toys, and recognize family members' faces.

Building Effective Sentences

Effective Sentences Pre-Test

The next section of the book explores sentence varieties and structural issues such as sentence fragments and run-on sentences. Make any necessary corrections to eliminate the fragments and run-ons lurking in the following word groups. (If the group is correct, write OK.)

1. We hope that you will be able to join us for lunch on Monday, we will meet in Dining Room B at 12:30.

2. The menu includes vegetarian stir fry and other healthy options. So that you don't need to feel guilty about what you eat.

3. During the meal, employees will have many opportunities to meet others who work here. But in different departments.

4. Some employees remember a labour dispute that ended in a strike three years ago, regrettably, some of the wounds from that battle have yet to heal.

5. However, some strikers reported that walking a picket line gave them the unexpected opportunity to become far better acquainted with their coworkers.

6. In many employment situations, strikes are considered part of the working conditions unionized employees save money from every paycheque for their personal strike fund.

7. So-called white collar workers are uneasy about going on strike. Although sometimes it may be necessary in order to force honest nego-tiation from both sides.

8. Non-union personnel often find themselves caught in the middle. When they have to cross a legal picket line that is made up of close friends and co-workers.

9. Although strikes are rarely beneficial to either side. In some workplaces, the threat of a work stoppage encourages more open contract negotia-tions.

10. Legislation designates some workers "essential" even though they belong to a union, these individuals are not allowed to participate in a withdrawal of services.

Introduction to Sentence Structure

Sentence structure refers to the way sentences are built using words, phrases, and clauses.

Phrases are word groups without subjects and verbs.
Clauses are word groups with subjects and verbs.

A *dependent clause* has a subject and a verb but an incomplete idea.

An *independent clause* has a subject and a verb and conveys a complete idea.

Clauses are the most important because they make statements—they tell who did what (or what something is) in a sentence.

Look at the following sentence, for example:

We bought oranges at the farmer's market on Queen Street.

It contains ten words, each playing its own part in the meaning of the sentence. But which of the words together tell who did what? *We bought oranges* is correct. That word group is a clause. Notice that *at the farmer's market* and *on Queen Street* also link up as word groups but don't have somebody (subject) doing something (verb). Instead, they are phrases to clarify *where* we bought the oranges.

Importantly, you could leave out one or both of the phrases and still have a sentence—*We bought oranges*. However, you cannot leave the clause out. Then you would have just *At the farmer's market on Queen Street*.

IMPORTANT!

Every sentence must contain at least one independent clause.

Learning about the structure of sentences helps you control your own. Once you know more about sentence structure, you can understand writing errors and learn how to correct them.

Among the most common errors in writing are fragments and run-ons.

Here are some fragments:

Wandering around the mall all afternoon.

Because I tried to do too many things at once.

By interviewing the applicants in groups.

They don't make complete statements—not one has a clause that can stand by itself. Who was *wandering*? What happened *because you tried to do too many things at once*? What was the result of *interviewing the applicants in groups*? These incomplete sentence structures fail to communicate a complete thought.

In contrast, here are some run-ons:

Computer prices are dropping they're still beyond my budget.

The forecast calls for rain I'll wait to wash my car.

A truck parked in front of my driveway I couldn't get to school.

Unlike fragments, run-ons make complete statements, but the trouble is they make *two* complete statements; the first *runs on* to the second without correct punctuation. The reader has to go back to see where there should have been a break.

> Fragments don't include enough information, and run-ons include too much.

Fragments and run-ons confuse the reader. Not until you get rid of them will your writing be clearer and easier to read. There is no quick, effortless way to learn to avoid errors in sentence structure. First you need to understand how clear sentences are built. Then you will be able to avoid these common errors in your own writing.

Identifying Clauses

Many sentences you write contain more than one clause. Conveying your ideas clearly often means building sentences containing two or more word groups with separate subjects and verbs.

Every clause contains a subject and a verb. However, you'll need to know the difference between the two kinds of clauses: independent and dependent. A dependent clause alone should not be punctuated as a sentence.

Here's why: An independent clause has a subject and a verb and expresses a complete idea. A dependent clause also has a subject and a verb, but its idea is incomplete because it begins with a dependent word (or words) such as

after	since	where
although	so that	whereas
as	than	wherever
as if	that	whether
because	though	which
before	unless	whichever
even if	until	while
even though	what	who
ever since	whatever	whom
how	when	whose
if	whenever	why

Whenever a clause begins with one of these dependent words, it is a dependent clause (unless it's a question, which would end with a question mark). If we take an independent clause such as

We ate dinner together.

and put one of the dependent words in front of it, it becomes a dependent clause and can no longer stand alone:

After we ate dinner together ...

Although we ate dinner together ...

As we ate dinner together ...

Before we ate dinner together ...

Since we ate dinner together ...

That we ate dinner together ...

When we ate dinner together ...

While we ate dinner together ...

With the added dependent words, these do not make complete statements. They leave the reader expecting something more. Therefore, these clauses can no longer stand alone. Each would depend on another clause—an independent clause—to make a sentence. The dependent clauses in the sentences below are underlined with a broken line.

After we ate dinner together, we went to the evening seminar.

We went to the evening seminar *after* we ate dinner together.

The speaker didn't know *that* we ate dinner together.

While we ate dinner together, the restaurant became crowded.

PUNCTUATION TIP:

Always place a comma after an opening dependent clause.
Example:

When he moved, his leg muscles ached.

(The comma prevents the reader from misreading the first clause as *When he moved his leg muscles.*)

Note that sometimes the dependent word is the subject of the dependent clause:

Theirs is the house that was remodelled last month.

The children understood what was happening.

Sometimes the dependent clause is in the middle of the independent clause:

The house that was remodelled last month is theirs.

The events that followed were confusing.

And sometimes the dependent clause is the subject of the entire sentence:

> What you do also affects me.

> Whichever they choose will be best for them.

> How it looks doesn't mean anything.

Also note that sometimes the *that* of a dependent clause is omitted.

> I know *that* you can tell the difference between red and green.

> I know you can tell the difference between red and green.

> Did everyone get the classes *that* they wanted?

> Did everyone get the classes they wanted?

The word *that* doesn't always introduce a dependent clause. It may be a pronoun and serve as the subject of the sentence.

> That was a big mistake.

> That is my book.

That can also be a descriptive word.

> That movie makes me cry every time.

> I will take him to that restaurant tomorrow.

E X E R C I S E S

Underline the subjects once and the verbs twice in both the independent and the dependent clauses. Then put a broken line under any dependent clauses. Some sentences may have no dependent clauses, and others may have more than one.

Exercise 1

> **1.** I am not a big talker in school.

> **2.** Whenever a teacher asks me a question in class, I get nervous.

3. When I know the answer, I usually find the courage to speak.

4. If I don't know the answer, I look up at the ceiling as if I am thinking about it.

5. Usually, the teacher calls on someone else before I finish "thinking."

6. Obviously, when I take a public speaking class, I must talk sometimes.

7. In my last public speaking class, the assignment was to give a speech that demonstrated some sort of process.

8. The speech that I gave explained how crêpes suzettes are made.

9. Since I work at a French restaurant, I borrowed a crêpe pan to use in my demonstration.

10. The crêpes cooked quickly, and the teacher and students were so busy eating them that I didn't have to say much at all.

Exercise 2

1. Many of us remember when microwave ovens were first sold to the public.

2. People worried about whether they were safe or not.

3. Before we had the microwave oven, we cooked all of our food over direct heat.

4. At first, it was strange that only the food heated up in a microwave.

5. And microwave ovens cooked food so much faster than ordinary ovens did.

6. We had to get used to the possibilities that the microwave offered.

7. Since they are fast and don't heat up themselves, microwave ovens work well in offices, in restaurants, and on school campuses.

8. People who are on a budget can bring a lunch from home and heat it up at work.

9. Now that the microwave oven is here, we can even make popcorn without a pan.

10. As each new technology arrives, we wonder how we ever lived without it.

Exercise 3

1. When Canadians gather at sporting events, everyone sings "O Canada" while the Canadian flag proudly flies overhead.

2. "O Canada" is the song that Canada has chosen as its national anthem.

3. After Calixa Lavallée composed the music, the song was first performed at a banquet for skaters in Quebec City on June 24, 1880.

4. Adolphe-Basile Routhier wrote the French version, which he called "Chant national."

5. It was translated into English by Stanley Weir, who was a schoolteacher in Toronto.

6. Though French Canadians sang the anthem widely, English Canadians did not use it until the end of the 19th century.

7. When it gathered in 1967, the Parliament approved "O Canada" as the Canadian national anthem.

8. The words, which were altered somewhat after parliamentary debate, became official through the National Anthem Act, which was passed on June 27, 1980.

9. Canada's flag was hotly debated from Confederation to 1965, when the flag with the single red maple leaf became official.

10. Before that time, the Red Ensign was used for Canadian ceremonies, whether Canadian nationalists liked it or not.

Source: Adapted from *The Canadian Encyclopedia,* s.v. "O Canada."

Exercise 4

1. Many of us wouldn't mind shedding a few pounds from time to time.

2. There are a number of dieting problems that can leave you back at square one or worse.

3. For example, when you decide to lose weight, you need to be well prepared.

4. As part of your preparation, you should consider your long- and short-term goals before you commit to a specific action.

5. When some individuals begin a program, they pick the wrong course of action or have unrealistic expectations.

6. It's easy to become disappointed and frustrated if those expectations aren't met.

7. Skipping meals and not eating for long periods of time are common mistakes that you need to avoid.

8. When you go off your diet, the body's higher resting metabolic rate may drop.

9. Then your body will not be able to burn calories as quickly as it did before.

10. Since so many commercials, advertisements, and articles promise fast and easy ways to lose pounds, who knows which to believe?

Source: Adapted from Joanna Lavoie, "5 Weight-Loss Mistakes," CanadianLiving.com. Reprinted with permission from the author.

Exercise 5

1. Tina, my twin sister, got a job that requires late-night hours.

2. The hours that I like the best are between six and eleven in the morning.

3. Now Tina sleeps until noon because she works all night.

4. When she comes home from work, our whole family is asleep.

5. Since Tina works all night and sleeps all day, I rarely see her.

6. Our dad thinks that Tina works too hard.

7. Our mom believes that Tina's new hours are a good challenge for her.

8. Yesterday, Tina's boss asked me if I wanted a job like Tina's.

9. I am not sure when I will find the right job for me.

10. Whenever I do find a good job, it will be during the day.

PROOFREADING EXERCISE

Underline the subjects once, the verbs twice, and put a broken line under the dependent clauses in these paragraphs from *The Moon* by Isaac Asimov.

We can think about an eclipse of the Sun in another way. Since sunlight cannot pass through the Moon, the Moon casts a shadow. The shadow is cone-shaped. It usually does not touch the Earth. But sometimes it moves across the Earth. When that happens, there is an eclipse. Inside the small place where the shadow touches, people can see a total eclipse. There is darkness. In places that are near the shadow, people can see only a partial eclipse. Farther away from the shadow, people can see no eclipse at all.

The Moon's shadow makes a circle when it touches the Earth. The circle moves as the Moon does. So an eclipse of the Sun can be seen in one place for only a few minutes.

SENTENCE WRITING

Write ten sentences about your morning routine (getting up, getting ready for school or work, eating breakfast, etc.). Try to write sentences that contain both independent and dependent clauses. Then underline your subjects once and your verbs twice, and put a broken line under your dependent clauses.

_____

_____

_____

_____

_____

_____

_____

_____

_____

_____

Correcting Fragments

Groups of words that fail to contain the three essential components of a sentence—subject, verb, complete thought—are incomplete pieces or sentence fragments. Here are a few examples:

Just ran around hugging everyone in sight. (no subject)

Paul and his sister with the twins. (no verb)

Nothing to do but wait. (no subject and no verb)

After Tang went to the market. (dependent clause)

In general, sentence fragments fall into one of two categories. *Phrase fragments* are groups of words that fail to contain a complete subject, a complete verb, or either. Such word groups qualify as fragments because they are missing one or more of the three essential sentence components.

Dependent clause fragments are a more deceptive type. As you learned only a few pages ago, every clause has a subject and a verb. However, a dependent clause makes no sense on its own because it begins with a dependent warning word. The existence of a dependent word at the beginning of a clause means that the word grouping is missing the most important sentence structure element: a complete idea.

Here are some examples of both types of fragments:

Just ran around hugging everyone in sight. (phrase fragment with no subject)

Paul and his sister with the twins. (phrase fragment with no verb)

Nothing to do but wait. (phrase fragment with no subject or verb)

After Tang went to the market. (dependent clause fragment, incomplete idea)

PHRASE FRAGMENTS

Phrases by definition are word groups without subject and verbs, so whenever a phrase is punctuated as a sentence, it is a fragment. Three categories of phrases cause the most difficulties:

ing phrases

Hoping to see my mother.

Correction: <u>Juan</u> <u>was</u> <u>hoping</u> to see my mother. (add a subject and complete the verb)

to phrases

> To be drafted into the National Hockey League.

> Correction: <u>Martin</u> <u>wanted</u> to be drafted into the National Hockey League. (add a subject and a verb)

prepositional phrases

> Under the starry skies in Nunavut.

> Correction: Even during the winter, sled <u>dogs</u> <u>sleep</u> outside under the starry skies in Nunavut. (add a subject and verb)

Proofread your written work carefully to eliminate any phrase fragments. Sometimes you can add the phrase onto a related sentence either before or after it. Other times, you will need to supply the missing words so that the phrase becomes a complete idea.

E X E R C I S E S

Exercise 1

Each of the numbered groups of words below contains a phrase fragment. Using what you already know about sentence structure, correct each by adding missing components to create an independent clause or by joining the fragment to an already existing complete sentence.

1. Deciding to further her education by attending college. Maiya discovered the process was a lengthy and confusing one.

2. Unlike many prospective students, she easily tackled the task of choosing a program. Without any help from her friends or family members.

3. Unfortunately, getting an adequate student loan wasn't nearly so easy. Because of the lack of youth employment opportunities during the summer.

4. As a result, her loan application form considerably overestimated the amount of the personal finances. Available to her at the beginning of the school year.

5. After speaking with the college's financial aid officer. Maiya decided to appeal the loan amount.

6. Arriving early on registration day without her birth certificate, her social insurance card, or any government-issued photo identification. She quickly became frustrated by long line-ups and huge delays.

7. After an exhausting day in several lengthy lines, including at the bank as well as at the college. Maiya finally clutched her official registration form and timetable.

8. Unfortunately, she had been too tired at the end of registration day to locate the classrooms. Displayed on her timetable.

9. On the first day of classes, after a desperate search down several corridors. Maiya was dismayed at her inability to find her first class's location.

10. Trying to stay calm and be rational. She finally returned to the financial aid office and asked its staff for directions.

Exercise 2

Some—but not all—of the following word groups are sentences. The others suffer from incomplete sentence structure. Put a period after each of the sentences. Make any fragments into sentences by assuring that each has a subject and an adequate verb.

1. My car's compact disc player is difficult to use while driving

2. The discs reflecting the sunlight and shining in my eyes

3. The old CD ejects from the slot with a hissing sound

4. Nowhere to put it while getting the new one

5. Then inserting the new CD without touching its underside

6. Fumbling with those flat plastic cases can be really frustrating

7. One case for the old one and one case for the new one

8. Meanwhile I am driving along

9. Not paying any attention to the road

10. I hope I don't hit anything

SENTENCE WRITING

Transform the following sentence fragments into sentences by adding the missing elements. Remember that each of your results should include a subject and a verb and convey a complete idea. Try to create 10 sentences that will tell a single story.

1. playing video games all night instead of studying for my test

_____

2. to reach the next level and beat my friend

_____

3. the weapons and coins needed

_____

4. since Nintendo's original Mario Brothers game was released nearly twenty-five years ago

_____

5. difficult to decide among all the gaming options

_____

6. whether PS3, Xbox, iPhone, or the new Palm Pre

_____

7. to entertain gamers of every age

_____

8. going online to play against others

_____

9. in other provinces and even other countries and continents

_____

10. never winning, but sometimes coming close

_____

DEPENDENT CLAUSE FRAGMENTS

As you learned in the previous section, a dependent clause has a subject and a verb but doesn't communicate a complete idea because of a dependent word found at the beginning. To correct a dependent clause fragment, either remove the dependent word or add an independent clause in front of or behind the dependent one.

FRAGMENT
    While <u>some</u> of us <u>worked</u> on our journals.

CORRECTED
    <u>Some</u> of us <u>worked</u> on our journals. (removed dependent word)

or

    While <u>some</u> of us <u>worked</u> on our journals, the fire <u>alarm</u> <u>rang</u>. (added an inde-
    pendent clause)

Are fragments ever permissible? Fragments are sometimes used in advertising and in other kinds of writing. But such fragments are used by professional writers who know what they're doing. These fragments are used intentionally, not in error. Until you're an experienced writer, stick with complete sentences. Especially in college and university writing, fragments should not be used.

EXERCISES

Exercise 1

Each of the numbered groups of words below contains one dependent clause fragment. First, find the dependent word and then **combine** the two word groups to create a sentence. (Capitalize and punctuate appropriately. Refer to the Punctuation Tip on page 108.)

  1. My friends and I always go hiking in the fall. Although we risk running into cool, wet weather.

  2. Crisp air and gloriously coloured maple leaves remind us to take advantage of the last decent weather. Before winter blusters in with its storms and frigid temperatures.

  3. We sometimes need to bundle up with layers of clothing that we can shed. If we generate too much heat during our hike.

  4. Since we particularly enjoy wilderness hikes. We jump into our van and drive 45 minutes to our favourite spot.

  5. This location features a lovely path. That snakes beside a rushing river.

  6. One of my classmates always packs a delicious picnic lunch. Because the hike increases our appetite.

7. We are often visited by three or four inquisitive squirrels. As we are eating our lunch.

8. Some folks call these visitors "chipmunks." Even though a chipmunk is an entirely different animal.

9. For nearly ten years, we've been sharing our picnic lunches at the same location with an identical number of squirrels. Who might be members of the same family.

10. Each year the squirrels seem less and less nervous at our presence. When we arrive at our traditional picnic site.

Exercise 2

Correct each dependent clause fragment by eliminating its dependent word or by attaching the dependent clause to the independent clause before or after it.

1. Thrift stores, yard sales, and flea markets have become very popular places to shop. Because they sell items that are not available anywhere else as cheaply.

2. Most thrift stores benefit charities. Which use the profits to help people in need.

3. Although the styles of clothing and furniture found in thrift stores are often outdated. Many people prefer the old styles over the new.

4. Modern shelving units are made of particle board or plastic, but thrift store shoppers can find more substantial ones. Which are made of solid wood or thick metal.

5. There are also famous stories of people becoming rich. Because they visited yard sales and flea markets.

6. One man bought a framed picture for a few dollars at a flea market. Since he liked the frame itself but not the picture.

7. When he returned home. He removed the picture from its frame and found the signature of a famous artist.

8. At a yard sale, a woman bought a small table. Which she later discovered was worth half a million dollars.

9. Of course, collectors always shop at these places. Where they hope to find treasures like rare cookie jars, pens, paintings, records, toys, and others objects of value.

10. In a way, shopping at thrift stores, yard sales, and flea markets is a kind of recycling. Which is something that benefits everyone.

SENTENCE WRITING

Each of the numbered groups of words below contains one dependent clause fragment. Using what you already know about sentence structure, **add** the necessary independent clause to each in order to create a sentence. (Capitalize and punctuate appropriately. Refer to the Punctuation Tip on page 108.)

1. whenever the first snowstorm hits

_____

2. although the weather reports give adequate notice

_____

3. unless their cars are equipped with ice tires

_____

4. while those cars without winter tires slide through intersections

_____

5. because there are so many traffic accidents

_____

6. when the snow continues to fall

_____

7. until the lanes on the highway can no longer be seen

_____

8. if drivers are unfamiliar with the roadway

_____

9. until snowplows and other winter maintenance equipment clear the snow

_____

10. how driving habits must change from season to season

_____

FRAGMENTS — COMBINED EXERCISES

Exercise 1

Some of the word groups below are sentences, but others are either phrase or dependent clause fragments. Change all fragments into complete sentences. Since the word groups are linked, remember that you could decide to tack a fragment onto a complete sentence immediately before or after it.

1. Canada's oldest trees may not be in the old-growth forests of British Columbia but in trees in fossilized form in New Brunswick.

2. A forest of 345-million-year-old trees sticks out of a rock face.

3. Outside Sussex, New Brunswick, about sixty-five kilometres from Saint John.

4. A geology curator with the New Brunswick Museum found the fossilized forest.

5. While he was looking for roadside fish fossils six years ago.

6. The curator's first impression was that the outcrop was odd.

7. Then he saw it was a whole forest.

8. Standing on end, sideways, and extending on and off the road for ten kilometres.

9. Researchers have identified more than seven hundred trees.

10. Which were mostly mosslike plants that grew to twenty metres high.

Source: Adapted from "Highway Construction Reveals Ancient Forest in New Brunswick." October 27, 2004. Reprinted with permission.

Exercise 2

Some of the word groups below are sentences, but others are either phrase or dependent clause fragments. Change all fragments into complete sentences. Since the word groups are linked, remember that you could decide to tack a fragment onto a complete sentence immediately before or after it.

1. Kaitlyn's father recently purchased a used car. After saving his money for over a year.

2. Now he is looking for a good mechanic because the car won't start. At least not in damp weather.

3. The dealership doesn't offer extended warranties on used vehicles.

4. Unless they have been regularly serviced by authorized service technicians.

5. Routine maintenance is critical to ensure a car's performance. Including regular oil changes and other inspections.

6. Kaitlyn is hoping to locate a good mechanic for her father. Because he has always tried to help her.

7. Generally, the hourly rate of independent licensed mechanics is over $65. Resulting in an expensive bill unless the problem is easy to identify and quick to repair.

8. One of my neighbours is a student in the motive power program at school. Where cars are serviced as part of the students' hands-on learning activities.

9. I know the school is always looking for vehicles. Especially those with complicated electrical problems.

10. I'll tell Kaitlyn about this program. So that she can follow up on this possibility.

PROOFREADING EXERCISE

Find and correct the five phrase and dependent clause fragments in the following paragraph.

Shark attacks have been on the rise. We've all heard the heartbreaking news stories. Of people on their honeymoons or children playing in only a few feet of water being attacked by sharks. Movies like *Jaws* and *Open Water* make us wary and scared. When we watch them. But their effects fade over time, and we forget about the risks. Of entering the habitats of dangerous animals. Experts try to convince us. Saying that sharks and other powerful species are not targeting human beings on purpose. To a shark, a person is no different from a seal or a sea turtle. Facts such as these prompt many of us to think twice. Before we take a dip in the ocean.

Correcting Run-On Sentences

Any word group having a subject and a verb is a clause. As we have seen, the clause may be independent (able to stand alone) or dependent (unable to stand alone). If two independent clauses are written together without proper punctuation between them, the result is called a run-on sentence. Here are some examples.

Lester now lives in Kenora however he was born in the Maritimes.

My best friend is very talented he auditioned for the *Canadian Idol* show.

Run-on sentences can be corrected in one of four ways.

1. Make the two independent clauses into two sentences.

Lester now lives in Kenora. However, he was born in the Maritimes.

My best friend is very talented. He auditioned for the *Canadian Idol* show.

2. Connect two closely related independent clauses with a semicolon.

Lester now lives in Kenora; however, he was born in the Maritimes.

My best friend is very talented; he auditioned for the *Canadian Idol* show.

When a connecting word such as

also	however	otherwise
consequently	likewise	then
finally	moreover	therefore
furthermore	nevertheless	thus

is used to join two independent clauses, the semicolon comes before the connecting word, and a comma usually comes after it.

Cellular phones are convenient; however, they can be intrusive.

Earthquakes scare me; therefore, I couldn't live in California.

We travelled to London; then we took the "Chunnel" to France.

The college recently built a large new library; thus students have more quiet study areas.

> **NOTE:** The use of the comma after the connecting word depends on how long the connecting word is. If it is only a short word, like *then* or *thus*, the comma is not necessary.

3. **Connect the two independent clauses with a *comma* and a *FANBOYS* word (*FANBOYS* is a word created using the first letters of seven small joining words: *for, and, nor, but, or, yet, so*).**

Lester now lives in Kenora, but he was born in the Maritimes.

My best friend is very talented, so he auditioned for the *Canadian Idol* show.

Each of the *FANBOYS* has its own meaning (for example, *so* means "as a result," and *for* means "because").

Swans are beautiful birds, *and* they mate for life.

Students may register for classes by phone, *or* they may do so in person.

I applied for financial aid, *but* (or *yet*) I was still working at the time.

Beth doesn't know how to use a computer, *nor* does she plan to learn.

Before you put a comma before a *FANBOYS*, be sure there are two independent clauses. The first sentence that follows has two independent clauses. The second sentence is merely one independent clause with two verbs, so no comma should be used.

The snow began falling at dusk, and it continued to fall through the night.

The snow began falling at dusk and continued to fall through the night.

4. **Make one of the clauses dependent by adding a dependent warning word (such as *since, when, as, after, while*, or *because* — see p. 107 for a full list).**

Lester now lives in Kenora although he was born in the Maritimes. (independent clause followed by dependent clause without punctuation)

Although Lester now lives in Kenora, he was born in the Maritimes. (opening dependent clause and comma introduce the independent clause)

Because my best friend is very talented, he auditioned for the *Canadian Idol* show. (opening dependent clause and comma before the independent clause)

WAYS TO CORRECT RUN-ON SENTENCES

I = Independent Clause   **D** = Dependent Clause

Option 1.   **I. I.** (punctuate as two separate sentences)

Option 2.   **I; I.** (use semicolon to link closely related independent ideas)

Option 3.   **I, FANBOYS I.** (link independent ideas with a small joining word: *for, and, nor, but, or, yet, so*)

Option 4.   **D, I or ID.** (change one of the independent clauses into a dependent one)

EXERCISES

Exercises 1 and 2

CORRECTING RUN-ONS WITH PUNCTUATION

Most—but not all—of the following sentences are run-ons. If the sentence has two independent clauses, separate them with correct punctuation. For the first two exercises, *don't create any dependent clauses*; use only a period, a semicolon, or a comma to separate the two independent clauses. Your answers may differ from those at the back of the book depending on how you choose to separate the clauses.

Exercise 1

1. Nearly everyone yawns but few understand the dynamics of yawning.

2. One person's yawn often triggers another person's yawn.

3. Yawning clearly seems to be a contagious activity.

4. Scientific studies of yawning verify this phenomenon and also explain the reasons for it.

5. Groups of people do similar things for they are acting somewhat like herds of animals.

6. During times of transition, such as getting up from or going to bed, members of a family or a dorm full of roommates synchronize their activities through yawning.

7. The yawning helps the group act as one so it minimizes conflict.

8. There are a few misconceptions about yawns one of them has to do with oxygen levels.

9. Some people explain yawning as the body's way to increase oxygen intake.

10. Surprisingly, studies show no changes in yawning patterns due to levels of oxygen in fact, research subjects inhaling pure oxygen yawned the same number of times as those breathing normally.

Source: Adapted from *Discover*, June 2001.

Exercise 2

1. I am writing a research paper on Margaret Laurence she was one of Canada's most celebrated novelists and a pioneer in the world of Canadian literature.

2. She was born in Neepawa, Manitoba, in her novels *The Stone Angel, A Jest of God, The Fire-Dwellers*, and *The Diviners*, the town was called "Manawaka."

3. Laurence was encouraged to write by Jack McClelland he also published the works of other Canadian writers such as Mordecai Richler and Farley Mowat.

4. Margaret and her husband, Jack, briefly lived in England then they moved to Africa.

5. She became very interested in European–African relations as a result her early books, *This Side Jordan* and *The Tomorrow-Tamer*, deal with this issue.

6. Her husband wanted her to be a traditional wife and mother but Margaret wanted to be a full-time writer.

7. When they divorced, she had to support herself and her children with her writing.

8. Laurence received her first Governor General's Award for her masterpiece *The Stone Angel.*

9. Twice her books were condemned or banned in schools yet today they are taught as Canadian classics.

10. In 1986, she was diagnosed with inoperable and fatal lung cancer several months later she took her own life.

Source: Adapted from James King, *Margaret Laurence* (Toronto: Alfred A. Knopf, 1997).

Exercises 3 and 4

CORRECTING RUN-ONS WITH DEPENDENT CLAUSES

Most—but not all—of the following sentences are run-ons. Correct any run-on sentences by making one of the clauses dependent. You may change the words. Use a dependent word (such as *since, when, as, after, while, because,* or the others listed on p. 107) to begin the dependent clause. In some sentences you will want to put the dependent clause first; in others you may want to put it last (or in the middle of the sentence). Since various words can be used to start a dependent clause, your answers may differ from those suggested at the back of the book.

Exercise 3

1. On summer evenings, people around the world enjoy the sight of little lights they are flying around in the air.

2. Most people know the glowing insects as fireflies they are also called lightning bugs and glowworms.

3. Glowworms are unique they don't fly.

4. The term *fireflies* is a little misleading they are not technically flies.

5. Lightning bugs are beetles they have special substances in their bodies.

6. These substances make them glow these substances are luciferin and luciferase.

7. The luciferin and luciferase combine with oxygen they produce a greenish light.

8. The light can be very intense people in some countries use caged fireflies as lamps.

9. In addition to their ability to light up, fireflies blink on and off.

10. Incredibly, groups of fireflies blink out of order at first they seem to coordinate their blinking within a few minutes.

Source: Adapted from *Current Science*, May 11, 2001.

Exercise 4

1. Glenn Gould died and Canada lost a great musician.

2. Gould was a sublime pianist he was also a composer of international fame.

3. If you are interested in classical piano music, you will know Glenn Gould's name.

4. He was a child prodigy he was put on the stage at a very young age.

5. He was fourteen years old and he became a soloist with the Toronto Symphony.

6. Gould began touring across Canada at age nineteen in later years he stopped performing in public.

7. While he is best known for his interpretations of Bach, he also played with great mastery the music of many other composers.

8. He was an eccentric and a loner few people knew much about his personal life.

9. The day after he turned fifty, he had a severe stroke and died.

10. Gould's music continues to live on he is no longer alive.

Source: Adapted from *Toronto Star*, November 16, 1999, D4.

Exercise 5

Correct the following run-on sentences using any of the methods studied in this section: adding a period, a semicolon, a semicolon + a transition word, or a comma + a *FANBOYS*, or using a dependent word to create a dependent clause.

1. There is a new way to find a date in Japan singles use vending machines to sell information about themselves to others.

2. Men provide personal details in packets to be sold in the machines first the men swear they are not married.

3. A woman chooses to purchase a packet for a couple of dollars in it she will find a picture of the man, his age, and his employment status.

4. The packets also include the men's phone numbers the women can use the numbers to contact the men they like.

5. The system seems to be working many of the couples are dating more than once.

6. A lot of Japanese businesspeople use the machines they do not have time to meet people in other ways.

7. Employees have little opportunity to socialize in Japan it is normal to stay at work until late into the evening.

8. A man might pay almost $50 to put many of his packets into the machines that doesn't mean that women will call him.

9. Japan is famous for its vending machines they are even used to sell meat and clothes.

10. Other countries might find it unusual to sell personal information in vending machines they seem to be working well as matchmakers in Japan.

Source: Adapted from *Fortune*, April 6, 1992.

REVIEW OF FRAGMENTS AND RUN-ON SENTENCES

If you remember that all clauses include a subject and a verb, but only independent clauses can be punctuated as sentences (since only they can stand alone), then you will avoid fragments in your writing. And if you memorize these six rules for the punctuation of clauses, you will be able to avoid most punctuation errors.

PUNCTUATING CLAUSES

I am a student. I am still learning.	(two sentences)
I am a student; I am still learning.	(two independent clauses)
I am a student; therefore, I am still learning.	(two independent clauses connected by a word such as *also, consequently, finally, furthermore, however, likewise, moreover, nevertheless, otherwise, then, therefore, thus*)
I am a student, so I am still learning.	(two independent clauses connected by *for, and, nor, but, or, yet, so*)
Because I am a student, I am still learning.	(dependent clause at beginning of sentence)
I am still learning because I am a student.	(dependent clause at end of sentence) The dependent words are *after, although, as, as if, because, before, even if, even though, ever since, how, if, in order that, since, so that, than, that, though, unless, until, what, whatever, when, whenever, where, whereas, wherever, whether, which, whichever, while, who, whom, whose, why.*

It is essential that you learn the italicized words in this table—know which ones come between independent clauses and which ones introduce dependent clauses.

EXERCISES

Each of the following contains a fragment or a run-on sentence or fails to punctuate clauses correctly. Use your understanding of subjects, verbs, and clauses to identify the problem area. Then make the necessary corrections.

Exercise 1

1. Lydia's father graduated from high school in the mid-sixties. When he was only sixteen years old.

2. Last September his class held its forty-fifth reunion and he decided to travel more than one thousand kilometres to participate in the special events.

3. His favourite part of high school was sports. Although the football coach rarely called upon him to hit the field.

4. At the reunion, members of the varsity football team hosted a special party, he was amazed to find that he remembered almost every team-mate's name.

5. "Dougie," the star quarterback, was a little guy. Who, at the time, stood up to the other players' armpits and weighed less than half as much as any player on the defensive team.

6. At the football team's special party, "Dougie" ran up to Lydia's father. Giving him a giant bear hug.

7. To his delight, even some of the most popular girls remembered his name, apparently he had made a larger impact on classmates than he had thought.

8. The reunion's dinner/dance gave Lydia's father the chance to sit and chat with others he remembered more dimly, nonetheless, the conversations were animated and filled with warm laughter.

9. To reconnect with his friends from so long ago and so far away provided him with new memories. To treasure for decades more.

10. Lydia says her dad acted like a teenager at the airport after his trip and she doubts that any other trip could match this one for excitement.

Exercise 2

1. A famous Canadian coffee and doughnut chain conducts a special annual contest. To give consumers added incentives to purchase the franchise's coffee.

2. Regular customers know the odds of winning. Therefore, likely doubling their coffee intake during the contest period.

3. Customers can win prizes such as cars, computer equipment, cash equipment, and the doughnut company's merchandise in a unique way. By rolling up the rims of specially marked coffee cups.

4. Even when they have their coffee served in a china mug in the restaurant itself. Purchasers get a cardboard contest cup in order to participate.

5. The effect on landfill sites must be notable. Because the cups are coated with a waxed substance and cannot be recycled.

6. Some in-store customers hesitate when offered the extra cardboard cup, after all, one of the reasons they choose to drink from china mugs is to minimize the negative environmental impact of the paper.

7. Although some geographical areas have more contest winners than others. This apparent advantage may be the result of easier store accessibility in some cities and provinces.

8. Some cities have five or more outlets of the same coffee and doughnut chain. So that caffeine addicts can have a regular supply of their favourite beverage.

9. Eager contest participants once had to buy a cup of coffee from one of the brand's hundreds of outlets in Canada and the United States, however, modern technology now makes anyone with Internet access eligible to play.

10. Without purchasing a single cup of the beverage, anyone can register online, and have a chance to claim a prize.

Exercise 3

1. Many scientists have blamed global warming for recent unusual weather patterns. That include more severe storms throughout the world.

2. Hurricanes in North America and floods throughout Europe are occurring. Making even the most skeptical person take notice.

3. To understand our planet's future. We need to study what climate changes have already taken place.

4. Glaciers are melting at an unprecedented rate, sea levels are rising, and annual temperatures are climbing. According to many climate studies.

5. The Canadian government has recently recognized, that the Northwest Passage may soon have open water year round.

6. Several other countries are beginning to take an interest in the Arctic's natural gas and mineral reserves. That have traditionally been locked away under tonnes of ice.

7. As the ice shield melts the sea levels rise, sometimes to alarming levels; around the world, many heavily populated cities sit at the current edge of oceans and seas.

8. The president of the Maldive Islands spoke at a recent session of the United Nations–sponsored climate summit, he predicted that his whole country would disappear below ocean water by the end of this century.

9. Canada is facing special global warming challenges. Like droughts in the Prairie provinces, rising sea levels along its three ocean borders, and reduced habitats for endangered species like the polar bear.

10. It took centuries for the world to get to its current state some feel that extravagant styles of living and manufacturing demands in developing countries have taken the environment over its tipping point.

Exercise 4

1. Shortly after the collapse of the world's economies in October 2008. The Canadian government introduced a tax credit plan for taxpayers who chose to make permanent improvements to their primary places of residence.

2. As a result, many Canadians elected to renovate their homes, and spent thousands of dollars to repaint rooms, refinish hardwood floors, and add decks.

3. As the Home Renovation Tax Credit program was rolled out, TV commercials showed enthusiastic homeowners making long-delayed improvements but the devil was in the details.

4. Although the minority party in power had announced the program months earlier. The public relations campaign kicked into high gear before the House of Commons had approved the measure.

5. Only people in the habit of reading fine print saw the very small "Subject to Parliamentary approval" line appearing in each commercial. As well as on all printed materials available at home building supply outlets.

6. It must have been a relief to the governing party when the opposition's threat to topple the government evaporated, after all, it would have been embarrassing to explain the situation in an election campaign.

7. When homeowners filed their 2009 income tax forms they were able to claim a portion of their renovation expenses as a tax credit.

8. As it turned out, the timing of this tax credit hugely benefited building contractors. Expecting low earnings as the result of the world's economic downturn.

9. Suddenly, roofers, painters, and other specialized tradespersons found themselves with more work than they could handle, whole neighbourhoods swarmed with pickup trucks belonging to contractors and their workers.

10. In fact, many residents couldn't locate a house painter to complete the necessary work within the program's time frame because all the painting contractors were too busy. Even to provide project estimates to homeowners.

Exercise 5

1. Hybrid cars have grown considerably in popularity. Since Toyota's Prius first arrived on the North American market in 2001.

2. The Prius has grown from a compact to a midsize car, and now shares the market with hybrid SUVs and trucks.

3. Generally, consumers buy this car. Because it offers exceptional mileage and eco-friendly low emissions.

4. Toyota's development of the Prius took less than two years. From concept to production.

5. Every little detail is assessed, for example, the weight of the engine and other components is minimized to reduce the power requirements.

6. In the newest version, even the sunroof serves multiple purposes; when the car is parked in the summer sun, its solar panel provides power to a small fan. That keeps air circulating and provides a cooler interior.

7. Toyota developed the first hybrid technology. Blending gasoline and battery power.

8. Although the Prius has competitors at several levels from both domestic and foreign automakers. The technology for electric hybrids varies.

9. Battery power alone will operate over only a short distance, an infra-structure of many battery recharging stations must be built to act as the electrical equivalent of gasoline stations.

10. A recharging station would allow a driver whose vehicle's battery is running low on charge to exchange it for a fully charged one and be on his or her way in moments, however, the establishment of these recharging stations isn't going to happen overnight.

PROOFREADING EXERCISE

Rewrite the following paragraph, making the necessary changes so that there will be no fragments or run-on sentences. (There are ten areas that need revision.)

The shiny black sports car zipped through the heavy rush hour traffic. Changing lanes without signalling, tailgating the car immediately in front of it, acting as though he owned the road. The signs of an impatient driver. When it approached the intersection with the red traffic light. The car paused only long enough to allow the light to turn green. The driver quickly accelerated, however, another car was entering the intersection at the same time. The sports car slammed into it. Metal screeched, glass broke. Both cars were immobilized but fortunately no one was hurt badly. Still, all the time that the driver had "saved" was lost now it would be at least forty-five minutes before the police arrived. To investigate the accident. If eyewitnesses stayed to give their statements. Likely the sports car driver would get a ticket, then he would need to pay a large fine. And higher premiums for his auto insurance.

SENTENCE WRITING

Write a sample sentence of your own to demonstrate each of the six ways a writer can use to punctuate two clauses. You may model your sentences on the examples used in the preceding review chart.

_____

_____

_____

_____

_____

_____

_____

_____

_____

Exploring Sentence Variety

Combining independent and dependent clauses in a variety of patterns allows the writer to show relationships between ideas.

1. A *simple sentence* contains just one independent clause (I).

> Lester visited me last summer.

> Lester moved to Halifax last September but visited me in August. (The two verbs share the same subject, so there is only one independent clause.)

2. A *complex sentence* combines one independent clause with at least one dependent clause (I + D or D + I). Look for more than one subject–verb pair but only one complete thought.

> When the bat in the back of my barn occasionally swoops down on me, I am always surprised.

The first clause doesn't convey a complete thought, so *When the bat in the back of the barn occasionally swoops down on me* is a dependent clause.

> Lester moved to Halifax after he visited me in August.

Note that the independent clause appears first in this two-clause sentence. *after he visited me in August* is an incomplete thought, so it is a dependent clause.

> The correct punctuation for a complex sentence is determined by the order of the clauses. Look at the box below and compare its rules to the sentences above.

PUNCTUATING COMPLEX SENTENCES

Option 1.   I D. (independent clause followed by dependent)

Option 2.   D, I. (dependent first, independent clause following)

---

3. A *compound sentence* combines two independent clauses (I + I).

> The <u>bat</u> in the back of my barn occasionally <u>swoops</u> down on people, but <u>it</u> never actually <u>attacks</u>.

> <u>Lester</u> <u>has lived</u> most of his life on the West Coast; however, <u>he</u> <u>prefers</u> the Maritime provinces.

Remember that when a sentence contains two complete thoughts, placing only a comma between them will not be enough. As the box below indicates, you will need either a semicolon or a comma with a *FANBOYS* word.

PUNCTUATING COMPOUND SENTENCES

Test: **I. I.** (punctuate as two separate sentences)

Option   **I; I.** (use a semicolon to link closely related independent ideas)

Option   **I, *FANBOYS* I.** (use a comma plus a small joining word: *for, and, nor, but, or, yet, so*)

When you have a sentence with two clauses, use the test in the chart above to see if you have a compound sentence. Can each clause stand alone as a separate sentence? If so, you can also use other options from the box above to punctuate your sentence correctly.

Try this example:

> The diamond sparkled on the woman's finger the ring must have cost a fortune. (There are two clauses here. *The diamond <u>sparkled</u> on the woman's finger* is the first; *the <u>ring</u> <u>must have cost</u> a fortune* is the second.)

If you place a period between the two, you discover that both clauses are independent; each has a <u>subject</u> + <u>verb</u> and expresses a complete thought.

> The <u>diamond</u> <u>sparkled</u> on the woman's finger. The <u>ring</u> <u>must have cost</u> a fortune.

Because these two ideas are so closely related, you could also choose to place a semi-colon between them:

> The diamond sparkled on the woman's finger; the ring must have cost a fortune.

Finally, you could use a comma plus a *FANBOYS* word to join these two clauses. (Note that *so* means the same as *therefore*.)

> The diamond sparkled on the woman's finger, so the ring must have cost a fortune.

4. A *compound-complex sentence* combines a simple sentence with a complex sentence. At least two clauses will be independent; another will be dependent.

> The bat in the back of my barn occasionally swoops down on people, and although he never attacks visitors, he certainly frightens them.

> After Lester moved to Halifax, his mother phoned me; she seemed very pleased with his decision.

Bottom line: If your sentence contains more than one clause, identify the type of clause each is and then use the punctuation strategies outlined in the text boxes in this section.

EXERCISES

Identify each sentence as *simple, complex, compound,* or *compound-complex.*

Exercise 1

1. Canadians face an increased burden if they raise their children and care for their aging parents at the same time.
2. The burden includes more complicated personal schedules and less pay, according to a recent report by Statistics Canada.
3. One-third of middle-aged Canadians are part of this so-called Sandwich Generation, and more are expected to join their ranks.
4. With baby boomers getting older and fertility rates low, older family members will increasingly need care from people still raising their children.
5. The numbers in the Statistics Canada report show that 712,000 people between the ages of forty-five and sixty-four were caregivers to two generations.

6. These numbers are based on Statistics Canada's 2002 General Social Survey.

7. As members of the Sandwich Generation juggle responsibilities, their lives are increasingly busy and stressful.

8. According to the Statistics Canada survey, fifteen percent of these individuals reduced their work hours; another twenty percent changed their schedules after they took on the extra responsibilities.

9. More alarmingly, seventy percent admitted to high levels of stress.

10. The responsibility of caring for elderly parents falls mostly to women; while male caregivers report spending thirteen hours a month providing care to elderly relatives, women spend thirty hours.

Source: Adapted from "'Sandwich Generation' Expected to Grow," CBC.ca, September 28, 2004.

Exercise 2

1. Earthquakes are often followed by numerous aftershocks especially when the original quake is large.

2. Aftershocks are defined as earthquakes that occur after the main quake and in the same area.

3. Usually, aftershocks are smaller than the original earthquake is, but occasionally an aftershock may be strong enough to be felt throughout the area and may cause additional damage.

4. Structures already weakened in the original earthquake are the most likely to sustain damage from aftershocks.

5. Aftershocks are most common immediately after the first earthquake; their average number per day decreases rapidly as time passes.

6. In general, the larger the original earthquake is, the longer its aftershocks will be felt.

7. Aftershocks tend to occur near the original quake, but since the exact geographic pattern of the aftershocks varies from earthquake to earthquake, their locations are not predictable.

8. Again, the size of the initial earthquake is important; larger quakes generate aftershocks over wider areas.

9. The vast majority of aftershocks occur in an area close to the first shock.

10. A magnitude six earthquake may have aftershocks up to sixteen to thirty-two kilometres away while a magnitude seven earthquake may have aftershocks as far as fifty to eighty kilometres away.

Source: Adapted from "Aftershock Probability Report," Southern California Seismic Network (TriNet), September 30, 2004.

PROOFREADING EXERCISE

The paragraph below is written without any punctuation. Break the content into clauses and insert the appropriate punctuation. Use a variety of the sentence types you have learned about. (Hint: You will find it helpful to label each clause by its type and then analyze the combinations in your sentences. Consult the answer key to verify your punctuation and to confirm the types of sentences you have built.)

In this computer era most people have viewed many PowerPoint presentations while not all these presentations are ineffective they seem to fall into one of three categories poorly organized presentations are usually created by individuals whose understanding of this method of presentation is weak or non-existent at the other extreme presentations by PowerPoint showoffs usually demonstrate more graphics skills than ideas although most of us get really confused when speakers clutter up their slides with too much material the showoffs can't get enough action and content the good presentations lie somewhere in the middle the presenter limits each slide to just five bullets or one picture while these basic guidelines protect audiences from the other two extremes most people soon get bored seeing slide after slide with the same pattern and after a while all good PowerPoint presentations look alike.

Effective Sentences Progress Test

Test yourself on how much you have learned about sentence structure. Study the following word groups. Apply the necessary correction to eliminate any run-on or fragment. Check your answers in the answer key before taking the Post-Test.

1. Our new booklet is enclosed, an up-to-date price list will be sent to you within the next two weeks.

2. Although the strike has officially ended. We do not expect to resume production until the first of next month.

3. Ms. Yin is exploring the benefits of computer time-sharing; she believes that time-sharing will prove economical for the company.

4. The Stanton Company is not planning to expand its sales force. Because it expects sales to decrease for the next two years.

5. However, Stanton is upgrading its assembly line, the improvements will allow the company to reduce its workforce to just two shifts from its current three.

6. Transportation costs increased nearly twenty-three percent during the past year; so product prices had to be increased.

7. The company wants all its customers to know the ingredients of its products, therefore, every item shipped contains a detailed label.

8. The warehouse will be closed for inventory next week. Although the warehouse manager and her assistants will be at work.

9. During the inventory period, delivery trucks will be re-routed to the second plant. Which is located thirty kilometres north of Regina.

10. Next summer, staff can expect plant shutdowns at all locations. To allow recalibration of the machinery.

Effective Sentences Post-Test

Test yourself on how much you have learned about sentence structure. Study the following word groups. Apply the necessary correction to eliminate any run-on or fragment.

1. A parliamentary democracy like Canada's offers fascinating options. For voters who take the time to watch Parliament at work.

2. Even though voters in many parts of the country can choose from as many as six different official parties. Many Canadians don't recognize most of these parties as legitimate options.

3. Some official parties represent regions of the country, as a result, not all parties have candidates running in every riding.

4. The Bloc Québécois, for example, offers candidates only in the province of Quebec. Because the party's primary goal is to protect the French language and the culture of that province.

5. Francophone voters in New Brunswick or Northern Ontario might be just as concerned about these issues. Which affect their daily lives.

6. In fact, only three Canadian political parties are generally viewed as national in scope, specifically, the Liberal, Conservative, and New Democratic parties have historically fielded candidates in every riding.

7. However, the Green Party tried to have a candidate in every federal riding. In the last election.

8. With the exception of the Bloc, the smaller parties understand the importance of being seen as nationally representative, however, in a country as vast as Canada, it is difficult to build a political party.

9. Sometimes, Liberal members of Parliament have been elected, when two or more other parties ran opposing candidates who split the right-of-centre vote.

10. In 2003, the Canadian Alliance Party and the Progressive Conservative Party merged to form the Conservative Party of Canada. Although there were differences between the two parties' positions on several issues.

PART 4

Keeping the Message Clear

Clarity Pre-Test

Some rules of grammar usage are designed to ensure that the writer's message is clear. Making the subject agree with its verb, choosing the correct pronoun, keeping sentence elements balanced, and choosing wording carefully are habits that every good writer develops so that the reader doesn't have to guess at the meaning. In the sentences below, isolate problems that make the message unclear. Write your corrections in the spaces between sentences.

1. When the developers explained the area plans to other members of the Planning Committee, they were confused.

2. The plan for recommended ski hill changes are being debated at the next council meeting.

3. Discussions at that meeting will involve city staff, the representatives elected to council, and what interested citizens have to say.

4. Everyone in the sporting community are wondering if the city's plans will include revitalizing the city-owned ski hill, which had to close last winter because the equipment was outdated.

5. Do either of you snowboard?

6. The hill might attract a lot more attention if us taxpayers supported adding two special runs for snowboarders.

7. Currently the ski hill has a bunny run, an intermediate hill, and needs a challenging slope for those training for downhill competitions.

8. When the ski hill was first developed fifty years ago, it has only one bunny slope.

9. In an ideal world, there would be a lot of cooperation between taxpayers, politicians, and sport enthusiasts in making plans for sports complexes like this hill.

10. Louis Mayer, the manager of Leisure Activities, says his brother skis at a hill in another city now, which makes him very unhappy.

11. Nobody expected the new plan, which took nearly a year to prepare, to be so complicated, expensive, and attracting so much controversy.

12. Planning the new development is one thing; to make it all happen is another.

13. My city councillor, who supports the proposal, warns that no other councillor is as positive about it as her.

14. Therefore, she hopes skiers like you and your sister will attend one of the several public meetings about the ski hill and voice your ideas.

15. The truth is that there is two kinds of people in the city: the majority who love winter sports and a smaller number who hate them.

16. If we skiers, snowboarders, and the people who want a sled run don't attend these meetings, the plan will not gain acceptance in spite of the fact that we form the majority.

17. Please encourage everyone not only to attend a meeting but also to contact their councillor to support reopening the hill.

18. None of my other friends are a skier, but each of them understands the benefits of a winter sports complex in a city this size.

19. For example, the senior gentleman who lives across the street from me learned to ski on that hill; him and his wife will attend the meeting to show their support.

20. Just between you and me, some children in my neighbourhood fear that no one cares about the future of the hill as much as them.

Introduction to Keeping the Message Clear

Knowing the essential components of a sound sentence and understanding the way clauses work to convey ideas are only two considerations in sentence structure. Writers must also ensure that the sentences they build clearly convey ideas. Part 4 describes some of the most common problems that can undermine the clarity of your message and shows you how to correct the errors associated with them.

Maintaining Subject–Verb Agreement

As we have seen, the subject and verb in a sentence work together, so they must always agree. Different subjects need different forms of verbs. When the correct verb follows a subject, we call it subject–verb agreement.

The sentences below illustrate the rule that *s* verbs follow most singular subjects but not plural subjects.

One turtle walks.	Three turtles walk.
The baby laughs.	The babies laugh.
A good leader listens to the people.	Good leaders listen to the people.
One child plays.	Many children play.

And the following sentences show how forms of the verb *be* (*is, am, are, was, were*) and helping verbs (*be, have,* and *do*) are made to agree with their subjects.

This puzzle is difficult.	These puzzles are difficult.
I am surprised.	You are surprised.
He was sleeping.	They were sleeping.
That class has been cancelled.	Those classes have been cancelled.
She does not want to participate.	They do not want to participate.

Always Singular

The following words are always singular and take an *s* verb:

"ONE" WORDS	"BODY" WORDS	OTHERS
one	anybody	each
anyone	everybody	either
everyone	nobody	neither
no one	somebody	
someone		

Someone <u>feeds</u> my dog in the morning.

Everybody <u>was</u> at the concert.

Each <u>does</u> her own homework.

Remember that prepositional phrases often come between subjects and verbs. You should ignore these interrupting phrases, or you may mistake the wrong word for the subject and use a verb form that doesn't agree.

Someone from the apartments <u>feeds</u> my dog in the morning. (*Someone* is the subject, not *apartments*.)

Everybody on the list of celebrities <u>was</u> at the concert. (*Everybody* is the subject, not *celebrities*.)

Each of the twins <u>does</u> her own homework. (*Each* is the subject, not *twins*.)

SPECIAL CASES

Part or Portion Subjects

The words *some, any, all, none,* and *most* are exceptions to the rule of ignoring prepositional phrases. These words can be singular or plural, depending on the words that follow them in prepositional phrases.

Some of the apple <u>was</u> rotten. (subject is part of the singular word, *apple*)

Some of the apples <u>were</u> rotten. (subject is part of the plural word, *apples*)

Is any of the *paper* still in the supply cabinet? (part of singular)

Are any of the *pencils* sharpened? (part of plural)

All of her *work* has been recorded. (part of singular)

All of her *songs* have been recorded. (part of plural)

Subjects Joined by "Or"

When a sentence has more than one subject joined by *and*, the subject is plural.

Two glazed doughnuts and an onion bagel were sitting on the plate. (The subject words are joined by *and*, so the subject is plural. The helping form of the verb agrees.)

But when two subjects are joined by *or*, the subject word closer to the verb determines the verb form.
In the following two sentences, notice how the verb changes to agree with the subject word closest to it:

The doughnuts *or* the bagel was her breakfast. (bagel was)

The bagel *or* the doughnuts were her breakfast. (doughnuts were)

Reversed Order Sentences

In most sentences, the subject comes before the verb. However, in some cases, the subject follows the verb. Always identify subjects and verbs carefully.

Over the building flies a solitary flag. (the flag, not the building, flies)

Over the building fly two flags. (the flags, not the building, fly)

There is a good reason for my actions. (reason is)

There are good reasons for my actions. (reasons are)

EXERCISES

Underline the verbs that agree with the subjects of the following sentences. Remember to ignore prepositional phrases, unless the subjects are *some*, *any*, *all*, *none*, or *most*. Check your answers ten at a time.

Exercise 1

1. There (is, are) a celebratory sight that occurs around the end of June.

2. From balconies and flagpoles, in windows and doorways (fly, flies) many gaily coloured rainbow flags.

3. Not everyone (know, knows) what these flags (stands, stand) for.

4. No, they (is, are) not flags in preparation for Canada's birthday.

5. A parade with elaborate floats and exquisite costumes (are, is) part of the celebration.

6. Neither the police nor the citizens (seem, seems) to mind the intense crowds that form on the sidewalks to watch the people in the parade (go, goes) by.

7. Certain areas of the city (are, is) cleared of all traffic.

8. Even the mayor and other officials (take, takes) part in the frivolity.

9. Regardless of their sexual orientation, people of all ages (has, have) waited all year to watch this colourful event.

10. Can you guess how many cities in Canada (has, have) Gay Pride Parades?

Exercise 2

1. Banff National Park in the Rockies (is, are) one of Canada's most popular parks.

2. This parkland (was, were) set aside by the federal government in 1885 to preserve the sulphur hot springs for public use.

3. Glaciers from thousands of years ago (clings, cling) to the upper mountain slopes, creating breathtaking scenery.

4. Cougars, wolves, moose, elk, and two types of bear (makes, make) Banff National Park their home.

5. Forests of evergreens (softens, soften) the slopes of the Banff Rocky Mountains.

6. For visitors on all budgets, there (is, are) campgrounds, resorts, and even a first-class hotel.

7. Either hiking or skiing (is, are) available for most of the months of the year.

8. Hiking trails (radiate, radiates) from the Banff townsite.

9. The Banff Centre for the Arts (overlook, overlooks) the ski resort of Banff and the Banff Springs Hotel.

10. Participants in the program (enjoy, enjoys) the wilderness setting combined with the finest modern facilities in the arts.

Source: Adapted from *The Canadian Encyclopedia,* s.v. "Banff."

Exercise 3

1. A group of scientists (is, are) looking into the sensation that we (call, calls) déjà vu.

2. Déjà vu (is, are) the feeling that we (is, are) repeating an exact experience that (has, have) happened before.

3. Part of the odd sensation (is, are) that we (is, are) aware of the illogical part of déjà vu while it (is, are) happening.

4. One theory of Sigmund Freud's (was, were) that déjà vu (take, takes) place when a real experience (connect, connects) us with our unconscious thoughts.

5. Another of the psychiatrists studying déjà vu (believe, believes) that our previous experiences (is, are) stored like holographic images.

6. And déjà vu (happen, happens) when a new experience closely matches the 3-D memory of an old one.

7. The most recent theory (hypothesize, hypothesizes) that two different parts of the brain (control, controls) memory and familiarity.

8. One part (give, gives) us access to individual clear memories.

9. The other part (is, are) responsible for vague feelings of familiarity.

10. Experts in the field of psychiatry now (think, thinks) that the brain (produce, produces) déjà vu when this familiar feeling (activate, activates) during a brand-new experience.

Source: Adapted from *Scientific American,* September 2002.

Exercise 4

1. No one in my film class (has, have) ever seen *2001: A Space Odyssey* before, except me.

2. All of them (has, have) heard of it, but none of them (has, have) actually watched it.

3. Most of my friends outside of school (love, loves) old movies, especially science fiction ones like *Slaughterhouse Five* and *Fahrenheit 451.*

4. Each of these sci-fi movies (make, makes) its own point about the human situation.

5. But everybody I know (say, says) *2001: A Space Odyssey* makes the biggest point of all.

6. One of my roommates (think, thinks) that it is the greatest movie ever made.

7. I believe that either it or *Fahrenheit 451* (is, are) the best, but I (hasn't, haven't) decided which one yet.

8. Now George Orwell's famous year 1984 (has, have) passed.

9. And each of us (look, looks) back at the shocking events of the real year 2001.

10. No one really (know, knows) what surprises await us in the future.

Exercise 5

1. Three million Canadians (is, are) blind or visually impaired and (requires, require) books in an alternative format such as Braille or audio.

2. Today, less than five percent of published literature in Canada (is, are) available in such formats, but the CNIB Library (exists, exist) to address barriers to access to print information.

3. The Library (is, are) currently undertaking a complete digital transformation of its infrastructure and services, and some of these services (is, are) being offered for the first time.

4. This transformation of the Library's materials (is, are) leading to the first digital library of its kind; many libraries for the blind from all over the world (is, are) watching this project with great interest.

5. With over 60 000 titles in its collection, including more than 300 000 individual talking book copies, the CNIB Library conversion (doubles, double) the size of the collection and (allows, allow) clients to access materials faster and in better ways than ever before.

6. The Library's clients across Canada (requests, request) nearly two million accessible items and (makes, make) more than 50 000 inquiries to reader advisors every year.

7. Twenty percent of new books added to the collection every year (is, are) children's titles, and the Library (maintains, maintain) the world's second-largest collection of music in Braille.

8. Canada Post or the website (is, are) used to make the requested item available, although some of the audio items (is, are) even available over the phone.

9. Many of the other countries in the world (funds, fund) comprehensive library service for blind or visually impaired citizens; in fact, there (is, are) no other G8 countries without government-sponsored programs.

10. Along with forty other nonprofit libraries for the blind, the Canadian National Institute for the Blind Library (belongs, belong) to the international DAISY (Digital Audio-based Information SYstem) Consortium, which (is, are) creating world standards for the next generation of digital audiobooks.

Source: Adapted from *About the CNIB Library for the Blind,* 2005, Canadian National Institute for the Blind (http://www.cnib.ca/library/general_information/about_lib.htm).

PROOFREADING EXERCISE

Find and correct the ten subject–verb agreement errors in the following paragraph.

My courses for this academic year are really challenging. Each of the classes are difficult in a different way. Some of them requires us to learn on our own in labs. And the others demand that students carefully follows the minute instructions of the professor. The assignments given by my geography instructor, for example, is harder than I expected. Everybody in the class have to prepare a scale model of a mountain range. All of the models so far have looked the same. But one of the models were a little out of scale, and the instructor failed it. The other students and I has decided to work together so that none of us makes the same mistake. I guess that all of this hard work are worthwhile. My instructors says it helps prepare us for our future careers.

SENTENCE WRITING

Write ten sentences in which you describe the shoes you are wearing. Use verbs in the present time. Then go back over your sentences—underline your subjects once, underline your verbs twice, and be sure they agree.

_____

_____

_____

_____

_____

_____

_____

_____

_____

_____

Using Pronouns

Nouns name people, places, things, and ideas—such as *students, school, computers,* and *cyberspace.* Pronouns take the place of nouns to avoid repetition and to clarify meaning. Look at the following two sentences. Nouns are needlessly repeated in the first sentence, but the second uses pronouns.

> The boy's mother felt that the children at the party were too loud, so the boy's mother told the children that the party would have to end if the children didn't calm down.

> The boy's mother felt that the children at the party were too loud, so *she* told *them* that *it* would have to end if *they* didn't calm down.

In the second sentence, *she* replaces *mother*, *they* and *them* replace *children*, and *it* takes the place of *party*.

CHOOSING THE RIGHT PRONOUN

Of the many kinds of pronouns, the following cause the most difficulty because they include two ways of identifying the same person (or people), but only one form is correct in a given situation:

SUBJECT GROUP	OBJECT GROUP
I	me
he	him
she	her
we	us
they	them
who	whom

Use a pronoun from the Subject Group in two instances:

1. Before a verb as a subject:

> *He* is my cousin. (*He* is the subject of the verb *is.*)

> *He* is taller than *I.* (The sentence is not written out in full. It means "*He* is taller than *I* am." *I* is the subject of the verb *am.*)

Whenever you see *than* or *as* in a sentence, ask yourself whether a verb is missing at the end of the sentence. Add the verb in both speaking and writing, and then you'll automatically use the correct pronoun. Instead of saying, "She's smarter than (I, me)," say, "She's smarter than I *am*." Also, instead of "She is as tall as (he, him)," say, "She is as tall as he *is*."

2. After a linking verb (*is, am, are, was, were*) as a pronoun that renames the subject:

> The one who should apologize is *he*. (*He* is *the one who should apologize*. Therefore the pronoun from the Subject Group is used.)

> The winner of the lottery was *she*. (*She* was *the winner of the lottery*. Therefore the pronoun from the Subject Group is used.)

Use pronouns from the Object Group for all other purposes. In the following sentence, *me* is not the subject, nor does it rename the subject. It follows a preposition; therefore, it comes from the Object Group.

> My boss left a message for Rachael and *me*.

A good way to tell whether to use a pronoun from the Subject Group or the Object Group is to leave out any extra name (and the word *and*). By leaving out *Rachael and*, you will say, *My boss left a message for me*. You would never say, *My boss left a message for I*.

> My sister and *I* play chess on Sundays. (*I* play chess on Sundays.)

> *She* and her friends rented a limousine. (*She* rented a limousine.)

> We saw Joseph and *them* last night. (We saw *them* last night.)

> The teacher gave *us* students certificates. (The teacher gave *us* certificates.)

> The coach asked Raj and *me* to wash the benches. (The coach asked *me* to wash the benches.)

EXERCISES

Correct any errors you find in the writer's choice of pronouns in the following sentences.

Exercise 1

1. My father and me went camping over the long weekend.

2. Every time him and me have gone camping before, I have chosen where to stay and what to do.

3. We are careful to keep all receipts so that we can divide the expenses between him and I.

4. The one in charge of this trip was him.

5. Dad and I have different personalities, so him and I use different techniques when we go fishing.

6. Me, I'm always wanting to move to another location if we don't get a good catch within ten minutes of setting anchor.

7. Dad can plunk down in one spot for hours, enabling we companions to settle in for the long haul.

8. His method certainly has proven results; on this trip, he caught seven fish more than me every day.

9. I guess I am a lot less patient than him, but now I have learned how to stay in one spot and enjoy the moment.

10. In the future, I will leave all the big decisions about our camping trips up to he and Mother Nature.

Exercise 2

1. Ann is very active as a volunteer in the community because her mother and her serve as board members for several not-for-profit organizations.

2. Every fall, the local arts council sponsors a studio tour to highlight the work of local artisans like them and we potters.

3. Used to the quiet disarray of our studios, we are generally aghast when visitors make so much more noise than us.

4. Last fall, several of we potters decided to open just a single studio to the public tour.

5. Due to space limitations, though, the other club members and me soon discovered that we had to restrict the number of items on display and for sale.

6. Ann was able to find time to visit the shared studio we had established, and no other visitor was as enthusiastic as her.

7. Since her mother and her work with textiles, they don't know a lot about pottery.

8. The two women lingered over our displays even though the two of them must have had a more exhausting day than us.

9. To our delight, Ann's mother actually ended up purchasing one of my partner's best pieces, one that us club members had predicted was too expensive to attract a buyer at a local show.

10. Later, Ann told a friend and I that her mother couldn't take her eyes off the piece and had given it a place of honour in her home.

Exercise 3

1. At a town hall meeting last week, me and my sister heard about how to reduce the energy consumption in our home.

2. The speaker, a prominent environmentalist, certainly knew more about energy than us.

3. He suggested that homeowners' utility costs could be greatly reduced if only us energy consumers would follow some basic tips.

4. One of those tips included insulating water pipes if you and me want to save on heating costs.

5. Since the audience and me were using natural gas water heaters, the idea is to keep the incoming water from becoming too cold in the winter.

6. When we compared bills, I discovered that the man sitting next to me used nearly twice as much natural gas as me throughout last winter.

7. However, him and me had almost identical hydro bills for the same period.

8. In the audience was one of our neighbours, Bill; him and his wife Martha had already switched their incandescent light bulbs for compact fluorescent bulbs (CFBs).

9. Just between you and I, homeowners can save money far more effectively by purchasing Energy Star–rated appliances.

10. When we consumers decide to conserve energy, the biggest winners will be us.

Exercise 4

1. Probably the closest friends in our school are Rajih, Karyn, and me.

2. Karyn says that she likes the same music as us.

3. However, when we bought tickets to the folk music festival, Karyn wasn't excited about the relatively unknown new group her boyfriend Rajih and me wanted to see.

4. Perhaps the newer group was more exciting to we older listeners than her.

5. Rajih recently explained that Karyn thinks she is as good a judge of music as us.

6. The next time us friends decide to attend a concert, we should vote on what groups to see before the tickets are purchased.

7. Because there are only three of us, the ones who will make the decision will be Rajih and me.

8. Although me and Rajih are older than she, our musical tastes are broader than just the Beatles and the Rolling Stones.

9. Still, if anyone gives free tickets for a Stones concert to him or I, we will go.

10. My mother and father once told me that even when she and him were younger, they knew that Sir Michael Philip ("Mick") Jagger was going to be an influential rocker.

SENTENCE WRITING

On the lines below, write sentences using the indicated pronoun phrases correctly.

1. than we

_____

2. Sheila and her

_____

3. Bill and she

_____

4. among us

_____

5. she and I

_____

MAKING PRONOUNS AGREE

Just as subjects and verbs must agree, pronouns should agree with the words they refer to. If the word referred to is singular, the pronoun should be singular. If the noun referred to is plural, the pronoun should be plural.

Each concept car has its own advantage.
The pronoun *its* refers to the singular noun *car* and therefore is singular.

Both concept cars have their own advantages.
The pronoun *their* refers to the plural noun *cars* and therefore is plural.

The same rules that we use to maintain the agreement of subjects and verbs also apply to pronoun agreement. For instance, ignore any prepositional phrases that come between the word and the pronoun that takes its place.

The *box* of chocolates has lost *its* label.

Boxes of chocolates often lose *their* labels.

The *player* with the best concentration usually beats *her or his* opponent.

Players with the best concentration usually beat *their* opponents.

When a pronoun refers to more than one word joined by *and*, the pronoun is plural:

The *teacher* <u>and</u> the *tutors* eat *their* lunches at noon.

The *salt* <u>and</u> *pepper* were in *their* usual spots on the table.

However, when a pronoun refers to more than one word joined by *or*, then the word closest to the pronoun determines its form:

Either the *teacher* <u>or</u> the *tutors* eat *their* lunches in the classroom.

Either the *tutors* <u>or</u> the teacher eats *her* lunch in the classroom.

Today many people try to avoid gender bias by writing sentences like the following:

> If anyone wants help with the assignment, he or she can visit me in my office.
>
> If anybody calls, tell him or her that I'll be back soon.
>
> Somebody has left his or her pager in the classroom.

But those sentences are wordy and awkward. Therefore some people, especially in conversation, turn them into sentences that are not grammatically correct.

> If anyone wants help with the assignment, they can visit me in my office.
>
> If anybody calls, tell them that I'll be back soon.
>
> Somebody has left their pager in the classroom.

Such ungrammatical sentences, however, are not necessary. It just takes a little thought to revise each sentence so that it avoids gender bias and is also grammatically correct:

> Anyone who wants help with the assignment can visit me in my office.
>
> Tell anybody who calls that I'll be back soon.
>
> Somebody has left a pager in the classroom.

Probably the best way to avoid the awkward *he or she* and *him or her* is to make the words plural. Instead of writing, "Each actor was in his or her proper place on stage," write, "All the actors were in their proper places on stage," thus avoiding gender bias and still having a grammatically correct sentence.

E X E R C I S E S

In the following sentences, find and correct any pronouns that fail to agree with the nouns they represent. (Some of the sentences may have no error.)

Exercise 1

1. Many Canadian cities now feature restaurants focusing on a wide variety of foods from around the world; each of these dining spots serves their host country's favourite dishes.

2. When my family first immigrated to Canada, we were surprised to find many Chinese restaurants that served its dishes in an all-you-can-eat buffet format.

3. Any Canadian living in a large city like Toronto, Montreal, or Vancouver can eat exotic meals from any continent they choose.

4. At the small East Indian restaurant down the street, each customer ordering a hamburger is asked whether they want it served with hot or mild curry powder.

5. Still, a restaurant specializing in the cuisine of other countries used to find their financial survival was dependent upon offering some Canadian standards, like poutine and chicken strips.

6. For example, traditional Mexican restaurants have sprung up and then disappeared, not because their food was too spicy but because its menus didn't include pizza or spaghetti.

7. However, the newest restaurant in town features shrimp and alligator on its menu, and they seem to be doing good business.

8. The owners seized upon the Acadian experience in New Brunswick; it has made eating Cajun food fashionable.

9. However, when it comes to volume of customers, ethnic eating establishments are often financially successful only if it is in a small storefront location.

10. To attract families, American chain restaurants or a small local dining spot has a natural advantage because their menus feature food that children like.

Exercise 2

1. Either my partner or his sisters will soon need to make decisions about how best to care for his aging father Frank.

2. The three siblings are scattered across the world, but each knows their dad won't be capable of living alone much longer.

3. While two of the three can't visit Frank face-to-face, one sister tries to visit him as often as she can.

4. Because the other sister lives at the other end of the country, she and her brother call his or her father regularly to get up-to-date information about him.

5. Everyone in the family agrees that they have taken this man's lifelong independence for granted.

6. Unfortunately, a recent series of mini-strokes has taken their toll on his well-being.

7. A recent fall from a ladder or the mini-strokes have caused Frank to worry about their independence.

8. The three children have hired a personal support worker to attend Frank's home three times a day because each child lacks confidence that their dad is safe on his own.

9. Frank has always provided help to every family member who needed it; now they need to convince him that he needs his or her assistance.

10. A parent no longer able to live confidently on his or her own should discuss possible solutions with their children.

Exercise 3

1. Every individual should make a point of checking all medicine purchases with their pharmacist.

2. Some of the drugs on the market today carry labels that advise consumers not to use it with other specified medications.

3. When seeing a doctor, a patient should bring a list of all the medications they are currently taking.

4. Recently, a study revealed that certain vitamins or other seemingly harmless openly available pills were actually detrimental to a patient's health.

5. Still, an otherwise healthy person may not be aware that an over-the-counter drug can be harmful in their specific situation.

6. As individuals age and suffer from more disorders, he or she is more likely to need several prescriptions.

7. Each of my mother's prescription drugs has their own side effects.

8. Adult family members need to pay close attention to all medications, prescribed or not, taken by his or her loved ones.

9. Some individuals' parents refuse to allow his or her children to be immunized against standard childhood diseases.

10. However, recent studies seem to have proven beyond any reasonable doubt that a child who receives inoculations will not suffer later in their life from a serious disorder like autism.

Exercise 4

1. Each of the patients in the chronic care wing of a retirement home has a separate chart to indicate which treatments they are taking.

2. However, sometimes a chart maintained by retirement home staff members isn't as up-to-date as they ought to be.

3. Chronic care residents often need specialized and timely care if he or she is to live a meaningful life.

4. For example, if a resident fails to take a prescribed medication as ordered by the doctor, they might develop even more severe health issues.

5. Many older citizens prefer to live his or her final days in their own private homes.

6. Without supervision, however, issues like drug interactions, poor nutrition, and inadequate exercise can go unnoticed unless it causes fainting.

7. Although several individuals die every year from a drug interaction, the cause of his or her death might be difficult to determine without proper records.

8. Each of the deaths resulting from drug interaction is unnecessary; they could have been avoided.

9. When a relative moves into a hospital setting with registered nurses providing constant care, their drug interactions are more closely monitored.

10. Still, the lack of alternative care beds in most hospitals restricts its ability to look after patients with the care and thoroughness necessary.

Exercise 5

1. When selecting a computer, consumers often find the marketplace very confusing because they come with so many options.

2. A huge company like Microsoft has a huge portion of the market in their hands.

3. Linda and her brother have been contemplating his or her computer purchase for nearly six months; however, they really don't know much about computer basics.

4. The humorous Apple commercials appeal to each of them even though they know almost nothing about the differences between Apples and PCs.

5. Linda's boyfriend Amil is a real geek, but whenever he tries to explain computer terms like RAM and hard drive, their eyes glaze over.

6. They should listen carefully to him because no one understands their computer terminology better than he does.

7. Nonetheless, Amil's understanding is useless when he speaks to Linda or her brother because they need to acquire more basic information first.

8. Even the most confident computer users in class go to Amil when he or she has a question.

9. Amil is probably the most patient man I've ever met; when one of the computers in the lab crashed and lost all their files, he managed somehow to retrieve them.

10. Now, if either Linda or her brother listens to Amil about how to choose a computer, they will make a sounder choice.

MAKING CLEAR PRONOUN REFERENCES

A pronoun replaces a noun to avoid repetition, but sometimes the pronoun sounds as if it refers to the wrong word in a sentence, causing confusion. Be aware that when you write a sentence, although *you* know what it means, your reader may not. What does this sentence mean?

The students tried to use the school's computers to access the Internet, but they were too slow, so they decided to go home.

Who or what was too slow, and who or what decided to go home? We don't know whether the two pronouns (both *they*) refer to the students or to the computers. One way to correct such a faulty reference is to use singular and plural nouns:

> The students tried to use a school computer to access the Internet, but it was too slow, so they decided to go home.

Here's another sentence with a faulty reference:

> Sylvie told her mother that she needed a haircut.

Who needed the haircut—Sylvie or her mother? One way to correct such a faulty reference is to use a direct quotation:

> Sylvie told her mother, "You need a haircut."
>
> Sylvie said, "Mom, I need a haircut."

Or you could always rephrase the sentence completely:

> Sylvie noticed her mother's hair was sticking out in odd places, so she told her mother to get a haircut.

Another kind of faulty reference is a *which* clause that appears to refer to a specific word, but doesn't really.

> I wasn't able to finish all the problems on the exam, which makes me worried.

The word *which* seems to replace exam, but it isn't the exam that makes me worried. The sentence should read

> I am worried because I wasn't able to finish all the problems on the exam.

The pronoun *it* causes its own reference problems. Look at this sentence, for example:

> When replacing the ink cartridge in my printer, it broke, and I had to call the technician to come and fix it.

Did the printer or the cartridge break? Here is one possible correction:

> The new ink cartridge broke when I was putting it in my printer, and I had to call the technician for help.

E X E R C I S E S

In the following exercises, look for pronouns that are making unclear references to the nouns they represent. Then correct the problems to make the meaning clear to the reader.

Exercise 1

1. As is always the case with special events, this year's awards presentations weren't without its problems.

_____

2. The awards programs didn't arrive on time from the printers, and they misspelled several names.

_____

3. Although workers placed three hundred chairs in the hall late yesterday afternoon, they weren't clean at the time.

_____

4. As the ceremony began, a serious accident outside the hall involved a truck and an ambulance; its horn stuck and drowned out the introductions.

_____

5. At last night's event, the award recipients were seated beside the sponsors, but they didn't have name tags.

_____

6. Luanne won the President's Award, which was a real surprise.

_____

7. The winners hardly spoke to the sponsors at their tables because they were too uncomfortable.

_____

8. When Luanne's mother met the woman who organized the evening, she told her that her dress was elegant.

_____

9. The tables seated only eight people, but they were too close together.

_____

10. The award winners stayed after the ceremony for a group photo, which everyone enjoyed.

_____

Exercise 2

1. This summer, I ordered a set of patio furniture for our new deck, which arrived the next day.

_____

2. The set included a large glass-topped table, two mesh chairs, and two rockers, and they are exceptionally comfortable.

_____

3. The two types of chairs were listed with different prices before they went on sale at the end of the season.

_____

4. I asked two salesclerks about the difference, which seemed reasonable to me.

_____

5. Once satisfied that the sale price was being applied, I needed to select the method of payment for my purchase because it was a big one.

_____

6. Now that my bank's credit card uses "chip technology," I didn't even have to sign it.

_____

7. Instead, I swiped my credit card, entered my PIN on the transaction machine, and returned it to my wallet.

   _____

8. When I assembled the furniture set, one chair was clearly defective, so I had to return it to the retail store.

   _____

9. The clerk told his manager that he could probably get a replacement chair from the warehouse.

   _____

10. The whole return process took only half an hour, but it was worth all the effort.

    _____

Exercise 3

1. Earlier this month, our neighbours the MacNeils bought some new trees, but they were too tall for them.

   _____

2. The trees had so many branches that they appeared to be several years old.

   _____

3. Homeowners need specialized horticultural skills to plant mature trees, which most of them don't have.

   _____

4. When Bill MacNeil asked a member of the local horticultural society how to plant such trees, he was confused.

   _____

5. The horticulturalist told Bill that he would need expert advice.

_____

6. The root balls of these trees were beginning to dry out while they sat waiting for planting.

_____

7. Finally, the MacNeils asked my parents for help, which made my mother smile.

_____

8. Sandra MacNeil told my mother that she had a green thumb.

_____

9. Sandra and Mom quickly rented several pieces of equipment because they needed to move the trees.

_____

10. The preparation work was finished within a week, and each tree was carefully planted; Mom says it was a difficult job.

_____

Exercise 4

1. Lots of people who wear glasses can tell you horror stories about how they affected their lives.

_____

2. One sunny day at the beach, my brothers smashed my glasses when they ran across my towel.

_____

3. When the ophthalmologist took the lenses out of my glasses' frames, they broke.

_____

4. Apparently the life expectancy of any set of eyeglasses is far shorter than they advertise.

_____

5. Some very expensive glasses are now sold with insurance policies to protect the owner against their accidental breakage.

_____

6. When they went on a trip together, my sister told our aunt that she shouldn't sit on the bed.

_____

7. The hotel bed's duvet had designs the same colour as my sister's glasses, so they just disappeared into the fabric.

_____

8. When I travel, I try to put my glasses in a safe place at night, which isn't always easy.

_____

9. If people don't treat their glasses carefully, they may need to be replaced.

_____

10. Some people elect to wear flexible contact lenses, but they can pose a different set of problems.

_____

Exercise 5

1. Whenever Kareena puts gasoline into her mother's car, its smell gives her a headache.

_____

2. One brand seems just as bad as another, which is difficult to understand.

_____

3. Kareena and her mother haven't owned cars very long because they need too much attention.

_____

4. Prior to moving to Canada, the bicycle once served as the family's primary source of transportation, which helped with the family budget.

_____

5. India's Tata Motors, a car manufacturing company, has now introduced what is said to be the least expensive car in the world; it makes not just cars but also trucks.

_____

6. Still, neither Kareena nor her mother has much experience pumping gasoline into a vehicle, so it is unsettling because it's new.

_____

7. The problem doesn't have anything to do with a low octane level, either, because it is just as smelly with the highest priced gasoline.

_____

8. Possibly, other additives in the fuels cause the problem because they now sometimes include ethanol for environmental reasons.

_____

9. Some experts question the environmental benefits of ethanol because they haven't been proven entirely.

_____

10. Kareena is fortunate that her family's car is not fuelled by diesel; it has a distinct smell.

_____

PROOFREADING EXERCISE

The following paragraph contains errors in the use of pronouns. Find and correct the errors.

I told my cousin Miles a secret at our last family reunion, and as soon as I did, I knew it would get out. I forgot that Miles is six years younger than me when I told him that I was taking a job overseas. Right before I told him the secret, I said, "Now this is just between you and I, and you're not going to tell anyone, right?" He assured me that the only person he would talk to about it was me. I made the mistake of believing him. If I had taken out a full-page ad in the newspaper to print my secret and delivered it to my family, it could not have been spread around faster. Miles and I are still cousins, but him and me are no longer friends.

SENTENCE WRITING

Write ten sentences about a misunderstanding between you and someone else. Then check that your pronouns are grammatically correct, that they agree with the words they replace, and that references to specific nouns are clear.

_____

_____

_____

_____

_____

_____

_____

_____

_____

_____

Correcting Misplaced or Dangling Modifiers

To modify something, you often change whatever it is by adding something to it. You might modify a car, for example, by adding special tires. In English, *modifiers* are words, phrases, and clauses that add information to another part of a sentence.

Do you remember this book's discussion of sentence parts at the very beginning of Part 2: Knowing Sentence Essentials? Two sentence parts, *adjectives* and *adverbs*, act only as modifiers. An adjective changes the meaning or adds description to words identifying persons, places, things, or ideas. An adverb modifies or adds information to verbs, adjectives, and adverbs. A modifier, whether a single word or several words in length, always describes, so you might want to review the section on adjectives and adverbs in Part 2.

MISPLACED MODIFIERS

To do its job properly, a modifier needs to be in the right spot—and that's as close as possible to the word it describes. If you put new tires on the roof of your car instead of where they belong, an onlooker is going to be confused.

One-word modifiers can easily cause confusion. Check out the following four legitimate sentences where the placement of the modifier *only* changes the writer's meaning. (You'll find the meaning within parentheses at the end of each sentence.)

Only I am allowed to change the toner in that laser printer. (No one else is allowed.)

I am allowed only to change the toner in that laser printer. (I cannot, for example, add paper to the paper tray.)

I am allowed to change only the toner in that laser printer. (I am not allowed to change anything else.)

I am allowed to change the toner only in that laser printer. (I can't change the toner in any other machine.)

Notice that all four of the above sentences sound "right" even though the meanings of the four sentences are entirely different from one another. If you want your reader to understand exactly what you mean, each word needs to be placed in the right position.

Correcting Misplaced Modifiers

Be aware of modifiers in your sentences. To ensure that your reader will seamlessly understand your message, make sure that all modifiers are positioned as closely as possible to the words they are describing.

In the following sentence, the modifier is built of several words (a *phrase*) located too far away from the word it describes:

Swinging from tree to tree, we watched the monkeys at the zoo.

Was it *we* who were swinging from tree to tree? That's what the sentence says because the modifying phrase *Swinging from tree to tree* is next to *we*.

The modifying phrase needs to appear next to *monkeys*, like this:

At the zoo, we watched the monkeys swinging from tree to tree.

Longer misplaced modifiers are sometimes more noticeable since, as in the example above, the sentence's meaning will often seem amusing.

E X E R C I S E S

The sentences in the following exercises contain modifiers that appear to describe the wrong words because the modifiers are located in the wrong place in the sentences. Make the necessary changes to clarify the meaning of each sentence.

Exercise 1

1. My sister ran over a neighbour's cat by accident.
2. Weeping loudly, we thought the neighbour mistook her pet for a child.
3. Perhaps hoping to make some financial gain from the unfortunate situation, my sister was threatened with a lawsuit for thousands of dollars by the woman.
4. Complaining bitterly about how much money she had spent to get the cat neutered, my sister and I could only listen with disbelief to the angry woman.
5. Our whole family loves cats, but this one roamed the streets killing harmless little birds with no regrets.
6. Incapable of intentionally hurting any animal, let alone a family pet, I quietly suggested to my sister that she replace the neighbour's cat.

7. Offering to purchase a new cat, the neighbour suddenly stopped crying and smiled sweetly at my sister.

8. We adopted a cat for the neighbour with a fluffy tail.

9. Less than six weeks later, the new cat wandered away sadly.

10. After hearing our offer to help find her missing pet, we were astonished when the neighbour just shrugged her shoulders.

Exercise 2

1. Most people describe Robert Munsch as a master storyteller, especially children.

2. He makes his stories come alive with his sparkling eyes.

3. Munsch usually attracts children of all ages to shows on his storytelling tours.

4. At the Theatre Centre, Janine's granddaughter is begging her grand-mother to see Munsch.

5. Through a local radio station's contest, Janine hopes to win free tickets for the performance.

6. She's heard that these tickets will be awarded for front-row seats on the radio.

7. Munsch's performance will be the first time to see the difference between a story reader and a storyteller for many in the audience.

8. Seated on chairs next to him on stage, the characters in the stories Munsch is telling are transformed into the children he has selected from the audience.

9. Munsch has put smiles on listeners' faces and favourite stories on readers' lips over several generations.

10. Giggling, Munsch smiles at the children in the audience.

Exercise 3

1. Canada Day is a time to celebrate in many Canadian cities and towns on July 1.

2. In the park, families with picnic lunches spread out blankets with laughing children.

3. Greeting everyone with smiles, the summer season has begun for most individuals.

4. With their loud trumpets and drums, groups line up along the streets downtown to watch the marching bands.

5. Designed with tiny Canadian flags, spectators run after candies distributed by some marchers and floats.

6. With maple leaves, face painters use red theatre makeup to decorate children's faces.

7. The added benefit of a warm day puts everyone into a celebratory mood with blue skies.

8. Teens and young adults pack the parks for rock concerts wearing only lightweight clothes later in the evening.

9. Keeping their eyes on the skies, the Canadian Forces' Snowbirds acrobatic team thrills onlookers whenever it appears as part of the festivities.

10. As the sky darkens, fireworks produce ooh's and aah's from appreciative viewers with all colours and shapes.

Exercise 4

1. Citing the current worldwide economic situation, job security is not being offered by most employers.

2. One year after becoming manager, the company closed its doors, and my brother was without any job at all.

3. Seeing the fragile nature of their employment, call centres are experiencing a particularly high turnover of staff.

4. On the other hand, health care professionals can count on bright futures with aging patients.

5. Some disorders previously seldom encountered have become far more prevalent like Alzheimer's.

6. Older patients also present with a wider range of symptoms and conditions at family doctors' offices, after-hours clinics, and emergency rooms across the country.

7. Slowing down the economy, a significant role is played by the surging value of the Canadian dollar.

8. Compared to the U.S. dollar, the prices of manufactured goods aren't always reflecting the higher value of the Canadian dollar.

9. Facing near bankruptcy, North American taxpayers found their governments becoming significant shareholders in Daimler-Chrysler and General Motors.

10. Agreeing to provide stimulus funding, many mechanics, millwrights, and other skilled tradespersons found that their North American jobs were saved by the infusion of capital by governments.

Exercise 5

1. When doing the laundry this weekend, Rani found a ten-dollar bill going through the pockets of her brother's pants.

2. Smiling as she remembered her mother's rules for sorting clothes, the unexpected discovery delighted Rani.

3. At the age of six, the routine for preparing the family's laundry had been assigned to Rani.

4. Not only did Rani learn to check pockets for their contents, but she also learned to verify the washing instructions with tags stitched into clothing to avoid mishaps.

5. Now a mother herself, Rani knew her mother would be proud to see that the lessons had been so well learned twenty years later.

6. When she was a child, Rani couldn't remember ever finding anything except tissues and the occasional penny or nickel in anyone's pockets.

7. Carefully folded into quarters, she wondered why her brother didn't remember putting the bill into his pocket.

8. In the laundry room, Rajit learned his sister had found money in his pants pocket.

9. Whimpering quietly about plans to spend this money on their mother, Rani listened to Rajit without much sympathy.

10. A week earlier, Rajit was grateful that his sister had missed the twenty-dollar bill that somehow made it through the washing machine and dryer in his pants.

DANGLING MODIFIERS

Even more confusing are sentences in which a modifier appears without the word it is describing. With sentences like these, the reader is forced to make guesses at the meaning. Words and phrases that fail to identify clearly what they are describing are called *dangling modifiers*. Here is one example:

At the age of eight, my family finally bought a dog.

Obviously, the family was not eight when it purchased a dog. Nor was the dog eight. The phrase modifier *At the age of eight* is not describing any other word in the sentence.

Correcting Dangling Modifiers

One way to eliminate dangling modifiers is to turn them into dependent clauses. (See pp. 107–109 in Part 3: Building Effective Sentences for a review of dependent clauses.)

Look at how this method can be used to correct the previous sentence:

When I was eight years old, my family finally bought a dog.

In this sentence, because the clause has its own subject and verb (*I was*), there's no guesswork about who or what is eight years old.

Another possibility is to reword the rest of the sentence so that the word being modified appears beside what had previously been a dangling modifier.

Check out this sentence:

After a ten-minute nap, the plane landed.

Did the plane take a nap? If not, who did? When that information is not stated, the reader is forced to guess at the meaning.

After a ten-minute nap, I awoke just as the plane landed.

The corrected sentence opens with a modifier but continues by immediately inserting the word being modified.

In both these examples, the dangling modifier appears in the form of a prepositional phrase. Remember that, like all modifiers, dangling modifiers can also be single words or other multiple-word phrases.

The exercises that follow will be challenging. Take your time and remember to check your corrections with those found in the answer key.

E X E R C I S E S

Each of the sentences in the following exercises contains a dangling modifier that fails to describe clearly any other word in the sentence. Rewrite the sentence so that the meaning is clear. Remember that because your interpretation may be different, the correction in the answer key might not be the same as yours.

Exercise 1

1. When purchasing a new car, the vehicle's appearance is only one factor to take into consideration.

_____

2. Increasingly, due to their safety features, gasoline consumption, and technological options, decisions are trickier to make.

_____

3. Having access to only a few automotive dealerships, "oak tree mechanics" filled the service gap to make cars reliable in the 1960s.

_____

4. During trips, scenery was more important than a high-class sound system while driving leisurely down a deserted country road.

_____

5. Looking after routine repairs and breakdowns, many small rural towns had small service stations.

_____

6. Without being asked, these full-service stations cheerfully pumped gas, washed windshields, and checked oil levels on customers' cars.

_____

7. Selling well-equipped vehicles, owners were able to depend on full-sized spare tires along with jacks and other tools to change flat tires.

_____

8. Offering many varieties of scenery, Canadian automobile travellers can view everything from flat, waving fields of grain on the Prairies to lofty, majestic pine forests in northwestern Ontario to invigorating salt water waves against the rocks of Newfoundland.

_____

9. The splendid visual experiences in Canada during warmer periods of the year are completely eliminated by intimidating winter snow squalls and blizzards even when using only major highways.

_____

10. Especially while enjoying perfect weather and speeding along the Trans-Canada Highway to get from Point A to Point B in the shortest time possible, much of the beauty of the countryside is lost in a blur.

_____

Exercise 2

1. Unless paying attention, industrial accidents can easily happen in virtually any workplace.

_____

2. For example, roofing jobs can result in nasty tumbles from the tops of buildings without being tied off securely.

_____

3. Even when driving down a residential street, a boom truck can snag on low overhead hydro lines and be electrocuted.

_____

4. Studying workplace health and safety, new employees and those with many years of experience are the two categories of employees particularly susceptible to workplace accidents.

_____

5. At a young age, on-the-job health and safety training doesn't seem critically important.

_____

6. However, working for the first time, some experts say that many employers fail to give appropriate instructions.

_____

7. Interested in saving money for the future, high-risk employment opportunities quickly build healthy bank accounts to pay college or university expenses.

_____

8. Routine safety rules can become boring and repetitive after several years in the same workplace.

_____

9. With a work history of scooping minerals from the earth for several years, safety procedures may be either forgotten or ignored.

_____

10. Hearing the siren announcing a mining accident, the production operations come to a stop in order to focus on rescuing those trapped.

_____

Exercise 3

1. After test-driving several cars, my first vehicle purchase was a Chevrolet Impala.

_____

2. At the age of twenty-one, the car seemed to include all my favourite features.

_____

3. Worried at my lack of mechanical skills, the only technology onboard involved reading the owner's manual.

_____

4. Fortunate that the used-car dealer had managed to provide one with the sale, some of the manual answered questions about the car's proper operation and troubleshooting procedures.

_____

5. Not a natural reader, the manual still offered several pleasant surprises.

_____

6. The car was certainly clean and smooth running at the dealership when talking with the salesperson.

_____

7. Not knowing, the car's first problem was that it already had a leaky gas tank.

_____

8. Full of gas, I drove home from the dealer's lot.

_____

9. After sitting in my driveway all night, I couldn't drive to work the following morning.

_____

10. At the age of twelve, my boss said I shouldn't be surprised at the problem.

_____

Exercise 4

1. Confused by media reports, H1N1 flu vaccination clinics were scheduled to open in early November 2009.

_____

2. The vaccines available in Canada came in two forms after learning about the reactions of some patients.

_____

3. Although called swine flu, consumers were quickly reassured that eating pork products carried no increased health risk.

_____

4. Not wanting to inject vaccines unnecessarily, some children likely did not get the shot.

_____

5. Young children were, however, identified as a group that suffered the most severe symptoms and required the most intensive hospitalized care while studying the disease's characteristics.

_____

6. After determining risk levels through the trials, clinics were moved up by at least two weeks.

_____

7. Visiting a doctor's office, after-hours clinic, or emergency room, the waiting rooms were completely filled regardless of the time of day.

_____

8. Especially listening to conflicting information, advice about who should get the vaccine was difficult to understand.

_____

9. Under the age of five, experts originally recommended two doses of the vaccine.

_____

10. Mutating each year, the virus in this year's H1N1 vaccination will likely become part of the seasonal flu vaccine in subsequent years.

_____

Exercise 5

1. One day after turning forty, my new car broke down in a hectic intersection during rush hour.

_____

2. Managing to bring all traffic to a complete stop, a nearby resident offered to call a tow truck for me.

_____

3. Becoming increasingly agitated, the traffic noises sounded louder and louder.

_____

4. Turning on the hazard lights when my car refused to start, other drivers began honking their horns.

_____

5. Zooming past my stalled car and coming close to hitting it, I watched in terror.

_____

6. Groaning with relief, a tow truck with blinking lights finally appeared to take charge of the situation.

_____

7. Pushing my car to the side of the road, the other drivers could move more freely.

_____

8. While thanking the helpful neighbour who called the tow truck, unhappy drivers were distracting me.

_____

9. Forgetting his name, he might read my thank you letter in tonight's newspaper.

_____

10. After cooling down for almost half an hour, I was able to get started on the road again.

_____

PROOFREADING EXERCISE

Find and correct any misplaced or dangling modifiers in the following paragraphs.

I love parades, so last year my family and I went to Toronto to see the Caribana parade. It turned out to be even more wonderful than I expected.

Arriving one day before the festivities, the city was already crowded with tourists. Early the next morning, people set up lawn chairs on Lakeshore Boulevard. We didn't want to miss one float in the parade, so we found our own spot and made ourselves at home. When the parade began, I had as much fun watching the spectators as the parade itself. I saw children pointing at the breathtaking floats sitting on their parents' shoulders. Decorated extravagantly with feathers and sequins, I couldn't believe how beautiful the costumes were.

The crowd was overwhelmed by the sights and sounds of the parade. Marching and playing their instruments with perfect rhythm, everyone especially enjoyed hearing the steel drum bands. They must have practised the whole year to be that good.

My experience didn't end with the parade, however. After the last float had passed, I found a twenty-dollar bill walking up Yonge Street. Now hanging on my wall at home, I framed it as a souvenir of my Caribana experience.

Avoiding Shifts in Time and Person

In crafting multi-clause sentences or extended paragraphs, you will want to keep your eye on consistency and appropriateness of time frames (expressed by verb tense) and perspective (determined by the "person").

SHIFTS IN TIME

Verbs and their tenses (present, past, future) place actions in a time context. Use common sense to guide you. If you begin writing about a topic in past time, don't shift back and forth to the present unnecessarily. If you begin in the present, don't shift to the past without good reason.

Confusing shift in time:

Tom loved racing his Volkswagen GTI, and he wins lots of races.

Does Tom still race? (*loved* is in past tense)
If he doesn't race, how can he still win races? (*win* is in present tense)

Possible corrections:

Tom *loves* racing his Volkswagen GTI, and he *wins* lots of races. (present)

Tom *loved* racing his Volkswagen GTI, and he *won* lots of races. (past)

REQUIRED SHIFTS IN TIME

When I was just six years old, I did not know that all spiders have eight legs.

Here the first two verbs (*was* and *did know*) are written in the past tense, but the final verb (*have*) is in present. This shift is correct because spiders still have eight legs, but the writer is no longer six and has learned more about spiders.

Lu Kim is studying Canadian history and geography and was surprised to hear that the country's maple leaf flag design generated so much controversy in the 1960s.

Here the present tense has to be used with the first verb (*is studying*) to represent an action taking place right now. On the other hand, both the student's surprise and the controversy are in the past (*was, generated*).

Remember that shifts in time should be justified.

E X E R C I S E S

In the following sentences, make the necessary changes to eliminate unnecessary shifts in time.

Exercise 1

1. Studying the history of words helps readers because many words relied on the same root.

2. For example, when looking at words that contained "graph," the linkage between "graphics," "telegraph," and even "photograph" becomes obvious.

3. Many vocabulary-building exercises build on how well the reader understood the meanings of words' prefixes, roots, and suffixes.

4. Prefixes like "hyper" and "hypo" appear in many health science textbooks; they meant, respectively, "over" and "under."

5. Knowing the history of a word also helps in its spelling; some winners of spelling contests succeeded because they break words into several parts.

6. Using this method, such individuals are able to correctly spell a word they had never heard before.

7. On the other hand, some well-read individuals found it difficult to understand why some restaurants call a sandwich variety a "sub"; after all, "sub" as a prefix means "under."

8. To make matters worse, because "marine" means water, who wants a sandwich that was soaked under water?

9. Suffixes, additions to the ends of words, have special meanings and needed to be memorized.

10. Some websites offer a new word every day; the site's manager often provided not only pronunciation keys but also a quote using the day's word.

Exercise 2

1. To open savings, chequing, or investment accounts, Canadians choose from a limited number of financial institutions while Americans get these services from a huge number of banks, some of which had only a single local branch.

2. The Canadian Deposit Insurance Corporation, a Crown corporation, insures the first $100,000 of deposits in registered Canadian financial institutions; however, deposits in credit unions were backed by separate provincial insurance plans.

3. CDIC insurance extended to guaranteed investment certificates (GICs) with terms under five years, but the CDIC protection doesn't cover any accounts using foreign currency, even if the accounts are deposited with a registered institution.

4. Since 1967, few financial institutions have failed in Canada, and the last registered bank failure took place over a decade ago.

5. The Canadian federal government established a set of regulations governing registered banks and appoints an inspector of financial institutions, who has the power to close a financial institution.

6. Besides banks, the Canadian financial industry includes credit unions, who sold shares to their clients.

7. As shareholders, credit union account holders attend annual meetings and voted for directors to oversee the business.

8. Perhaps because they were relatively small and customer-oriented, credit unions trace their history to rural and agricultural areas.

9. Since most Canadians have chequing and savings accounts at the major banks, homeowners usually also kept their residential mortgages at banks.

10. Although credit unions offered competitive interest rates, these institutions have still failed to capture any major slice of the financial investment pie.

Exercise 3

1. As I was growing up in Southern California, I was always astonished at the huge influences that Mexico and California have on each other.

2. One of my best friends was born in El Monte, California, which he always called "Occupied Mexico."

3. Perhaps one of the most moving areas along the Pacific Ocean coastline is Border Field State Park, which, as its name suggests, marked the international border between Mexico and the United States.

4. Every weekend, farm labourers who came from Mexico to work the fields in California's lush valleys meet with other family members still in Tijuana, Mexico, at a flimsy fence on the border.

5. It always delighted me to watch these families as they share picnic lunches, exchange notes, and chat happily with one another while the sun beamed down on them and the ocean waves crashed onto the white beach nearby.

6. More recently, however, the U.S. Department of Homeland Security built a series of high walls on the border; the intent is to prevent illegal immigration, but the existence of these barriers means that these family outings are no longer possible.

7. To the north, the U.S./Canadian border is becoming less and less open than it once was.

8. Formerly allowing crossings from Canada with minimal documentation, the U.S. government announced in 2007 that airline passengers need passports.

9. Now, even travelling U.S. citizens on their way home are required to show a valid passport if they hoped to cross the border without trouble.

10. Perhaps the world has become a dangerous place, but many on both sides of the border didn't find it reasonable to make a grandmother remove her shoes for airport security.

PROOFREADING EXERCISES

In the two paragraphs that follow, correct any unnecessary shifts back and forth in time. Change the verbs to maintain one time frame, thus making the entire paragraph flow smoothly.

1. I am taking an art history class right now. Every day, we watched slide shows of great pieces of art throughout history. We memorized each piece of art, its time period, and the artists who created it. I enjoy these slide shows, but I had trouble remembering the facts about them. I always get swept away by the beautiful paintings, drawings, and sculptures and forgot to take notes that I could study from at home.

2. I enjoyed travelling by plane to Cuba. Even though I have to arrive three hours early at the airport, it didn't bother me. I watch all the people taking off their shoes for security. And once I am through to the boarding gates, I bought some food and relax until it was time to enter the plane. Before I board the plane, the passengers who were arriving walked off the ramp with all their carry-on luggage. They look tired but happy and well tanned from their visit to the island. Both of my flights were comfortable, and the flight attendants are so nice and cheerful. I liked the way the Cubana flight crew pump Calypso music through the cabin while we wait for take-off. Before I even touch Cuban soil, these signs convince me that this country offered a completely different lifestyle. No wonder the motto of Cuba's official airline translates to "Cuba's doorway to the world."

SHIFTS IN PERSON

To understand what "person" means when using pronouns, imagine a conversation between two people about a third person. The first person speaks using "I, me, my … "; the second person is called "you"; and when the two of them talk of a third person, they say "he, she, they…." You should never forget the idea of "person" if you remember it as a three-part conversation.

First person — *I, me, my, we, us, our*
Second person — *you, your*
Third person — *he, him, his, she, her, hers, it, its, they, them, their, one, anyone*

You may use all three of these groups of pronouns in a paper, but don't shift from one group to another without good reason.

Wrong: Few people know how to manage *their* time. *One* need not be an efficiency expert to realize that *one* could get a lot more done if *he* budgeted *his* time. Nor do *you* need to work very hard to get more organized.

Better: *Everyone* should know how to manage *his or her* time. *One* need not be an efficiency expert to realize that *a person* could get a lot more done if *one* budgeted *one's* time. Nor does *one* need to work very hard to get more organized.

          (Too many *ones* in a paragraph make it sound overly formal, and words such as *everyone* lead to the necessity of avoiding sexism by using *s/he* or *he or she,* etc. Sentences can be revised to avoid using either *you* or *one.*)

Best: Many of *us* don't know how to manage *our* time. *We* need not be efficiency experts to realize that *we* could get a lot more done if *we* budgeted *our* time. Nor do *we* need to work very hard to get more organized.

Often students write *you* in a paper when they don't really mean *you, the reader.*

You wouldn't believe how many times I saw that movie.

Such sentences are always improved by getting rid of the *you.*

I saw that movie many times.

E X E R C I S E S

Rewrite the following sentences to eliminate incorrect shifts in person.

Exercise 1

1. Diabetes is looming as a larger health problem for Canadians than ever before, especially if you have a first-degree relative (a parent or sibling) already diagnosed with this disease.

_____

2. An individual is also at increased risk for diabetes if they come from specific ethnic backgrounds.

_____

3. In general, diabetes appears in one of two forms (Type 1 or Type 2), and the medication a person takes is highly dependent upon which type of diabetes you have.

_____

4. You may also need to make some lifestyle changes in order to manage an individual's blood sugar levels in his or her blood.

_____

5. A diabetic is often advised to watch their diets very carefully and to exercise whenever they can.

_____

6. However, people who understand the risk factors know what symptoms he should monitor.

_____

7. Diabetics understand that too much exercise, for example, can dramatically lower your blood sugar level, causing you to sweat profusely.

_____

8. As well, an individual with diabetes needs to have a clear understanding of the types of medical problems they might encounter.

_____

9. Individuals with Type 1 diabetes have a good chance of developing medical problems related to his or her eyesight (glaucoma), liver, kidneys, and circulatory system.

_____

10. Many diabetics find that they feel much healthier once they look after yourself more carefully.

_____

Exercise 2

1. Visitors to the 2010 Winter Olympic Games in Vancouver, British Columbia, will face mounting challenges if you haven't already made arrangements for accommodations.

_____

2. A few homeowners are planning to sublet their residences via Internet advertisements, but none of these possibilities is easy to locate.

_____

3. It's amusing that after they fought so hard to earn the right to host the Games, a Vancouver resident would choose to leave town during the competitions.

_____

4. Part of each visitor's decision-making needs to be based on which venues and events they hope to attend.

_____

5. For example, the thousands of skating and hockey fans need to book their accommodations early so you can have easy access to the Richmond Olympic Oval or Canada Hockey Place venues.

_____

6. On the other hand, if you have your heart set on seeing the ski jumpers or bobsledders, viewers will need to make a three-hour winter drive up mountainous highways to get to Whistler and the events planned for that venue.

_____

7. Many individuals will finally decide that to save time and money, he will need to pick one type of Olympic sport and try to locate lodging close by.

_____

8. Others who enjoy surprises will probably elect to arrive in Vancouver and accept whatever accommodation you can find.

_____

9. If you don't feel comfortable taking chances, the only option is to make their reservations early.

_____

10. Even an individual who is forced to sleep in their cars during the Games is sure to find the atmosphere thrilling.

_____

Exercise 3

1. A person who is bit by an infected animal may not know a lot about rabies, but according to the World Health Organization (WHO), the disease is fatal once you develop its symptoms.

2. Many humans treated for rabies in North America are bitten by our own domestic pet after it has interacted with an infected wild animal like a fox.

3. Unfortunately, it's not at all unusual for a child to be bitten by their pet cat or dog who became infected when it took a hike through the woods.

4. A surprisingly large number of children in Canada suffer dog bites, but most people probably assume that the child somehow provoked the dog's anger.

5. However, when we make this assumption, people risk children not getting the medical attention they need to prevent the onset of the rabies virus.

6. Another possible reason for people's general lack of alarm is the belief that all responsible pet owners routinely keep your pets' rabies vaccinations up-to-date.

7. Parents, particularly in rural areas, need to make sure that family pets get such vaccinations because a rabid wild animal like a fox could have infected the otherwise friendly dog that bites your three-year-old child.

8. Sometimes, you can find rabies outbreaks even in larger cities when they don't enforce vaccination procedures.

9. To ensure that an individual is safe after being bitten or scratched, officials from Agriculture Canada can conduct tests to determine if the animal that bit you is infected with rabies.

10. These medical procedures need to be completed within twenty-four hours after you have received a bite because unless an autopsy can disprove the presence of rabies, health care providers will administer precautionary antiviral shots to injured individuals.

PROOFREADING EXERCISES

Each of the following paragraphs contains *unnecessary* shifts in person. When there is an unnecessary shift, revise the writing to eliminate the problem. Your corrections will make these paragraphs read smoothly.

1. I love travelling by train. The rocking sensation makes you feel so calm, and the clackety-clack of the railroad ties as we ride over them sounds like a heartbeat to me. I also enjoy walking down the aisles of all the cars and looking at the different passengers. Whole families sit together, with children facing their parents. I notice that the kids like to ride backward more than the adults. The food that you eat in the dining car is expensive, but it is always fancy and delicious to my taste buds. My favourite part of the train is the observation car. It is made of glass from the seats up so that we could see everything that we pass along the way.

2. People, especially those who have money, are sometimes wasteful. We exhibit wastefulness in different ways. Restaurants throw out a lot of food every day. Homeowners water our lawns for too long and let the excess run down your street. People cleaning out their garages discard their clothes and furniture when you could recycle these items by giving them to charities. When you think about it, individuals can reuse and recycle so much of what we consume. We should be particularly alarmed whenever people fail to think of second lives for items you plan to discard. I plan to buy large bags to store the items that you would usually toss into the garbage. Even if we pay more attention to the excess packaging on the products we purchase, consumers can go a long way to helping out others as well as the planet.

Correcting for Parallel Structure

Your writing will be clearer and easier to read and understand if you use parallel construction. That is, when you include any kind of list, put the items in similar form. If you write

> My favourite ice cream flavours are rocky road, heavenly hash, and the green ice cream with chocolate chips in it.

the sentence is awkward. The items don't all have the same form. But if you write

> My favourite ice cream flavours are rocky road, heavenly hash, and mint-chip.

then the items are balanced or parallel. They are all nouns because they are names of ice cream flavours. Or you could write

> I like ice cream with nuts, marshmallows, or chocolate chips.

Again the sentence has parallel structure because all three items in the list are nouns. Note how much easier it is to read the parallel sentences. Here are other examples.

LACKING PARALLEL CONSTRUCTION	**HAVING PARALLEL CONSTRUCTION**
I like to hike, to ski, and going sailing.	I like to hike, to ski, and to sail. (all "to____" verbs)
The office has run out of pens, paper, ink cartridges, and we need more toner, too.	The office needs more pens, paper, ink cartridges, and toner. (all nouns)
They decided that they needed a change, that they could afford a new house, and wanted to move to Calgary.	They decided that they needed a change, that they could afford a new house, and that they wanted to move to Calgary. (all dependent clauses)

The supporting points in an outline should always be parallel. In the following brief outlines, the supporting points in the left-hand column are not parallel in structure. Those in the right-hand column are parallel.

NOT PARALLEL	**PARALLEL**
Food Irradiation	Food Irradiation
I. How is it good?	I. Benefits
A. Longer shelf life	A. Extends shelf life
B. Using fewer pesticides	B. Requires fewer pesticides
C. Kills bacteria	C. Kills bacteria

    II. Concerns   II. Concerns

        A. Nutritional value   A. Lowers nutritional value

        B. Consumers are worried   B. Alarms consumers

        C. Workers' safety   C. Endangers workers

Using parallel construction will make your writing more effective. Note the effective parallelism in these well-known quotations:

A place for everything and everything in its place.

Isabella Mary Beeton

I have been poor and I have been rich. Rich is better.

Sophie Tucker

The more the data banks record about each of us, the less we exist.

Marshall McLuhan

A Canadian I was born; a Canadian I will die.

John G. Diefenbaker

E X E R C I S E S

Most—but not all—of the following sentences lack parallel structure. In some, you will be able to cross out the part that is not parallel and write the correction above. Other sentences will need complete rephrasing.

Exercise 1

1. Children's fears were featured in the Healthy Living section of a recent issue of a popular newsmagazine.

2. The article is written for adults, but the subject of the article is young children.

3. It explains that many kids have become frightened by information about global warming and also mentions other environmental concerns.

4. Children are watching the same scary news stories, and they see the same upsetting images that adults see.

5. One animated movie, the sequel to Ice Age, called The *Meltdown,* even tells the story of flooding and destruction caused by melting ice.

6. Some children suffer very strong reactions of fear, and they feel helpless when they encounter such information.

7. Others ignore or they don't seem bothered by the same troubling pictures and stories.

8. The article makes an interesting point about the connection between today's children and their parents; as kids, some of today's parents were panicked by the idea of nuclear war, and now their children worry about the changing of the climate.

9. All these issues pose serious concerns for the future, but children need help dealing with them.

10. Parents can take steps to help children cope by pointing out the positive aspects of nature, limiting small children's exposure to frightening images or information, and adults should find ways to help their children to take positive action.

Exercise 2

1. Taking driving lessons was exciting, but I also considered it nerve-racking.

2. I was ready to learn how to start the car, to manoeuvre, and hopefully how to bring the car to a stop.

3. Between lessons, I read driving manuals, watched videos about driving, and I even practised the hand signals and turn indicators.

4. My instructors taught me, tested me, and were encouraging to me.

5. Each one had a tip or two to share about driving.

6. Finally, my teachers decided that I had learned enough, and I was probably ready to take the test for my driver's licence.

7. I arrived at the testing location, waited in the lobby for a few minutes, and then I heard someone call my name.

8. Throughout the test, I started, manoeuvred, and stopped like a professional driver.

9. The man who tested me said that I knew the rules, and he thought I must have had good teachers.

10. I took a box of cookies to my driving school to thank everyone for helping me become a good driver.

Exercise 3

1. I like coffee, and I sort of like tea.

2. I've heard that coffee is bad for you, but drinking tea is good.

3. It must not be the caffeine that's bad because coffee has caffeine and so does tea.

4. I heard one expert say that it's the other chemicals in the coffee and tea that make the difference in health benefits.

5. All teas are supposed to be healthy, but the healthiest is green tea supposedly.

6. Unfortunately, green tea is the only type of tea I don't like.

7. I love orange pekoe tea with tons of milk and a ton of sugar too.

8. I was really surprised to find out that all tea leaves come from the same plant.

9. I know that all coffee comes from coffee beans, but it shocked me to find out that green tea and orange pekoe are both made with leaves from the *Camellia sinensis* plant.

10. Maybe I'll give green tea another try since it could improve my health.

Exercise 4

1. There are many coincidences in the lives of the members of my family.

2. My mother and father were both born on July 1, and I was born on Canada's birthday.

3. My mother was named Sarah Louisa at birth; my cousin's first name is Louisa, and her middle name is Sarah.

4. My mother was twenty-four when she had her first baby, and her sister-in-law was pregnant at the time.

5. Therefore, my cousin and I are the same age.

6. When my father was in high school, he had three jobs: waiter, babysitter, and he delivered newspapers.

7. To earn extra money, I often deliver newspapers, work in a restaurant, and I get money for babysitting for my neighbour.

8. Sometimes my cousin and I will meet accidentally at the movies, and we wore the same shirts.

9. Is this just a coincidence or have we something in common?

10. My cousin and I both hope to become veterinarians: I study science at school, and she is doing a volunteer job at an animal shelter this year.

Exercise 5

Make the following list parallel.

1. I've made a list of eight basic steps I can follow to improve my writing.

2. First, I need to accept that my writing needs work and I can make it better if I try.

3. Second, a lot of progress can be made by just cutting out wordy expressions.

4. Third, working on my vocabulary will also help a lot.

5. Fourth, I need to proofread my papers more carefully.

6. Fifth, my sentences should be different lengths, some short and others should be longer.

7. Sixth, I've been told that I use the passive voice too much and that I should use the active voice instead.

8. Seventh, budgeting my time will allow a first draft to sit for a while before I revise it.

9. Finally, always look at the overall structure of a paper when I revise, not just the words and sentences.

10. By following these eight steps, I hope to become a better writer.

SENTENCE WRITING

Write ten sentences that use parallel structure in a list or a pair of objects, actions, locations, or ideas. You may choose your own subject or describe a process that you carry out at your job.

_____

_____

_____

_____

_____

_____

_____

_____

_____

_____

Avoiding Clichés, Awkward Phrasing, and Wordiness

CLICHÉS

A cliché is an expression that has been used so often it has lost its originality and effectiveness. Whoever first said "light as a feather" had thought of an original way to express lightness, but today that expression is worn out. Most of us use an occasional cliché in speaking, but clichés have no place in writing. The good writer thinks up fresh new ways to express ideas.

Here are a few clichés. Add some more to the list.

the bottom line

older but wiser

last but not least

in this day and age

different as night and day

out of this world

white as a ghost

sick as a dog

tried and true

at the top of their lungs

the thrill of victory

one in a million

busy as a bee

easier said than done

better late than never

Clichés lack freshness because the reader always knows what's coming next. Can you complete these expressions?

the agony of ...

breathe a sigh of ...

lend a helping ...

the early bird ...

raining cats and ...

time flies when ...

been there ...

worth its weight ...

Clichés are expressions too many people use. Try to avoid them in your writing.

Awkward Phrasing

Another problem—awkward phrasing—comes from writing sentence structures that *no one* else would use because they break basic sentence patterns, omit necessary words, or use words incorrectly. Like clichés, awkward sentences might *sound* acceptable when spoken, but as polished writing, they are usually unacceptable.

Awkward

There should be great efforts in terms of the cooperation between coaches and their athletes.

Corrected

Coaches and their athletes should cooperate.

AWKWARD

During the experiment, the use of key principles was essential to ensure the success of it.

CORRECTED

The experiment's success depended on the application of key principles.

AWKWARD

My favourite was when the guy fell all the way down the ship as it sank.

CORRECTED

In my favourite scene, a man fell all the way down the sinking ship's deck.

WORDINESS

Good writing is concise writing. Don't say something in ten words if you can say it better in five. "In today's society" isn't as effective as "today," and it's a cliché. "At this point in time" could be "presently" or "now."

Another kind of wordiness comes from saying something twice. There's no need to write "in the month of August" or "9 a.m. in the morning" or "my personal opinion." August *is* a month, 9 a.m. *is* morning, and anyone's opinion *is* personal. All you need to write is "in August," "9 a.m.," and "my opinion."

Still another kind of wordiness comes from using expressions that add nothing to the meaning of the sentence. "The point is that we can't afford it" says no more than "We can't afford it."

Here is a sample wordy sentence:

The construction company actually worked on that particular building for a period of six months.

And here it is after eliminating wordiness:

The construction company worked on that building for six months.

WORDY WRITING	CONCISE WRITING
actual fact	fact
advance planning	planning
an unexpected surprise	a surprise
at a later date	later
at this point	now
basic fundamentals	fundamentals

blue in colour	blue
but nevertheless	but (or nevertheless)
combine together	combine
completely empty	empty
down below	below
each and every	each (or every)
end result	result
fewer in number	fewer
free gift	gift
in order to	to
in spite of the fact that	although
just exactly	exactly
large in size	large
new innovation	innovation
on a regular basis	regularly
originally from	from
past history	history
rectangular in shape	rectangular
refer back	refer
repeat again	repeat
serious crisis	crisis
sufficient enough	sufficient (or enough)
there in person	there
two different kinds	two kinds
very unique	unique

E X E R C I S E S

Exercise 1

Rewrite the following sentences to eliminate clichés and awkward phrasing.

1. I like to shop around before I buy something.

2. Three or four different stores is not unusual for me to go to.

3. I always keep my eye on the bottom line.

4. I can save $100 on one item with this foolproof method.

5. Stranger things have happened.

6. Prices may vary significantly on the exact same merchandise.

7. But buying at the right time is easier said than done.

8. Once I waited so long for a sale on a computer that I was left empty-handed.

9. There is a real feeling of satisfaction I get when I do find a bargain though.

10. Looking for good prices is my bottom line.

Exercise 2

Cross out words or rewrite parts of each sentence to eliminate wordiness. Doing these exercises can almost turn into a game to see how few words you can use without changing the meaning of the sentence.

1. I received an unexpected surprise in the mail today.

2. It came in a small little box that was square in size and brown in colour.

3. I discovered as I looked at the mailing label that it had been sent by someone in Cape Dorset.

4. I had a hard time figuring out whether or not I knew anyone in Cape Dorset.

5. After I thought about it for a long period of time, I kind of remembered that our old neighbours who used to live next door had moved to Cape Dorset.

6. Due to the fact that I had been good friends with their son Josh, I figured that it must be Josh who was the one who sent the mysterious box.

7. Sure enough, as I saw what it was that was inside the box, I knew for sure that Josh had sent it to me.

8. Josh must have remembered that I collect many different kinds of souvenir snow globes from all the places that I have travelled to in my life.

9. Inside this particular package, there was a large size snow globe with a white polar bear and a man riding on a sled pulled by dogs across the snow and a nameplate that said the words *Cape Dorset* in letters that were red.

10. There was a whole bunch of plastic snow that made the whole thing look like a snowy blizzard was going on when I shook it back and forth.

Exercise 3

Revise the sentences in the remaining exercises to eliminate any *clichés, awkward phrasing,* and *wordiness.*

1. In today's society, many shoppers at the supermarkets are on the look-out for organic meats and vegetables.

2. In fact, they don't draw the line at fresh foods; these same shoppers' eyes light up whenever they see an organic label on a can or any other package.

3. I know this for a fact since I work as an employee at the supermarket in the middle of the busiest section of town.

4. It's not only people with a lot of money who want the foods grown without pesticides and hormones.

5. It's just about everybody who walks in the door.

6. I guess that what's going on is that people are taking a good long look at their lives and caring about their children's eating habits, too.

7. I do have to admit that the organic eggs I buy taste pretty good when you get right down to it.

8. Knowing that the eggs come from happy, free-ranging chickens makes me feel good about eating them.

9. Of course, the bottom line for some people will always be price.

10. If organic foods cost more than traditionally grown foods, some of the shoppers are going to keep passing them by on the supermarket shelves.

Exercise 4

1. In this day and age, it's hard to find a place that is really and truly old-fashioned.

2. Black Creek Pioneer Village is that kind of place; it's near Canada's Wonderland, but in my personal opinion, these two amusement parks are as different as night and day.

3. First of all, the original Pioneer Village was settled by pioneer families, many of whom were Pennsylvania German farmers who came to Canada in the early nineteenth century.

4. Pioneer Village was a real settlement for the pioneers and has been restored and is shown as it was in the 1860s.

5. The creators of Black Creek Pioneer Village were able to re-create the old village and the past with more than thirty-five carefully restored 1860s' shops and homes.

6. Talk about old-fashioned; Pioneer Village also has a blacksmith, a cabinet maker, and other tradespeople with whom people can talk to about their crafts.

7. There are even an old doctor's house, Roblin's Mill and water wheel, a local schoolhouse, and other authentic homes and shops that people can see during their visit to the past.

8. Pioneer Village is staffed with many hosts dressed as if they were right out of the 1860s who are more than happy to guide guests through a part of Canadian history.

9. And if that's not enough, people can even take a ride on a horse-drawn wagon just as the pioneers did in the olden days.

10. There is a wide variety of activities offered throughout the year including demonstrations of village trades and home crafts, a pioneer festival in September, and special Christmas celebrations in December.

Sources: http://www.trca.on.ca/bcpv.html; http://www.nfb.ca/FMT/E/MSN/15/15338.html.

Exercise 5

1. The other day I had to stay home from work because I was as sick as a dog with the flu.

2. I told my boss that one day of complete and utter rest would make me feel much better, but that was easier said than done.

3. I had forgotten that on Thursdays nearly every house on the block has its gardeners come to take care of the plants and trees in the yards.

4. Each and every one of them always uses a power leaf blower and a tree-trimming saw to get the work done.

5. The noise around the neighbourhood made my head spin, and I couldn't get to sleep for the life of me.

6. I tried watching television in order to drown out the noise and put me to sleep.

7. That was like jumping out of the frying pan into the fire; the shows on daytime TV were really hard to take.

8. Once the gardeners finished, I finally got to go to sleep at about 3 p.m. in the afternoon.

9. It was better late than never.

10. I got just about sixteen hours of sleep, felt better, and was as happy as a clam to be back at work the next day.

PROOFREADING EXERCISES

The following student paragraphs contain examples of clichés, awkward phrasing, and wordiness. Revise the paragraphs so that they are concise examples of Standard Written English. When you're done, compare your revisions with the sample answers at the back of the book.

1. Technologies in this day and age are getting more and more advanced. All of the friends that I have have cell phones with cameras in them. Anyone who doesn't have one is just not up with the times. For instance, my friend was getting robbed, and he took a picture of the guy who robbed him and of his truck as he

was driving away from the scene of the crime. And when the police got there, my friend showed them the picture on his phone screen, and they sent out a description of the truck and the man who robbed my friend. They arrested him in just a few hours. When it came to the trial, if my friend hadn't had his cell phone with the camera in it, it would have just been my friend's word against the man's.

2. I've been trying to help my small son finish his first-grade homework every night, but that's easier said than done. Of course, I think that he is the smartest kid in the world, but getting him to show it takes a lot of hard work. When I do get him to sit down in front of his workbooks, he will work for a few minutes on them and then run off as soon as my back is turned. I try to tell him that when I was his age, I got in big trouble if I didn't do my homework. Unfortunately, my son's teacher just doesn't give him a sticker for that day if he doesn't do his. Stickers don't do the trick as motivators. I hope with all my heart that my son will learn the value of keeping up in school.

Clarity Progress Test

In the following sentences, use what you have learned in the previous section to identify and then correct problems that may make the writer's message unclear. Remember that this family of errors includes mistakes in subject–verb agreement, choice of pronoun, parallel structure, and wordiness. Write your corrections in the spaces between sentences.

1. My father often asks my brother if he understands the difference between traditional and non-traditional gender roles.

2. Dad's understanding of roles was developed in the 1950s, when men and women have clearly defined responsibilities in their lives.

3. In this day and age, many roles, especially in the home, make moms and dads as alike as peas in a pod.

4. Before the war, men always found good, hearty meals on the table when they arrived home after a hard day's work, which was a reasonable expectation for that generation.

5. For example, a wife and mother very seldom gave much thought to careers or schooling because their job was to look after the home and the children.

6. However, comparing my mother and father, Mom saw the coming major changes in societal roles more quickly and clearly than he.

7. During the war, she was one of many wives who exchanged their cooking pans and laundry baskets to complete high school, obtain technical training, or to find employment outside the home.

8. I doubt if any of these women thought they were creating a new society, but they certainly were.

9. Within a short period of time, many women found themselves bringing home the bacon and experiencing the challenge of making major decisions for their entire families.

10. After the war ended, many women discovered that the husbands returning from the fields of battle expected them to return to their pre-war roles.

11. Each of my mother's friends had worked outside the house during the war and were confused about how to use the skills they had acquired.

12. Some mothers never did return to full-time homemaking, which is why working mothers are no longer viewed as non-traditional.

13. In the '60s and '70s, the feminist movement declared women to be equal to their male partners economically, politically, and even in the area of sex.

14. Feminists faced a particularly bitter uphill battle in the workplace, where women's salaries lag considerably behind their male counterparts'.

15. While allowing women to work outside the home, society had built new expectations of where they could work, how they could work, and even the salaries they could expect.

16. Even today, one of my daughters, a mining technologist, earn only two-thirds of the rate paid to a male co-worker doing the same job, having the same experience and credentials, and working for the same employer.

17. Some women insist that the definition of traditional/non-traditional domestic roles for women have just moved into the workplace.

18. Everyone with the same qualifications and job descriptions should feel that they are being fairly treated when it comes to calculating rates of pay.

19. While the last half century has brought many changes to women's roles in the home and workplace, there is still many unaddressed issues.

20. Me and my daughters now take our college and university educations and our high-paying jobs for granted, but these privileges have been extended to women for only a relatively short time.

Clarity Post-Test

Use what you have learned in Part 4 (Keeping the Message Clear) to identify and then correct problems in the following sentences. Remember that this family of errors includes mistakes in subject–verb agreement, pronoun choice, parallel structure, and wordiness. In the sentences below, isolate problems that may make the message fuzzy. Write your corrections in the spaces between sentences.

1. When applying for a job, many applicants take time to provide information about his or her community activities and leisure-time activities.

2. Some employers appreciate getting this information right at the beginning, which is why so many résumé consultants suggest including it.

3. Each of the human resource managers at my husband's company admit that they use such information to predict whether an applicant is well-suited for a particular position.

4. For example, when the job requires exceptional leadership abilities, a history of team skills, particularly as a captain, indicates that the applicant is respected by others, can influence those in his or her environment, and he or she is more likely to have a positive attitude.

5. On the other hand, for a job with tight deadlines, applicants must exhibit the ability to set and meet them consistently without direct supervision.

6. Even when two applicants have identical academic qualifications and related employment experiences, one of the candidates have the type of personal skills necessary to get the job done more effectively.

7. My husband's boss, Ms. Flanders, says she hired him because he clearly had more social skills than her.

8. The skills she is referring to was acquired when my husband and I took several ballroom dancing courses in our spare time.

9. In part, his job requires him to build client trust through casual conversations, and he certainly is great at phoning clients, discussing their immediate and long-term requirements, and listening skills.

10. Our daughter's career couldn't be more different because her supervisor, Mrs. Benton, thinks she is better at keeping records than at speaking with clients.

11. Mrs. Benton probably wouldn't be surprised to hear that Mindy spends most of her leisure hours reading books, doing crossword puzzles, or to balance her chequebook.

12. Some activities in the community also offers the side benefit of allowing individuals to network with other community leaders.

13. Then, when these individuals have a question or need advice, they can ask them.

14. During my high school and university years, I read lots of books and newspapers, but it's something I don't seem to have time for anymore.

15. My older sister, who dreamed of writing for a newspaper, lost interest after hearing our mother describe being a good wife and mother as the only important job in her life.

16. Between you and I, my sister would have made a wonderful journalist.

17. Both my younger sisters became artists, and although they don't make a lot of money, they seem a lot happier than me.

18. Perhaps they spend more time doing what they think is most important, like volunteering at the hospital and they donate their artwork to charity.

19. Neither of my sisters have a husband, children, or a full-time job.

20. But each of their résumés are packed with exciting achievements accomplished outside employment or academic environments.

Punctuating Correctly

Punctuation Pre-Test

In written messages, pieces of punctuation serve as guideposts for the reader. Some—periods, question marks, exclamation points—signal the end of an idea. Others (like the dashes in the previous sentence or the parentheses in this one) isolate part of the sentence so that the reader can identify information as not essential to the message. Punctuation also includes quotation marks to show the exact words of a speaker. The comma works in several ways to give the reader help in unpacking ideas. In the sentences below, circle problem areas that can be corrected by inserting, removing, or changing a piece of punctuation or by changing the capitalization of a word. Write your corrections in the spaces between sentences.

1. When the guest speaker entered the room went quiet.

2. The speaker's topic was going to be an interesting and important one, understanding it would be necessary to pass the provincial exam.

3. Ms. Saunders the dean of the School of Trades and Mr. Whitehorse the college president were on the podium with the speaker.

4. When Ms. Saunders introduced Bill Lee, she said that "he had worked in the skilled trades for over twenty years."

5. My friends and I wondered if Mr. Lee had to attend university or college?

6. In his introductory remarks, Mr. Lee explained his background, which included attending and being expelled from our college.

7. He was he explained the type of student who assumed he would learn all the important skills once he finally landed an apprenticeship.

8. Unfortunately, in the 1980s, getting an apprenticeship was easier said than done and although he personally visited one possible employer after another, he kept losing opportunities to those with certification from a Trades Institute or College.

9. Finally he decided to return to school with a new focus, and a revised opinion of education's importance to his future success.

10. Lee's experience is typical of many, who flooded into the skilled trades in the late 1980s.

11. The economic recession as well as the relative youth of the trades' work force at the time, meant there were fewer employment opportunities.

12. Once he returned to his shop classes, however he discovered that many other students didn't have the same motivation and understanding that he had.

13. Terrified of computers he was puzzled and irritated, when classmates surfed the Internet instead of listened to the instructor.

14. And were the students ever loud.

15. Could he have been like them when he first attended college.

16. He finally overcame his fear of computers by getting a tutor practising keyboarding skills during his spares and taking a course called Introduction to Keyboarding.

17. Once employed in industry he discovered that virtually every job required some level of computer competency.

18. Later, he became a computer-based training instructor with the Province of Alberta's well-known apprenticeships online program.

19. "There were two courses I felt I would never use after college graduation, Lee admitted to the audience, they were english and computers."

20. Now however he depends heavily on both to teach other tradespeople how to do their jobs.

Period, Question Mark, Exclamation Point, Semicolon, Colon, Dash

Every mark of punctuation should help the reader. Here are the rules for six marks of punctuation. The first three you have known for a long time and probably have no trouble with. The one about semicolons you learned when you studied independent clauses (p. 123). The ones about the colon and the dash may be less familiar.

Put a period (.) at the end of a sentence and after most abbreviations.

The students elected Ms. Daniels to represent the class.

Tues.   etc.   Jan.   Ph.D.   Ave.

Put a question mark (?) after a direct question but not after an indirect one.

Will the exam be an open-book or a closed-book test? (direct)

I wonder if the exam will be an open-book or a closed-book test. (indirect)

Put an exclamation point (!) after an expression that shows strong emotion. Use it sparingly.

Finally! It's spring!

Put a semicolon (;) between two independent clauses in a sentence *unless* they are joined by one of the connecting words *for, and, nor, but, or, yet, so.*

My mother cosigned for a loan; now I have my own car.

Some hairstyles go in and out of fashion; however, every style relies on a good cut.

Remember: To be sure that you are using a semicolon correctly, see if a period and capital letter can be used in its place. If they can, you are putting the semicolon in the right spot.

My mother cosigned for a loan. Now I have my own car.

Some hairstyles go in and out of fashion. However, every style relies on a good cut.

Put a colon (:) after a *complete statement* that introduces something: one item, a list, a direct question, or a quotation that follows.

The company announced its Employee of the Month: Minh Tran. (The sentence before the colon introduces the name that follows.)

In London, we plan to visit the following famous sites: the Tower of London, Piccadilly Circus, and Madame Tussaud's Wax Museum. (Here *the following famous sites* ends a complete statement and introduces the list that follows, so a colon is used.)

In London, we plan to visit the Tower of London, Piccadilly Circus, and Madame Tussaud's Wax Museum. (Here *we plan to visit* does not end a complete statement, so no colon is used.)

All the kids in the class were wondering about the same thing: why is the sky blue? (Here *All the kids in the class were wondering about the same thing* is a complete statement that introduces a direct question, so a colon is used.)

All the kids in the class were wondering why the sky was blue. (Here *All the kids in the class were wondering* is not a complete statement, so a colon is not used.)

Thoreau had this to say about time: "Time is but the stream I go a-fishin in." (*Thoreau had this to say about time* is a complete statement. Therefore, a colon comes after it before adding the quotation.)

Thoreau said, "Time is but the stream I go a-fishin in." (*Thoreau said* is not a complete statement. Therefore, a colon does not come after it.)

Use a dash (—) to indicate an abrupt change of thought or to emphasize what follows. Use it sparingly.

I found out today—or was it yesterday?—that I have inherited a fortune.

We have exciting news for you—we're moving!

E X E R C I S E S

Exercise 1

Add any necessary semicolons, colons, and dashes to the sentences in this exercise. The commas and end punctuation are correct and do not need to be changed.

1. You've likely seen one of those inflatable jumping rooms at a community festival sometimes, they can be found in a home's front yard during a child's birthday party.

2. These jumpers are popular for several reasons children can have fun playing with their friends, adults can keep an eye on many children at once, and everyone gets lots of exercise.

3. Several years ago, a freak accident occurred on a beach it involved an inflated castle-shaped bouncer, a few brave adults, and several lucky children.

4. As the kids bounced around and squealed with pleasure, a strong gust of wind—a whirlwind, according to many accounts lifted the castle straight up into the air.

5. When the wind released its hold on the castle, the structure came crashing down all but two of the children were knocked unconscious instantly.

6. The castle bounced on the sand once before flying into the sky and landing at least fifty metres into the water.

7. As the castle flew into the air the second time, another child dropped out of it, luckily he was unhurt.

8. Many adults both lifeguards and others jumped in to save the two-year-old girl who remained inside the castle.

9. One man was able to reach her in time incredibly she was not seriously hurt.

10. A sunny day, laughing children, an inflatable castle everyone on the scene agreed that a tragedy had been narrowly avoided.

Exercise 2

Add the appropriate end punctuation to the sentences in this exercise. The existing commas and semicolons are correct and do not need to be changed.

1. My friend Kristine and I arrived early for work yesterday; it was a very important day

2. We had worked late the night before perfecting our presentation—wow, what a job

3. The boss had given us an opportunity to train our colleagues in the use of a new computer system

4. I wondered how the other workers would react when they heard that we had been chosen to teach them

5. Would they be pleased or annoyed

6. Kristine and I worked hard on the slide show of sample screens from the program

7. Kristine thought that our workshop should end with a test—what a horrid idea

8. I knew that our fellow employees—at least some of them—would not want us to test them

9. By the time we ended our presentation, we both realized that I had been right

10. Wouldn't you prefer that your coworkers see you as an expert, not a know-it-all

Exercise 3

Add any necessary periods, question marks, exclamation points, semicolons, colons, and dashes to the sentences in this exercise.

1. People have not stopped inventing mousetraps in fact, there are more than four thousand different kinds.

2. Some are simple however, some are complicated or weird.

3. Nearly fifty new types of machines to kill mice are invented every year.

4. The most enduring mousetrap was designed by John Mast it is the one most of us picture when we think of a mousetrap a piece of wood with a spring-loaded bar that snaps down on the mouse just as it takes the cheese used as bait.

5. Mast created this version of the mousetrap over a century ago since then, no other mousetrap has done a better job.

6. There is a long list of techniques that have been used to trap mice electricity, sonar, lasers, super glues, etc

7. One mousetrap was built in the shape of a multi-level house with several stairways however, its elaborate design made it impractical and expensive.

8. In 1878, one person invented a mousetrap for travellers it was a box that was supposed to hold men's removable collars and at night catch mice, but it was not a success.

9. Can you imagine putting an article of clothing back into a box used to trap a mouse what an awful idea.

10. Would you guess that Toronto's longest running play for decades was *The Mousetrap*, which was based on a story of the same title by Agatha Christie

Exercise 4

Insert any necessary semicolons, colons, dashes, and the appropriate end punctuation (period, question mark, exclamation point) in the sentences in the following two exercises.

1. Who would have thought that educators were a nomadic group

2. In 1899, Frontier College was founded by Alfred Fitzpatrick and a group of university students their aim was to make education available to the labourers in the work camps of Canada

3. Labourer–teachers were trained and sent to the camps there they worked alongside the labourers during the day and taught reading and writing to them at night

4. Frontier College was also involved in encouraging Canadians to take up farming a woman by the name of Margaret Strang offered her tutorial and medical services for those who were interested at a model settlement at Edlund, Ontario

5. The Department of National Defence made an agreement with Frontier College, which placed labourer–teachers in Depression relief camps to provide recreation and tutoring

6. Some other projects that labourer–teachers were involved in were constructing the Alaska Highway, working in rail gangs after World War II, tutoring new Canadians, and working in long-term community development projects in northern settlements

7. In the mid-1970s, Frontier College enlarged its focus to include urban frontiers volunteers began working in prisons and with street youth, ex-offenders, and people with special needs

8. More than a decade ago, Frontier College began doing work with children, teens, and families, while at the same time developing the workplace literacy program called Learning in the Workplace

9. The original idea to help out those isolated in work camps across Canada has changed a great deal since Frontier College's founding in 1899, but it continues to be an important aspect in today's education system

10. In 1999, Frontier College celebrated its centenary 100 years of teaching and learning in Canada

Source: Adapted from http://www.frontiercollege.ca.

Exercise 5

1. Do you believe in ghosts

2. On Aug 14, 1999, the body of a young man was found on the Yukon and BC border by three teachers who went hunting for the day

3. The man he was named Kwaday Dan Sinchi by the Champagne and Aishihik First Nations was found on a northern BC glacier

4. Though the First Nations people in the area believed he was as old as ten thousand years, test results showed the remains to be about 550 years old

5. Discovered along with the hunter were various artifacts a hat, a robe made of animal skins, and spear tools

6. Radiocarbon dating was done on two samples the hat and the cloak The results are considered to be ninety-five percent accurate

7. The "ghost" is believed to be a hunter who is estimated to have lived between the years 1415 and 1445, about the time Henry V was king of England and the Black Plague ravaged Europe

8. This means the hunter died more than three hundred years before the first known European contact on the northwest coast however, it is still not known if he is an ancestor of the Champagne or Aishihik First Nations

9. Scientists say that there are only two certainties the "ghost" is a young male, and he was on a trading route between the coast and the interior

10. The remains, which are now in the care of the Royal British Columbia Museum in Victoria, BC, will be studied for further historic information

Source: Adapted from "Do you believe in ghosts?" *Toronto Star,* September 29, 1999.

PROOFREADING EXERCISE

Can you find the punctuation errors in this student paragraph? They all involve periods, question marks, exclamation points, semicolons, colons, and dashes. Any commas used within the sentences are correct and should not be changed.

The ingredients you will need for a lemon meringue pie are: lemon juice, eggs, sugar, cornstarch, flour, butter, water, and salt. First, you combine flour, salt, butter, and water for the crust and bake until lightly brown then you mix and cook the lemon juice, egg yolks, sugar, cornstarch, butter, and water for the filling. Once the filling is poured into the cooked crust; you whip the meringue. Meringue is made of egg whites and sugar! Pile the meringue on top of the lemon filling; place the pie in the hot oven for a few minutes, and you'll have the best lemon meringue pie you've ever tasted.

SENTENCE WRITING

Write ten sentences of your own that use periods, question marks, exclamation points, semicolons, colons, and dashes correctly. Imitate the examples used in the explanations if necessary. Write about an interesting assignment you have done for a class, or choose your own topic.

_____

_____

_____

_____

_____

_____

_____

_____

_____

_____

Comma Rules 1, 2, and 3

Commas and other pieces of punctuation guide the reader through sentence structures in the same way that signs guide drivers on the highway. Imagine what effects misplaced or incorrect road signs would have. Yet students often randomly place commas in their sentences. Try not to use a comma unless you know there is a need for it. Memorize this rhyme about comma use: _when in doubt, leave it out._

Among all of the comma rules, six are most important. Learn these six rules, and your writing will be easier to read. You have already studied the first rule (on page 124).

1. Put a comma before _for, and, nor, but, or, yet, so_ **(remember them as the** _**FANBOYS**_**) when they connect two independent clauses.**

The neighbours recently bought a minivan, and now they go everywhere together.

Linda wrote a letter today, but she forgot to mail it.

She was recently promoted, so she has moved to a better office.

Remember: If you use a comma alone between two independent clauses, the result is a run-on.

The ice cream looked delicious, it tasted good too. (run-on)

The ice cream looked delicious, and it tasted good too. (correct)

Before using the comma with a *FANBOYS*, be sure you are connecting two independent clauses. The following sentence is a single independent clause with one subject and two verbs. Therefore, no comma should be used.

The ice cream looked delicious and tasted good too.

2. Use a comma to separate three or more items in a series.

Students in the literature class are reading short stories, poems, and plays.

On Saturday I did my laundry, washed my car, and cleaned my room.

Occasionally, writers leave out the comma before the *and* connecting the last two items of a series, but it is more common to use it to separate all the items equally. Some words work together and don't need commas between them even though they do make up a kind of series.

The team members wanted to wear their brand-new green uniforms.

The bright white sunlight made the room glow.

To see whether a comma is needed between words in a series, ask yourself whether *and* could be used naturally between them. It would sound all right to say *short stories and poems and plays*; therefore, commas are used. But it would not sound right to say *brand-new and green uniforms* or *bright and white sunlight*; therefore, no commas are used.

When writing an address, insert a comma after every item, including the last:

Mail your response to 107 Aberdeen Street, Fredericton, New Brunswick, E3B 1R6, before the end of the month.

If a full date appears, place a comma after the day of the month and another after the year:

My sister was born on September 25, 1972, in a small prairie town.

However, if the day of the month is absent, no series comma is necessary:

My sister was born in September 1972 and graduated from the University of Manitoba.

3. **Put a comma after an introductory expression (it may be a word, a phrase, or a dependent clause) or before a comment or question that is tacked on at the end.**

Finally, he was able to get through to his insurance company.

During his last performance, the actor fell and broke his foot.

Once I have finished my homework, I will call you.

He said he needed to ruminate, whatever that means.

The new chairs aren't very comfortable, are they?

E X E R C I S E S

Add commas to the following sentences according to the first three comma rules. Some sentences may not need any commas, and some may need more than one. Any other punctuation already in the sentences is correct. Check your answers after the first set.

Exercise 1

1. Whenever I ask my friend Nick a computer-related question I end up regretting it.

2. Once he gets started Nick is unable to stop talking about computers.

3. When I needed his help the last time my printer wasn't working.

4. Instead of just solving the problem Nick went on and on about print settings and font choices that I could be using.

5. When he gets like this his face lights up and I feel bad for not wanting to hear the latest news on software upgrades e-mail programs and hardware improvements.

6. I feel guilty but I know that I am the normal one.

7. I even pointed his problem out to him by asking, "You can't control yourself can you?"

8. He just grinned and kept trying to fix my printer.

9. Nick always solves my problem so I should be grateful.

10. When I ask for Nick's help in the future I plan to listen and try to learn something.

Exercise 2

Add commas according to the first three comma rules.

1. I've been reading Helen Keller's autobiography and I have learned a lot more about her.
2. I originally thought that Keller was born deaf and blind but I was wrong.
3. When she was just under two years old Keller became ill with a terrible fever.
4. The family doctor believed that Keller was dying and prepared her family for the worst.
5. Not long after the doctor shared his fears with her family Keller recovered from her fever.
6. Unfortunately this sudden illness left Keller without the ability to see to hear or to speak.
7. The only tools that Keller had left were her sense of touch her active mind and her own curiosity.
8. With her teacher Anne Sullivan's constant assistance Keller eventually learned to read to write and to speak.
9. Keller was lucky to have so many people who loved and cared for her.
10. In my opinion Helen Keller was an amazing person and her story inspires me to do my best.

Exercise 3

1. Over fifty years ago weavers and spinners in Ontario met to form a provincial organization.
2. The Ontario Handweavers and Spinners (OHS) offers educational programs to fibre artists fibre hobbyists basket makers recreational spinners and weavers at every level of skill.
3. Weaving and spinning were once thought of as tasks for older women but today's fabric world has gone high-tech.

4. As they plan a project modern weavers plot their designs with the assistance of a computer program.

5. My image of a weaver doesn't include her sitting in front of a computer screen but times have obviously changed.

6. Several wonderful weaving websites are now available to the general public for the art of weaving seems to be experiencing an unexpected renaissance.

7. Local weaving guilds sponsor wildly popular "sheep to shawl" competitions in which local shepherds shear a sheep spinners clean card and spin the resulting wool and weavers work feverishly to construct a shawl.

8. Even for those who don't weave watching one of these competitions is very exciting.

9. All the steps of the shawl production process are carefully choreographed so the final product is a true group effort.

10. Because many younger adults have never been taught to spin or weave the OHS has an important role to play.

Exercise 4

1. When asked about what makes Canada unique respondents have a wide variety of answers and sometimes amusing comments.

2. Some mention the Wawa goose or Niagara Falls and others immediately think of the beaver or the maple leaf.

3. One constant Canadian icon is ice hockey and almost everyone around the world acknowledges Canadian excellence in this sport.

4. As a result it was interesting to hear that soccer has recently surpassed ice hockey as the sport played by more Canadians than any other.

5. When one considers the high cost of hockey this shift is probably no big surprise.

6. Parents have been moaning for years about the price of hockey equipment ice and travel time and coaching clinics.

7. Teams in most junior leagues are heavily backed financially by team sponsors for their monetary support keeps the leagues alive.

8. After the season is over the shin and shoulder pads are stored away carefully beside the hockey helmets and sticks until next season's play.

9. Unfortunately many youngsters grow so much during the intervening summer that they need larger-sized equipment by the opening whistle of the next season's first game.

10. Many parents and sponsors are facing external financial challenges this year so players and teams can expect reduced financial support.

Exercise 5

1. Gold is amazing isn't it?

2. Unlike metals that change their appearance after contact with water oil and other substances gold maintains its shine and brilliant colour under almost any circumstances.

3. When a miner named James Marshall found gold in the dark soil of California in 1848 the gold rush began.

4. Though few people are aware of it the first gold in Canada was found in small deposits in central Nova Scotia and the Eastern Townships of Quebec.

5. Harry Oakes developed the deepest gold mine in North America at Kirkland Lake Ontario.

6. Beginning with the Fraser River Gold Rush in 1858 a series of gold discoveries in British Columbia transformed the colony's history.

7. During the famous Klondike Gold Rush the huge influx of people searching for gold prompted the Canadian government to establish the Yukon Territory in 1898.

8. Canada was the world's third largest gold producer but remained far behind South Africa and Russia.

9. Some people have become rich directly because of gold and some have become rich indirectly because of gold.

10. For example if it had not been for the gold rush Levi Strauss would not have had any customers and the world would not have blue jeans.

Sources: Adapted from *Smithsonian,* July 1998; *The Canadian Encyclopedia* (Edmonton: Hurtig, 1985).

PROOFREADING EXERCISE

Apply the first three comma rules to the following paragraph:

When Niels Rattenborg studied the brains of mallard ducks he made an interesting discovery. Rattenborg wondered how ducks protected themselves as they slept. The ducks slept in rows and these rows were the secret to their defence. To his surprise Rattenborg found that the two ducks on the ends of the row did something special with the sides of their heads facing away from the row. Instinctively the ducks on the edge kept one eye open and one half of their brains awake as they slept. The rest of the ducks slept with both eyes closed and both sides of their brains inactive. The two guard ducks were able to frame the ducks in the middle watch for danger and sleep almost as soundly as their neighbours.

Source: Adapted from *Discover,* May 1999.

SENTENCE WRITING

Combine the following sets of sentences in different ways using all of the first three comma rules. You may need to reorder the details and change the phrasing. Compare your answers with those at the back of the book.

I like to swim.

I have never taken lessons.

The alarm rings.

I get up and get ready for school.

He is currently an elementary school teacher.

He was a math tutor in college.

He worked as a ski instructor.

Tricia and James are equal partners in their business.

Both of them are practical.

They are both organized.

Both of them graduated from university.

_____

_____

_____

_____

_____

_____

_____

_____

_____

Comma Rules 4, 5, and 6

The next three comma rules all involve using a pair of commas to enclose information that is not needed in a sentence—information that could be scooped out of the sentence without affecting its meaning. Two commas are used—one before and one after—to signal unnecessary words, phrases, and clauses.

4. Put commas around the name of a person spoken to.

Did you know, Danielle, that you left your backpack at the library?

We are pleased to inform you, Mr. Chen, that your application has been accepted.

5. Put commas around expressions that interrupt the flow of the sentence (such as *however, moreover, therefore, of course, by the way, on the other hand, I believe, I think*).

I know, of course, that I have missed the deadline.

They will try, however, to use the rest of their time wisely.

Today's exam, I think, is only a practice test.

Read the preceding sentences aloud, and you'll hear how those expressions interrupt the flow of the sentence. But sometimes such expressions flow smoothly into the sentence and don't need commas around them.

Of course he checked to see if their plane had been delayed.

We therefore decided to stay out of it.

I think you made the right decision.

Remember that when one of the previous words joins two independent clauses, that word needs a semicolon before it. It may also have a comma after it, especially if there seems to be a pause between the word and the rest of the sentence (see p. 123).

The bus was late; *however*, we still made it to the museum before it closed.

James is improving his study habits; *therefore*, he is getting better grades.

I spent hours studying for the test; *finally,* I felt prepared.

Thus words like *however* or *therefore* may be used in three ways:

- as an interrupter (commas around it)

- as a word that flows into the sentence (no commas needed)

- as a connecting word between two independent clauses (semicolon before and often a comma after)

6. **Put commas around additional information that is not needed in a sentence.**

Such information may be interesting, but the subject and main idea of the sentence would be clear without it. In the following sentence

Lin Chow, who organized the workshop, will introduce the speakers.

the clause *who organized the workshop* is not needed in the sentence. Without it, we still know exactly who the sentence is about and what she is going to do: *Lin Chow will introduce the speakers.* Therefore, the additional information is set off from the rest of the sentence by a pair of commas to show that it could be left out. But in the following sentence

The woman who organized the workshop will introduce the speakers.

the clause *who organized the workshop* is needed in the sentence. Without it, the sentence would read, *The woman will introduce the speakers*. We would have no idea which woman. The clause *who organized the workshop* couldn't be left out because it tells us which woman. Therefore, commas are not used around it. In the sentence

Hamlet, Shakespeare's famous play, has been made into a movie many times.

the additional information *Shakespeare's famous play* could be left out, and we would still know the main meaning of the sentence: *Hamlet has been made into a movie many times*. Therefore, the commas surround the added material to show that it could be omitted. But in the sentence

Shakespeare's famous play *Hamlet* has been made into a movie many times.

the title of the play is necessary. Without it, the sentence would read, *Shakespeare's famous play has been made into a movie many times*. We would have no idea which of Shakespeare's famous plays was being discussed. Therefore, the title couldn't be left out, and commas are not used around it.

The trick in deciding whether additional information is necessary is to say, "If I don't need it, I'll put commas around it."

EXERCISES

Surround any "scoopable" elements with commas by applying Comma Rules 4, 5, and 6 to the following sentences. Any commas already in the sentences follow Comma Rules 1, 2, or 3. Some sentences may be correct.

Exercise 1

1. People who own cats know that these pets often bring their owners unwelcome surprises.

2. Cats bring dead mice or birds to their owners and expect them to be pleased.

3. Cats become confused when their owners react angrily not happily to these "presents."

4. Desmond Morris renowned animal expert explains this misunderstood behaviour in his book *Catwatching*.

5. Morris explains that the cats who most frequently bring prey to their owners are female cats without kittens.

6. These cats have a strong instinct to teach their kittens how to hunt for food.

7. In the absence of kittens, these cats treat their owners as the next best thing kitten replacements.

8. The first step in the process of teaching "kittens" how to hunt and the one cat owners hate most is sharing the results of the hunt with them.

9. The owners' reaction which usually involves yelling and disappointment should include praise and lots of petting.

10. Cat owners who do understand their pets will be flattered next time they see what the cat dragged in.

Exercise 2

1. Paula who left at intermission missed the best part of the play.

2. Anyone who left at intermission missed the best part of the play.

3. Our teacher posted the results of the test that we took last week.

4. Our teacher posted the results of the midterm which we took last week.

5. The math teacher Mr. Simon looks a lot like the English teacher Mr. Simon.

6. Mr. Simon the math teacher looks a lot like Mr. Simon the English teacher.

7. My clothes dryer which has an automatic shut-off switch is safer than yours which doesn't.

8. An appliance that has an automatic shut-off switch is safer to use than one that doesn't.

9. Students who ask a lot of questions usually do well on their exams.

10. John and Brenda who ask a lot of questions usually do well on their exams.

Exercise 3

1. One of the weirdest competitions on earth the Wife Carrying World Championships takes place in Finland once a year.

2. These load-carrying races which may have begun as training rituals for Finnish soldiers have become popular all over the world.

3. Each pair of participants made up of one man and one wife has to make it through an obstacle course in the shortest time possible.

4. The wife half of the team has to weigh at least 49 kilos (108 pounds).

5. She does not have to be married to the man who carries her; she can indeed be someone else's wife or even unmarried.

6. The wife-carrying course includes two sections a part on land and a part in water.

7. The contest rules are few: make it to the finish line first, have fun, and don't drop the wife along the way.

8. The wife-dropping penalty which is fifteen seconds added to the pair's time is enough to disqualify most couples.

9. Contest officials allow one piece of equipment a belt that the man can wear so that the wife has something to hold on to during the race.

10. The winning couple wins a prize, but the coveted title Wife Carrying World Champion is reward enough for most.

Sources: Adapted from http://www.sonkajarvi.fi; *Sports Illustrated for Kids,* July 2003.

Exercise 4

1. England's Prince Charles has two sons William and Harry.

2. William is the son who will someday inherit the throne.

3. William whose full name is His Royal Highness Prince William Arthur Philip Louis of Wales was named after William the Conqueror.

4. The princes' grandmother Queen Elizabeth II will pass the crown to her son Charles who will then pass it on to William.

5. William who was born in 1902 stands over six foot tall and has become as popular as a movie star.

6. He appears overwhelmed by the attention of the girls who throw him bouquets decorated with their phone numbers.

7. William exchanged e-mails with Britney Spears but as far as I know never met her in person.

8. William is well read and intelligent; however he is also athletic and fun-loving.

9. Polls from the mid-1990s showed that the majority of British citizens favoured William as the next king instead of his father.

10. It will probably be many years before William takes on his future title which will be King William V.

Source: Adapted from *Biography Magazine,* October 1998.

Exercise 5

1. Guy Laliberté the creator of the world renowned Cirque du Soleil has never recognized limits in his lifetime.

2. Laliberté is for example one of only a handful of civilians who have flown into space.

3. He was already well known for his creativity which appears to have no boundaries.

4. Pictures showing him boarding the International Space Station with his signature red clown nose beamed into houses everywhere remember?

5. This citizen of the world hosted a show from space about the importance of clean water a problem he has identified as a global issue.

6. The program which was available in every time zone as the International Space Station passed over it earned Laliberté even more respect.

7. Laliberté who is a member of the Order of Canada personally organized countless shows for activists on the ground.

8. This effort didn't come cheaply however as the cost to Laliberté for his flight to the International Space Station aboard a Russian Soyuz mission was over $35 million.

9. Canadians can take pride in the contributions that have already been made by this talented entrepreneur and philanthropist and can hope for a better world because of Laliberté's efforts to fight poverty wherever it exists on Planet Earth.

10. To the Canadian who laughs and makes the rest of us chuckle along, all we can say is "Thanks Guy!"

PROOFREADING EXERCISE

Surround any "scoopable" elements in the following paragraph with commas according to Comma Rules 4, 5, and 6.

Two types of punctuation internal punctuation and end punctuation can be used in writing. Internal punctuation is used within the sentence, and end punctuation is used at the end of a sentence. Commas the most important pieces of internal punctuation are used to separate or enclose information within sentences. Semicolons the next most important also have two main functions. Their primary function separating two independent clauses is also the most widely known. A lesser-known need for semicolons to separate items in a list already containing commas occurs rarely in college writing. Colons and dashes likewise have special uses within sentences. And of the three pieces of end punctuation—periods, question marks, and exclamation points—the period which signals the end of the majority of English sentences is obviously the most common.

SENTENCE WRITING

Combine the following sets of sentences in different ways using Comma Rules 4, 5, and 6. Try to combine each set in a way that needs commas and in a way that doesn't need commas. You may reorder the details and change the phrasing. Compare your answers with those at the back of the book.

Shrek is a very funny movie.
I have seen it several times.

I believe.
I will learn best in "hands-on" environments.

My friend has curly hair.
He sits in the back of the class.
He takes good lecture notes.

_____

_____

_____

_____

_____

_____

_____

_____

_____

_____

REVIEW OF THE COMMA

SIX COMMA RULES

1. Put a comma before *for, and, nor, but, or, yet,* and *so* when they connect two independent clauses.

2. Put a comma between three or more items in a series.

3. Put a comma after an introductory expression or before an afterthought.

4. Put commas around the name of a person spoken to.

5. Put commas around an interrupter, like *however* or *therefore.*

6. Put commas around unnecessary additional information.

PROOFREADING EXERCISE

Add the missing commas, and, in the brackets at the *end* of each sentence, identify which one of the six comma rules applies. Each of the six sentences illustrates a different rule.

I am writing you this note Helen to ask you to do me a favour. [   ] When

you get home from work tonight would you take the turkey out of the freezer?

[   ] I plan to get started on the pies the rolls and the sweet potatoes as soon as

I walk in the door after work. [   ] I will be so busy however that I might forget to thaw out the turkey. [   ] It's the first time I've made the holiday meal by myself and I want everything to be perfect. [   ] My big enamel roasting pan which is in the back of the cupboard under the counter will be the best place to keep the turkey as it thaws. [   ] Thanks for your help. Jim.

SENTENCE WRITING

Write at least one sentence of your own to demonstrate each of the six comma rules.

_____

_____

_____

_____

_____

_____

_____

_____

Quotation Marks and Underlining/Italics

Put quotation marks around a direct quotation (the exact words of a speaker) but not around an indirect quotation.

> The officer said, "Please show me your driver's licence." (a direct quotation)

> The officer asked to see my driver's licence. (an indirect quotation)

> John Keats said, "Heard melodies are sweet, but those unheard are sweeter."

> John Keats said that the melodies that can be heard are sweet, but those that cannot be heard are even sweeter.

If the speaker says more than one sentence, quotation marks are used before and after the entire speech.

> She said, "One of your brake lights is out. You need to take care of the problem right away."

If the quotation begins the sentence, the words telling who is speaking are set off with a comma unless, of course, a question mark or an exclamation point is needed.

"I didn't even know it was broken," I said.

"Do you have any questions?" she asked.

"Fire!" I yelled.

"Of course I'm interested in your proposal," she said.

"Yes, consider this just a warning," she said.

Each of the preceding quotations begins with a capital letter. But when a quotation is broken, the second part doesn't begin with a capital letter unless it's a new sentence.

"If you knew how much time I spent on the essay," the student said, "you would have given me an A."

"A chef might work on a meal for days," the teacher replied. "That doesn't mean the results will taste good."

Put quotation marks around the titles of short stories, poems, songs, essays, TV program episodes, or other short works.

I couldn't sleep after I read "Friend of My Youth," a short story by Alice Munro.

My favourite Gordon Lightfoot song is "Early Morning Rain."

We had to read George Orwell's essay "A Hanging."

Larry David's troubles in the "Trick or Treat" episode are some of the funniest moments in TV history.

***Italicize* titles of longer works such as books, newspapers, magazines, plays, record albums or CDs, movies, or TV or radio series.**

A Complicated Kindness is a novel by Miriam Toews.

I read about the latest discovery of dinosaur footprints in *Maclean's*.

Gone with the Wind was rereleased in movie theatres in 1998.

My mother watches CBC's *The National* every evening.

You may need to underline instead of italicizing if you are not using a computer. Just be consistent throughout any paper in which you use underlining or italics.

A Complicated Kindness is a novel by Miriam Toews.

I read about the latest discovery of dinosaur footprints in Maclean's.

Gone with the Wind was rereleased in movie theatres in 1998.

My mother watches CBC's The National every evening.

E X E R C I S E S

Punctuate the quotations, and underline or put quotation marks around each title.

Exercise 1

1. I am reading a book called Don't: A Manual of Mistakes & Improprieties More or Less Prevalent in Conduct and Speech.

2. The book's contents are divided into chapters with titles such as At Table, In Public, and In General.

3. In the section about table don'ts, the book offers the following warning: Don't bend over your plate or drop your head to get each mouthful.

4. The table advice continues by adding, Don't bite your bread. Break it off.

5. This book offers particularly comforting advice about conducting oneself in public.

6. For instance, it states, Don't brush against people or elbow people or in any way show disregard for others.

7. When meeting others on the street, the book advises, Don't be in a haste to introduce. Be sure that it is mutually desired before presenting one person to another.

8. In the section titled In General, there are more tips about how to get along in society, such as Don't underrate everything that others do or overstate your own doings.

9. Don't has this to say about books, whether borrowed or owned: Read them, but treat them as friends that must not be abused.

10. And one can never take the following warning too much to heart: Don't make yourself in any particular way a nuisance to your neighbours or your family.

Exercise 2

1. Have you been to the bookstore yet? Monica asked.

2. No, why? I answered.

3. They've rearranged the books, she said, and now I can't find anything.

4. Are all of the books for one subject still together? I asked.

5. Yes, they are, Monica told me, but there are no markers underneath the books to say which teacher's class they're used in, so it's really confusing.

6. Why don't we just wait until the teachers show us the books and then buy them? I replied.

7. That will be too late! Monica shouted.

8. Calm down, I told her, you are worrying for nothing.

9. I guess so, she said once she took a deep breath.

10. I sure hope I'm not wrong, I thought to myself, or Monica will really be mad at me.

Exercise 3

1. Women's Wit and Wisdom is the title of a book I found in the library.

2. The book includes many great insights that were written or spoken by women throughout history.

3. England's Queen Elizabeth I noted in the sixteenth century, A clear and innocent conscience fears nothing.

4. Nothing is so good as it seems beforehand, observed George Eliot, a female author whose real name was Mary Ann Evans.

5. Some of the women's quotations are funny; Alice Roosevelt Longworth, for instance, said, If you don't have anything good to say about anyone, come and sit by me.

6. If life is a bowl of cherries, asked Erma Bombeck, what am I doing in the pits?

244 Part 5 Punctuating Correctly

7. Some of the quotations are serious, such as Gloria Steinem's statement, The future depends on what each of us does every day.

8. Maya Lin, the woman who designed Washington D.C.'s Vietnam Veterans Memorial, reminded us, War is not just a victory or a loss.... People die.

9. Emily Dickinson had this to say about truth: Truth is such a rare thing, it is delightful to tell it.

10. Finally, columnist Ann Landers advised one of her readers The naked truth is always better than the best-dressed lie.

Exercise 4

1. Kurt Vonnegut, in his novel Slapstick, describes New York City as Skyscraper National Park.

2. The past is still, for us, a place that is not safely settled wrote Michael Ondaatje.

3. In her book The Mysterious Affair at Styles, Agatha Christie wrote Every murderer is probably somebody's old friend.

4. Swear not by the moon says Juliet to Romeo.

5. Pierre Trudeau told a U.S. audience Living next to you is like sleeping next to an elephant.

6. Norman Bethune stated The function of the artist is to disturb.

7. Writers are always selling somebody out Joan Didion observed.

8. The expression All animals are equal, but some animals are more equal than others can be found in George Orwell's novel Animal Farm.

9. A Swahili proverb warns, To the person who seizes two things, one always slips from his grasp!

10. Groucho Marx once remarked I wouldn't want to belong to any club that would accept me as a member.

Exercise 5

1. Ovid reminded us that we can learn from our enemies.

2. We know what a person thinks not when he tells us what he thinks said Isaac Bashevis Singer but by his actions.

3. The Spanish proverb El pez muere por la boca translated means The fish dies because it opens its mouth.

4. Ask yourself whether you are happy, and you cease to be so John Stuart Mill wrote.

5. A Russian proverb states Without a shepherd, sheep are not a flock.

6. Stephen Leacock felt The essence of humour is human kindliness.

7. St. Jerome had the following insight The friendship that can cease has never been real.

8. Oscar Wilde found In this world there are only two tragedies. One is not getting what one wants, and the other is getting it.

9. Self-respect observed Joe Clark permeates every aspect of your life.

10. Choose a job you love Confucius suggested and you will never have to work a day in your life.

PROOFREADING EXERCISE

Punctuate quotations, and underline or put quotation marks around titles used in the following paragraph.

It may be decided, sometime off in the future, that the sum of Douglas Coupland's literary contribution equals the two words he used for the title of his 1991 debut as a novelist. In Generation X, Coupland pointed and clicked onto the generation born in the late 1950s and the 1960s as it stared into the future and tried to figure out what was going to fulfill it there. If the book didn't attract universally favourable reviews, it was a resounding commercial success and made Coupland an instant spokesperson for his generation. It didn't matter so much that he didn't want the job—I speak for myself, he's said repeatedly, not for a generation. No, he'd been deemed a sociological seer and, like it or not, each of his subsequent novels—books like *Microserfs* (1995) and *Girlfriend in a Coma* (1998)—found itself judged less as fiction than as the words of an oracle between hard covers.

Source: Adapted from *Quill and Quire: Canada's Magazine of Books and News,* January 2000, Vol. 66, No. 1: 20.

SENTENCE WRITING

Write ten sentences that list and discuss your favourite songs, TV shows, characters' expressions, movies, books, and so on. Be sure to punctuate titles and quotations correctly. Refer to the rules at the beginning of this section if necessary.

_____

_____

_____

_____

_____

_____

_____

_____

_____

_____

Capital Letters

1. Capitalize the first word of every sentence.

Peaches taste best when they are cold.

2. Capitalize the first word of a direct quotation.

She said, "My brother never worked so hard before."

"He has finished most of his homework," she said, "but he still has a lot to do." (The *but* is not capitalized because it continues the same quotation and does not begin a new sentence.)

"Everyones loves English class," she said. "Maybe I'll change my program."
(*Maybe* is capitalized because it begins a new sentence.)

3. **Capitalize the first, last, and every important word in a title. Don't capitalize short prepositions (such as *in, of, at, with*), short connecting words, the *to* in front of a verb, or *a, an,* or *the*.**

I saw a copy of Darwin's *On the Origin of Species* at a yard sale.

The class enjoyed the essay "How to Write a Rotten Poem with Almost No Effort."

Shakespeare in Love is a comedy based on Shakespeare's writing of the play *Romeo and Juliet.*

4. **Capitalize specific names of people, places, languages, and nationalities.**

Roméo Dallaire	China	Louis Riel Trail
Iraq	Spanish	Japanese
Terry Fox	Fort Frances	Dundas Street

5. **Capitalize the names of months, days of the week, and special days, but not the seasons.**

March	Victoria Day	spring
Tuesday	Canada Day	winter
New Year's Eve	Labour Day	fall

6. **Capitalize a title of relationship if it takes the place of the person's name. If *my* (or *your, her, his, our, their*) is in front of the word, a capital is not used.**

I think Dad wrote to her.	*but*	I think my dad wrote to her.
She visited Aunt Sophia.	*but*	She visited her aunt Sophia.
We spoke with Grandpa.	*but*	We spoke with our grandpa.

7. **Capitalize names of particular people or things, but not general terms.**

I admire Professor Segsworth.	*but*	I admire my professor.
We saw the famous St. Lawrence River.	*but*	We saw the famous river.
Are you from the West?	*but*	Is your house west of the mountains?

I will take Philosophy 120 and English 100.	*but*	I will take philosophy and English.
She graduated from Sutter High School.	*but*	She graduated from high school.
They live at 119 Forest St.	*but*	They live on a beautiful street.
We enjoyed the Royal Ontario Museum.	*but*	We enjoyed the museum.

E X E R C I S E S

Add all of the necessary capital letters to the sentences that follow.

Exercise 1

1. mom and i have both decided to take classes next fall.

2. fortunately, in toronto we live near several colleges and universities.

3. classes at the community colleges usually begin in late august or early september.

4. we could easily drive to york university the university of toronto, ryerson university, humber college, george brown college, or sheridan college.

5. i want to take credit classes, and my mom wants to sign up for continuing education classes.

6. for instance, i will enroll in the academic courses necessary to transfer to a university.

7. these include english, math, science, and history classes.

8. my mother, on the other hand, wants to take non-credit classes with titles like "learn to play keyboards," "web pages made easy," and "be your own real estate agent."

9. mom already has a great job, so she can take classes just for fun.

10. i know that if i want to go to one of the colleges at the university of toronto, i will have to be serious from the start.

Exercise 2

1. Newfoundland and labrador, the youngest province in canada, joined confederation at midnight on march 31, 1949, little more than half a century ago.

2. Sixty years later, many newfoundlanders feel strongly that the real date was april 1, april fool's day.

3. The province is actually composed of the island of newfoundland and a section of land on the north american continent between quebec and the atlantic ocean coastline.

4. Along this easternmost coast, europeans caught their first view of the north american continent.

5. In the tenth century, viking explorers from iceland and greenland settled briefly in the north of the island of newfoundland.

6. Nearly five hundred years later, a venetian navigator, john cabot, sailed on a voyage of discovery for henry vii of England and discovered new lands, including a "new isle," in 1497.

7. Canada's tenth province's economic, political, and cultural history has been checkered, especially since world war II.

8. The nearby provinces of nova scotia, new brunswick, and prince edward island combined have a smaller land mass, but due to rugged terrain and climate, less than 0.01% of newfoundland and labrador's vast land area is farmed.

9. Postsecondary educational opportunities are limited; the memorial university of newfoundland in st. john's, was founded in 1925 as memorial university college and made the province's only university by a special act of the house of assembly in 1949.

10. The economic outlook turned exceptionally bleak when the cod fishery was banned by the federal government's department of fisheries, but more recently, the province found riches under the sea in the hibernia oil fields and in substantial reserves of reserves of nickel in voisey's bay.

Exercise 3

1. Imagine an ocean on the prairies and mountains higher than the himalayas in ontario.

2. That's part of the picture unveiled by lithoprobe, the name of a twenty-year examination of canada's ancient geological history.

3. Since 1984, more than eight hundred university, government, and industry scientists, led by dr. ron clowes, have been examining the movements of ancient continents, oceans, and islands.

4. "underneath the surface of alberta, we found a subsurface mountain range," reported dr. clowes, a professor of earth and ocean sciences at the university of british columbia.

5. Even more spectacular was the evidence that there was once an ocean the size of the pacific under modern day saskatchewan and manitoba.

6. The results of the lithoprobe study provide a map of canada's origins.

7. From the maritimes through the prairies to the west coast and from the great lakes to the arctic ocean, the study maps a view of the country eighty kilometres deep and six thousand kilometres wide.

8. The scientists used special trucks called "dancing elephants" to create seismic waves by coordinated bouncing on a pad.

9. The waves are reflected back from the earth, but the reflections vary, depending on what the waves hit.

10. The study is providing data on the process that might lead the volcano in mount st. helens, washington, to erupt again.

Source: Adapted from "Dancing Elephants Help Chart Prehistoric Canada." October 8, 2004. http://www.cbc.ca. Reprinted with permission.

Exercise 4

1. i grew up watching *the wizard of oz* once a year on tv before video stores like blockbuster even rented movies to watch at home.

2. i especially remember enjoying it with my brother and sisters when we lived on maple drive.

3. mom would remind us early in the day to get all of our homework done.

4. "if your homework isn't finished," she'd say, "you can't see the munchkins!"

5. my favourite part has always been dorothy's house dropping on one of the wicked witches and her feet shrivelling up under the house.

6. the wicked witch of the west wants revenge after that, but dorothy and toto get help from glinda, the good witch of the north.

7. glinda tells dorothy about the emerald city and the wizard of oz.

8. on their way, toto and dorothy meet the scarecrow, the tin man, and the cowardly lion.

9. together they conquer the witch and meet professor marvel, the real man who has been pretending to be a wizard.

10. the ruby slippers give dorothy the power to get back to kansas and to auntie em and uncle henry.

Exercise 5

1. In spring 2004 viewers of the cbc tv series *the greatest canadian* nominated ten individuals for the title: frederick banting, alexander graham bell, don cherry, tommy douglas, terry fox, wayne gretzky, sir john a. macdonald, lester b. pearson, david suzuki, and pierre trudeau.

2. Macdonald, the first prime minister, united the french and the english and facilitated the construction of the canadian pacific railway.

3. Under pearson's leadership in the 1960s, the canada pension plan, a national healthcare system, the bilingualism and biculturalism commission, a national labour code, and the maple leaf flag were introduced.

4. Pierre trudeau, the most contemporary prime minister to make the list, worked to promote bilingualism, stamp out quebec separatism, and patriate the canadian constitution and charter of rights.

5. The winner of the title greatest canadian was the late tommy douglas, five-term saskatchewan premier, who is credited as being the "father of medicare."

6. After bell patented the invention and staged a demonstration of the telephone at the centennial exhibition in philadelphia, pennsylvania, in 1876, he went on to form the bell telephone company in 1877.

7. A contemporary ambassador of science, david suzuki taught at the university of alberta and university of british columbia before moving his teaching out of the classroom and into the media as host of "suzuki on science," "quirks and quarks," and, most recently, "the nature of things."

8. Known as the man who discovered insulin, frederick banting brought new hope to diabetics the world over, earned a knighthood in the british crown, and was awarded canada's first-ever nobel prize in medicine.

9. Another medical hero was terry fox, whose marathon of hope to collect funds for cancer research is reenacted every year across the country.

10. Don cherry, the outspoken host of cbc's hockey night in canada, and wayne gretzky, the greatest scorer in nhl history and winner of four stanley cups, represented the sports world on the list of nominees.

Source: Adapted from *Top Ten Greatest Canadians.* CBC. December 10, 2004. http://www.cbc.ca/greatest/top_ten.

Punctuation Progress Test

Use the skills you've acquired in Part 5 to identify punctuation problem areas in the sentences below. Place a circle in any location that requires inserting, deleting, or changing a piece of punctuation. Write your corrections in the spaces between sentences.

1. Building large English vocabularies is one of the biggest challenges, facing many newcomers to Canada.

2. After immigrants learn a word's spelling they have to conquer the mysteries of English pronunciation.

3. One general rule is that a word becomes part of an individual's working vocabulary only when the person can: spell, pronounce, define, and use the word correctly in a sentence.

4. My best friend, who is from Sri Lanka tells me that she found dealing with word lists the most effective way to build her North American English vocabulary.

5. I've always wondered why English speakers from other parts of the world find Canadian English so difficult?

6. Unless he stops to think about it my neighbour from Britain still refers to gasoline as "petrol" and to the trunk of his car as the "boot."

7. Amazingly, he's been in Canada over a decade.

8. My teacher in grade 7 put a big emphasis on the importance of words, she told us that they were the building blocks of messages.

9. Miss Cutter, I think that was her name, clearly explained to us that recognizing a word in print didn't necessarily mean that we could include it in our vocabulary.

10. She urged us to find ways to make vocabulary building fun so I remember taping up small vocabulary cards all over the house.

11. Each card contained the following essential information, correct spelling, my own phonetic key to pronunciation, a definition, and a sample sentence using the word correctly.

12. When my mother protested about having so many cards cluttering the house I learned another important lesson: keep the task small.

13. I reduced the number of cards from fifty-two to no more than five at a time, then mastering the words was far easier.

14. My sister, who is four years younger than I am, suggested that I make a set of flash cards, like the ones she was using to learn her times tables.

15. What fun the two of us had studying together.

16. I also discovered that part of my difficulty in spelling; words could be traced to poor pronunciation.

17. These silly flash cards introduced many new words, at the same time, they helped me to improve my spelling and pronunciation.

18. For example, by saying the words correctly, I can easily spot the spelling difference between "pronunciation," and its verb form "pronounce."

19. Even though they appeared on my cards for months I still have to think twice about how to spell the past tense of the verb "occur" ("occurred") and its noun form ("occurrence").

20. Perhaps the most important lesson, was how many words were foreign to me even though I have spent my entire life surrounded by those who speak, read, and write in English.

Punctuation Post-Test

Use the skills you've acquired in Part 5 to identify punctuation problem areas in the sentences below. Place a circle in any location that requires inserting, deleting, or changing a piece of punctuation. Write your corrections in the spaces between sentences.

1. The Canadian health care system, a creation of government that has become a cultural icon is designed to protect all Canadians.

2. Through a complex web of doctors' offices, after-hours clinics, hospital emergency rooms, and paramedic care this country offers universal access to routine health care options.

3. Some Canadians take this accessibility for granted, and expect their health to be guaranteed.

4. Some individuals, my brother is one of them, require exceptional care that would cost hundreds of thousands of dollars in the United States.

5. Most people understand that no system is perfect especially a health care web as complicated and expensive as ours.

6. Some procedures require the attention of a team of health care professionals others, Canadians could likely look after themselves without placing a strain on the system's resources.

7. For example, my neighbour's little daughter was born with a heart defect and required immediate heart surgery at the hospital for sick children in Toronto.

8. Janine is now twelve years old but she still needs monitoring by a team of pediatric heart specialists.

9. Janine's mother Else is deeply concerned, because so many of the specialists they've seen over the past twelve years are now retiring.

10. Primary-care doctors, often referred to as family physicians, have patient rosters in the thousands, and can't spend the required time to keep their skills up-to-date or even to get to know their patients' needs well.

11. When my Niece gave birth last Spring to a lovely daughter, no doctor attended; instead, a midwife and a doula supervised the pregnancy and labour.

12. Whenever a community loses a doctor to death, retirement, or relocation that physician's patients must find another doctor or rely on after-hours clinics.

13. Some doctors find themselves so overworked that mistakes, some of them tragic!, can occur.

14. Everyone has a horror story or two to tell: about a relative or friend who received the wrong medication, got treatment for the wrong disease, or didn't get medical attention in time.

15. Can you imagine the nightmare of waking up to find out that the Surgeon had removed the wrong part.

16. Nurses, and pharmacists are increasingly taking up the workload once reserved for doctors.

17. As well as these front-line health care professions now include acupuncture, chiropractic, hypnosis, physical therapy, and naturopathy.

18. Regrettably, many of the services, offered by these individuals, are not covered by most provincial health care plans.

19. As a result, only those Canadians, who have extended health care plans through their employment, are likely to take advantage of these alternative health measures.

20. That means our society is leaving some Canadians without the same level of service—what a shame.

P A R T　6

Writing Well

What Is the Least You Should Know about Writing?

Until this point in the book, the focus has been on gathering the tools for effective communication. But having a computer and knowing how to use it doesn't guarantee that the user can create an effective document or build an informative spreadsheet. Nor does having a box holding all the necessary tools mean that a carpenter can build a beautiful house.

When you communicate, you certainly don't use just one word or even one sentence. Particularly in writing, you need blueprints that will allow your readers to understand the ideas you are communicating in paragraphs or in multi-paragraph units, such as reports, letters, essays, and summaries.

Like the earlier parts of the book, this section is designed to give you some familiarity and confidence in tackling effective communication. However, Part 6 is not designed to address all writing situations; it won't equip you with the skills to compose great essays, to write clear and concise technical reports, or to use the appropriate documentation style for your subject area.

Nonetheless, the book you're holding *will* give you the helpful overview necessary to tackle general writing tasks. By breaking the writing challenge into its most critical components, *The Least You Should Know about English* will make writing more logical and less intimidating. Reading this part of the book may also help you recall writing lessons that, while once learned, have been forgotten through disuse.

But what if your purpose for writing is more specific?

To learn about writing tips and techniques to meet more specialized writing challenges, you will want to consult a textbook with a writing focus. For example, the most recent edition of *The Canadian Writer's Workplace* by Gary Lipschutz et al. (Toronto: Nelson Education, 2009) or *Essay Essentials with Readings* by Sarah Norton and Brian Green (Toronto: Thomson-Nelson, 2006) include expanded discussions of the basics you will find in this book while maintaining the same Canadian flavour in their exercises.

A comprehensive writing textbook also describes research strategies and outlines documentation procedures. Most importantly, such a text will also devote a chapter to each of several different writing forms and purposes. These include description, narration, cause and effect, comparison/contrast, persuasion/argumentation, definition, process, and classification. If you will need to write business correspondence or technical reports, examine a book's table of contents to ensure that these topics are adequately covered.

> *TIP: Before purchasing any writing textbook, ensure that it outlines in detail strategies for the specific types of writing tasks you will be facing.*

Basic Structures

PARAGRAPHS

When you began working with this book, you focused on individual words. Then you learned how to link words together to form sentence structures so that your ideas would be clear to your readers. Logically, the next step is to discover how best to link sentences together. The smallest unit of combined sentences is called a *paragraph*. A typical paragraph centres on one idea, usually found in one sentence from which all other sentences in the paragraph radiate. Paragraphs generally contain several sentences, but no set number is required. And although a paragraph can stand alone, it more typically is used to build a piece of a larger written work, like a report or an essay.

As you build a paragraph, you will face three important questions:

- What is my main point in this paragraph?
- What information should I include to support that point?
- In what order should those supportive details appear?

Stating Your Main Point (Unity)

Every time you communicate, you have a central idea that you are trying to share with others. In face-to-face communication, you probably don't spend a lot of time choosing words to form that central idea. After all, when your listeners look at you and hear your voice, they can rely on the way you hold your head, your facial expressions your tone of voice, and other nonverbal clues about the point you are trying to make.

In written communication, though, neither you nor your readers can rely on any clues other than the words that appear on the printed page.

> *A topic sentence clearly states the main point of the paragraph.*

That's why many paragraph writers include a topic sentence in each of their paragraphs. A clear topic sentence offers two advantages: the writer is less likely to stray off-topic, and the reader gets a clear understanding of what the paragraph is all about.

The topic sentence does not have to be placed at the very beginning of the paragraph. In some paragraph patterns, it appears at the very end or in the middle. Occasionally, a paragraph's topic sentence is not stated but implied.

What's important is that the topic sentence has to state the writer's main point clearly, be broad enough to cover the sentences that will rely upon it for focus, and be narrow enough to allow details to be added.

Look at the following sentences, all of which are grammatically correct. Can you pick the one that could act as a topic sentence?

I jogged six kilometres yesterday. (This sentence doesn't make a point; it just states a fact.)

Eating well and exercising regularly are important factors in fighting obesity. (This sentence is too broad for a single paragraph.)

My sister has found that exercise helps control her weight. (This sentence is the best choice. A reader will be interested in hearing more, and the main idea is not too narrow.)

Exercise: Topic Sentences

In each of the paragraphs below, identify which sentence (if any) is serving as the paragraph's topic sentence.

1. Everyone loves the excitement of shopping for a new automobile. For most people, the fun begins with reading car reviews written by automotive journalists. Some reviewers provide every possible snippet of information that the potential buyer might need, from technical specifications to luxury trim options. After reading the reviews, consumers often find themselves watching TV auto commercials far more closely. The next step for most is a visit to dealerships to read all the literature and get behind the wheel for a test drive. During this step, motorists discover that the car the automobile reviewer raved about costs about $10 000 more than they can finance. At the end of the day, they will have learned the hard way that the realities of their budgets sometimes overrule their initial excitement.

(Topic sentence: _____)

2. If a text is misleading, the message readers receive is different from the message the writer intended, but the readers do not realize this. Although misleading passages are probably rare, they can be extremely hazardous because even though the readers are not getting the meaning intended, they are confident that they understand what the writer meant. If the document is a set of instructions, they will simply do what they think they were told to do. The writer's responsibility for clear writing can't be taken lightly.

(Topic sentence: _____)

3. Psychotherapists in Western cultures promote the ideas that people should be happy, that all change is possible, and that change is relatively easy. Eastern cultures, on the other hand, are more tolerant of conditions regarded as outside human control and have a less optimistic view of change. Western therapists want to fix problems, whereas Eastern therapists teach clients to live with and accept troubling emotions.

(Topic sentence: _____)

Providing Plenty of Supportive Details (Support)

Stating the main idea is generally not enough, especially in writing. In a conversation with a friend, you might be able to say, "I use exercise to control my weight." Likely the friend will understand enough about you to know if you belong to a gym or work out regularly. However, in more formal writing, your reader may be unable to understand the reasons behind your statement—and you won't be standing there to answer the reader's questions. The supportive details extend the length of a paragraph into several sentences.

> *Specific details **support**, **develop**, or **explain** the paragraph's main idea.*

In the example of the use of exercise to control weight gain, as this paragraph's writer, you could include information about what types of exercise you use, how much weight you have lost, or even when you knew the exercise was working. Notice that the paragraph would not, however, include details about health problems caused by obesity because those comments would be off-topic.

Which of the following sentences could be included in the above paragraph?

Ever since primary school, I have had weight problems. (This sentence provides historical information but doesn't focus on exercise.)

I enjoy going to the gym. (This statement isn't specific enough to support or explain the main idea of controlling weight gain.)

When I began visiting the gym three times a week, I quickly saw some positive results. (This one works best because it retains the main idea's focus on the use of exercise to control weight.)

Exercise: Main Ideas and Supportive Details

Look for the pattern in the phrases below. Notice that when you compare them, some are more general while others are specific examples. Using the outline template, arrange the phrases so that they show relationships and levels of importance.

Devoted Dogs	Talkative Tabbies	Lovable Pets	Curious Cats
Huggable Hounds	Sassy Siamese	Pampered Poodles	

(Topic) _____

(1st Support Point)   I. _____

    (example/specific detail)   A. _____

    (example/specific detail)   B. _____

(2nd Support Point)   II. _____

    (example/specific detail)   A. _____

    (example/specific detail)   B. _____

Keeping the Ideas Logically and Clearly Organized (Coherence)

As you grow into your writing, you'll discover that ideas are best expressed in organizational patterns. First, decide which pattern makes most sense in your paragraph. Some possibilities include Addition, Time or Space, Comparison/Contrast, Emphasis, and Cause/Effect. Then, include transitional words and phrases because they work like directional signs to help your reader see where your ideas are heading. Below are sample directional words used in each pattern.

Addition (showing equally weighted ideas)
for one thing, another, also

Time (showing the order of ideas from earliest to most recent)
first, second, next, then, finally

Space (relating details according to their order in some location)
  on the left, in the middle, near, next to, above, under

Comparison (showing similarities between previous idea and the next one)
  as well, like, in addition, similarly, for example

Contrast (showing differences between ideas)
  however, but, on the other hand

Emphasis (showing the relative importance of ideas)
  first of all, more/most importantly

Cause/Effect (showing how one support leads to the next)
  because, as a result, consequently

For example, one of the most obvious groups to learn is Time transitions. In a paragraph organized in this fashion, you could introduce the first significant supportive detail with a phrase like "the first" or "first of all," introduce the second detail with "next" or "then," and use "finally" in the sentence containing the last of the supportive details.

Look at the differences in the following two paragraphs. One of them has transitional (signal) words. The other does not.

Every variety of apple has a different appearance. Delicious apples have a solid dark red colour and an oval shape with five knobs on the bottom. They are a medium to large size. The Granny Smith variety of apples is bright green. Granny Smith apples have a round shape and a medium to large size.

Every variety of apple has a different appearance. Delicious apples, *for example,* have a solid dark red colour and an oval shape with five knobs on the bottom. *On the other hand,* the Granny Smith variety is bright green. *Like* Delicious apples, Granny Smith apples are medium to large in size; *however,* they have a round shape *as opposed to* an oval one.

Notice how the insertion of the italicized signal words transforms this paragraph so that it no longer appears as just a random list of sentences. The second paragraph's choice of signal words tells the reader that it is ordered in a Comparison/Contrast pattern.

Other Transitional Devices

Pronouns: Because pronouns refer to established nouns, the correct use of pronouns will link paragraph ideas.

Forceful repetition: Although most writers choose not to repeat words, purposefully repeating key words or phrases will link a paragraph's ideas.

> *Specific supportive details should appear in logical order.*
> *Transitional devices signal that order to your reader.*

Exercise: Transitions

Step 1: On a separate piece of paper, use the transitional words and phrases in the following sentences to sort them into a solid, well-organized paragraph.

Step 2: While rewriting the sentences, underline the words that helped you sort out the correct order.

- In the first place, most family physicians already have huge practices.

- Such burnout has several results: a reluctance to take on any new patients, a desire to take time off or retire prematurely, the decision to withdraw from hospital privileges, and sometimes a willingness to move to another area where the workload is less onerous.

- To illustrate this problem, statistics from the Sudbury District Health Unit indicate that the average Sudbury doctor maintains a practice with between four thousand and five thousand patients.

- Finding a family doctor in Northern Ontario is not an easy task.

- With an average age of fifty two, many family doctors are burning out under the strain of the work they are facing.

- For all these reasons, a newcomer to Sudbury is sure to face challenges in locating a family physician willing to take the person on as a new patient.

- Finally, Sudbury's family doctors often find themselves without specialists to whom patients with unique needs can be referred for more detailed diagnoses.

- A second problem is the age of those currently practising family medicine.

MULTI-PARAGRAPH COMPOSITIONS

When you find yourself needing to compose lengthier pieces of writing—such as personal letters, academic essays, technical reports, and other longer items—much of what you have learned about writing effective paragraphs still applies.

For example, any writing will focus on the author's main point; include details that support, develop, or explain that idea; and use a logical and clear pattern of organization.

Like any other large project, a longer writing job is most manageable when you break it into several smaller tasks. In general, a multi-paragraph writing job can be broken into seven smaller steps:

1. Pre-Writing (identifying your topic and its supports)

2. Identifying the Thesis (expressing your main idea)

3. Writing the Introductory Paragraph (catching the reader's interest)

4. Composing and Organizing Support Paragraphs (supplying interesting details)

5. Crafting a Final Paragraph (wrapping up)

6. Revising and Editing (making worthwhile changes)

7. Proofreading (eliminating embarrassing mistakes)

Step 1: Pre-Writing

Writing anything lengthy requires extra planning. Your reader will never see your pre-writing/planning efforts. However, investing time before you begin to write will make the actual writing process far easier and your written product far clearer. During pre-writing, you choose a topic and identify the main point you want to make about it, explore and evaluate pieces of supportive information, and group these details into categories that will form support paragraphs. In short, you design the long paper the same way an architect produces blueprints for a large house.

Because investing time at the pre-writing stage is guaranteed to produce clearer writing, you should investigate various pre-writing strategies. Some, like focused free writing, brainstorming, and simple listing, are more comfortable options for individuals who process their ideas in a linear (left to right, up to down, most to least important) fashion. Three-dimensional and visual individuals might find the clustering strategy more helpful. Look at the differences between the two styles:

Focused Free Writing (or Brainstorming)

Free writing is a good way to begin. When you are assigned a paper, try writing for ten minutes, putting down all your thoughts on one subject—golfing, for example. Don't stop to think about organization, sentence structure, capitalization, or spelling—just let the details flow onto the page. Free writing will help you see what material you have and will help you figure out what aspects of the subject to write about.

Here is an example:

Many individuals think of golfing as a pastime for only the well-to-do or the retirees with handsome pensions. after all, catching

a round of golf requires a fair amount of financial investment.
Even if you're only renting a set of clubs and heading out on the
greens once a week. If a person decides to make this a regular
hobby you will want to think about buying your own personalized
set of clubs. Plus a decent set of cleated shoes and maybe even
monogrammed golf balls. Another group that seems particularly
interested in this sport are teenagers and young adults although I
don't know how they can possibly afford to play on a regular
basis. Perhaps both generalizations are incorrect because I know
lots of middle aged people view golfing as an employment stress
reliever.

The result of this free writing session is certainly not ready to be typed and submitted. However, what did become clear was that you could focus this paper on how golfing, while costly, is an attractive pastime for people of various ages.

Clustering

Clustering is another way of thinking a topic through on paper before you begin to write. A cluster is more visual than free writing. You could cluster the topic of "going to the horse races," for instance, by putting it in a circle in the centre of a piece of paper and then drawing lines to new circles as ideas or details occur to you. The idea is to free your mind from the limits of sentences and paragraphs to generate pure details and ideas. When you are finished clustering, you can see where you want to go with a topic.

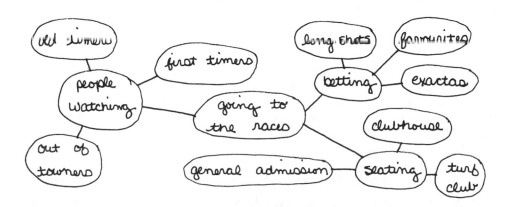

This cluster shows that the student has found three general aspects of attending the horse races: the variety of seating, types of bets, and groups of people to watch. This cluster might lead to another where the student chooses one aspect—groups of people to watch, for instance—and thinks of more details about it.

Step 2: Identifying the Thesis

No matter what you are writing, the most important thing to keep in mind is the idea you want to get across to your reader about the topic. You must have in mind a single idea that you want to express. In a paragraph, the sentence containing that idea is called a *topic sentence*; in an essay, it's called a *thesis statement*.

Once you have explored a topic through a pre-writing technique, you will likely have isolated the key message you want to make about the topic. "Despite its expense, golf is an attractive pastime for individuals of every age" and "The spectators at a racetrack are almost as entertaining to watch as the horses" are potential thesis statements for the pre-writing examples.

Whether you successfully craft a thesis statement at this point or later, what is important is that this one statement becomes the hub of the entire written work. All support paragraphs and their contents must relate directly to this sentence.

THESIS STATEMENT CHECKLIST

1. A thesis statement must be a sentence with a subject and a verb (not just a topic).

2. A thesis statement must be an idea that you can explain or defend (not just a statement of fact).

Exercise: Thesis Statements

Some of the following word groups represent thesis statements that you could further explain or defend. Others are only topics or facts that are too specific to develop into a multi-paragraph written essay. Write THESIS in front of each one that could be a thesis statement. In front of each that is too specific, write FACT.

1. We travelled to London last spring.

2. Some animals seem to be able to predict earthquakes.

3. Getting my first car took away my freedom.

4. Computer-generated movie characters can affect us in the same ways as real-life individuals.

5. Voice-recognition software is improving all the time.

6. Rivers of methane were recently found on Saturn's moon Titan.

7. Gasoline prices are rising again.

8. Travelling to other countries makes people more open-minded.

9. Vegetarians can suffer from health problems related to their diets.

10. Sharks have no bones in their body.

Step 3: Writing the Introductory Paragraph

An introductory paragraph poses special challenges. It will need to engage the reader's interest. It will identify your thesis statement—that is, the sentence that identifies the main idea you plan to develop in the multi-paragraph piece. Often, the introductory paragraph also prepares the reader for the important points you will make later.

To attract the reader's interest, open your paragraph with *an interesting example, a vivid image, a direct quotation, startling remarks or statistics, a problem,* or *a question.* Check out the following paragraph and identify which technique it uses to "grab" your interest.

> My brother, who has lived his whole life in Southern California, had seen the Milky Way only in photographs or via the Internet until he visited my farm in rural Saskatchewan. And he's not alone. <u>In most of North America, environmental issues have restricted many people's ability to view the full splendour of the night skies.</u> In highly developed areas, pollution, heat haze, and city lights all dim the natural beauty of the stars above.

For most Canadians, the idea that someone has never seen the Milky Way is surprising. As a result, a Canadian reader will likely be interested in reading the rest of this piece.

The third sentence (underlined) states the *thesis statement* (main idea). Then, the final sentence (broken underline) provides a glimpse at the major points to be developed in this paper. Such a sentence is called the *plan of development.* As in a paragraph, you will want to put supportive points in a logical order for your reader. If you are going to include a plan of development in your introductory paragraph, make sure that it lists the support points in the order in which your support paragraphs will appear.

INTRODUCTORY PARAGRAPH CHECKLIST

1. Engage the reader's interest.

2. Provide any necessary background information.

3. Express central idea in a thesis statement.

4. Identify main support points in plan of development (optional).

Step 4: Composing Support Paragraphs

Each support paragraph should follow the paragraph's guidelines of unity, support, and cohesion. Remember to include a topic sentence for each of these paragraphs and to organize the supportive details for the topic sentence in a logical fashion. But recall also that each support ("body") paragraph must relate specifically to the thesis statement you outlined in the introductory paragraph.

Because the introductory paragraph above includes a plan of development statement, your reader will likely expect three paragraphs dealing with the negative effects of environmental factors on nighttime skies: the first, with the effects of pollution, the second, with heat haze, and finally, with city lights. Note that the body paragraphs should appear in the order stated in the plan of development statement.

Transitional Sentences

Although each of these paragraphs should be sturdy enough to stand on its own and make sense, apply what you have already learned about transitional devices both within and between these paragraphs.

Longer pieces of writing will flow more smoothly if you include "linking" sentences that act as a bridge from one paragraph's main idea to the next paragraph's. These transitional sentences often rely on an "echo" technique, capturing the key phrases of the first paragraph and then adding a reference to the next main idea.

Take a look at the following two body paragraphs. Pay particular attention to the italicized sentences, which create bridges from one supportive paragraph to the next.

(Support paragraph 1: pollution)

(Support paragraph 2: heat haze)

Not only does industrial pollution dim the brightness of the night sky, but the heat haze in large metropolitan areas makes matters even worse. One problem is the result of overly dense populations. When individuals live in warrens, one atop the other, it's no surprise that when rush hour hits, the skies are alight with a shimmering glow as traffic backs up and exhaust pipes belch. As well, towering office buildings give off tons of emissions from the thousands of bodies, computers, and hydroelectrical power generators they hold. Those same buildings capture the daytime heat and offer no access to wind currents to remove its intensity.

(Support paragraph 3: city lights)

Besides the increasing pollution and heat haze experienced in larger metropolitan areas, glowing city lights overwhelm the natural light from the stars. Cities can be seen from many kilometres away because they cast an eerie glow in the night sky. In residential areas, street after street is ablaze with halogen and fluorescent bulbs, creating a darkly curtained night sky over residents' homes. Business districts maintain security by the heavy use of neon and other lighting. Highways are lit as bright as daylight. It's impossible for stars to compete with such powerful light sources.

> ### SUPPORT PARAGRAPH CHECKLIST
>
> **1.** Focus on one major support point, expressed in *topic sentence*.
>
> **2.** Provide plenty of supportive details for that point.
>
> **3.** Include logically organized specific details.
>
> **4.** Use linking transitional sentence to connect to next paragraph.

Step 5: Crafting a Final Paragraph

The final paragraph presents you with your last opportunity to impress your point upon your reader.

Final paragraphs usually take one of two approaches.

Summary Approach

A summary style uses the closing paragraph to remind the reader of the main idea and the supportive points outlined in the paper.

The following final paragraph for the "Night Skies" paper uses the summary style as a concluding paragraph:

> North Americans living in large cities have grown accustomed to the fact that their night skies appear empty of stars. The reasons for the darkened skies, from pollution to heat haze to city lights, can be directly traced to environmental issues. As a result, the constellations that our grandparents could easily pick out in the sky are no longer visible to many North Americans except as pictures in books or illustrations on Internet sites.

Notice that the thesis statement and the three major support ideas are repeated.

Conclusion Approach

A conclusion style uses the closing paragraph to encourage the reader to think about and apply the information in ways not discussed in the paper. Conclusion techniques include the following:

- Ask a question.
- Offer advice or suggest future action based on the paper's information.
- Look to the future with a generalized statement.
- Recommend solutions to a problem outlined.

Here's a conclusion-style final paragraph for the "Night Skies" paper:

> Because the cause of dimmed night skies can be directly traced to human activity, North Americans must resolve to find alternatives to the ways the environment is treated. If they don't, they risk losing not just the quality of nighttime skies but also of other national wonders once taken for granted.

This paragraph features the "look to the future" approach; notice that new ideas are introduced.

FINAL PARAGRAPH CHECKLIST

Select most appropriate closing style:

1. Summary style

    a. Repeat *thesis statement* and refer to main supports

2. Conclusion style

    a. Ask a question

    b. Offer advice, propose future action

    c. Look to future with generalized statement

    d. Recommend solutions to identified problem

Step 6: Revising and Editing

Building an effective multi-paragraph piece of writing is more than composing several separate paragraphs and then joining them together. Once you have written the paragraphs, you will want to view them from the perspective of the audience (your reader) and your purpose for writing.

It's at this stage where you need to ensure that your introductory paragraph contains a clearly stated main idea (expressed in a thesis statement), that the middle paragraphs offer plenty of specific details to develop this idea, and that the major and minor support sentences are organized logically and convincingly.

For example, because writing is a living, breathing exercise, you may discover that the support paragraphs would be more effective in a different order. Or you might notice at this point that one paragraph is too general and needs further details to back up its topic sentence. In any event, don't be so tied to your original work plan that you lose the flexibility necessary to make positive changes in wording, organization, and transitions.

Read the entire piece from start to finish from the perspective of your intended audience. Isolate any areas where better use of transitions will ensure a smoother read. Remember to check for unity (staying on topic), support (providing details or examples that develop or explain the main idea), and cohesion (organizing ideas in a logical pattern and using transitions to guide the reader from one point to another). Make changes in word choice when the vocabulary is too technical or otherwise inappropriate for your reader or purpose.

In short, at this stage, you want to question how effectively your piece is communicating your ideas to the individuals who will be reading them.

The writer of the piece on night skies may decide, as a result of preparing the paper, that the support paragraphs would be more effective if they appeared in a different order. Making such a decision will have an effect on the entire paper. The introduction's plan of development statement will need to reflect the new order. New "linking" sentences will have to be written to bridge the support paragraphs. Even in the concluding paragraph, the new organization needs to be taken into account.

While this may sound like considerable work, it really isn't. The revision and editing stage offers important opportunities to make the multi-paragraph piece stronger and more readable.

The following textbox contains a complete checklist to use when you are revising a multi-paragraph piece of writing. Follow it carefully, answering all the questions from the perspective of your potential reader.

REVISING CHECKLIST

INTRODUCTORY PARAGRAPH

Does it include …

1. an effective attention-getting device?

2. a clearly stated main idea (thesis statement)?

3. any necessary background information?

4. a plan of development statement with support points in correct order?

EACH SUPPORT PARAGRAPH

Does each have …

1. the major support point's main idea (topic sentence)?

2. all support details directly related to the paragraph's topic (unity)?

3. an adequate number of details and examples (support)?

4. a logical organization of supportive details (coherence)?

5. ample and appropriate transitional words and sentences?

CONCLUDING PARAGRAPH

1. Does it use the most appropriate style (summary or conclusion)?

2. If Summary style, does it contain an echo of the main idea and its major supports?

3. If Conclusion style, has the most effective closing technique been chosen?

> **OVERALL**
>
> **1.** Are word choice and vocabulary appropriate for audience and purpose?
>
> **2.** Do the body paragraphs (major support points) appear in the most logical order?
>
> **3.** Do the paragraphs flow together with the help of linking transitional sentences?

Step 7: Proofreading

The final step in any written work, regardless of its length, is a thorough sweep through the writing to ensure that it contains a minimum of grammatical and spelling errors and that it is correctly formatted. If you have completed the exercises in the first five parts of this book, you will be better able to recognize glaring problems in sentence structure, subject–verb agreement, and pronoun usage, for example. Apply the highest standards to your own writing. If it is allowed, you may also want to have another individual cast a careful eye over your work. The bottom line is that you have invested far too much time and energy in writing your paper to allow your ideas to be marred by easily avoidable errors.

This is also the moment when you need to ensure that the paper's format is correct. Do you need a title page? If not, where is your name to appear? Is the paper to be double-spaced? If you have done research to write the paper, what type of documentation style are you expected to use? Have you successfully addressed the assignment's other requirements in terms of number of pages or words?

A reminder about computer spell check and grammar check programs:

Never rely *only* on feedback from your computer's spell check (red underline) or grammar check (green underline) to catch and offer corrections for spelling and grammar errors.

Spell check programs check each word against a very limited dictionary, and any word in that dictionary is seen as correct. That means, for example, that the computer is often unable to recognize the difference between "past" and "passed" or "it's" and "its." Spell check will also not catch repeated words. Your human eyes are far more reliable proofreaders than the mechanical ones offered by your computer. The spell check program may work well as your first line of defence; that is, for your first sweep through for spelling problems. However, you will still need to hunt down spelling errors manually after that.

Grammar check programs can be very confusing and often offer incorrect solutions to nonexistent grammar "problems." Again, remember that computers can't do the thinking that you can. Instead of relying on a grammar check, apply what you have learned in the first five parts of this book.

Use the following Proofreading Checklist as a comprehensive guide to proof-reading your work and eliminating the most obvious errors.

Immediately following the checklist, you will find "Empty Night Skies," the completely revised and proofread final draft of the paper built over the course of this section. The underlined words and sentences were changed during the revision process when the writer decided to change the order of the supportive points. Italics are used to highlight the paper's *theis statement*, each supporting paragraph's *topic sentence*, and the *summary sentence* in the final paragraph. Other vocabulary and sentence structure changes were made to strengthen the work's flow and readability.

PROOFREADING CHECKLIST

SPELLING

Conduct the following:

1. Preliminary spell check sweep

2. Careful review of entire paper (Part 1: pp. 3–51)
   Words often confused
   Repeated words
   Possessives
   Contractions
   Other spelling problems

GRAMMAR

Check for any errors in the following categories:

1. Sentence structure (Part 3: pp. 114–125)
   Fragments (pp. 114–115, 117–118)
   Run-on sentences (pp. 123–125)

2. Subject–verb agreement (Part 4: pp. 146–148)

3. Correct pronouns (Part 4: pp. 154–155)

4. Pronoun agreement (Part 4: pp. 159–160)

5. Pronoun references (Part 4: pp. 164–165)

6. Misplaced or dangling modifiers (Part 4: pp.173–174, 178–179)

7. Shifts in time or person (Part 4: pp. 186–187, 190–191)

---

8. Parallel structure (Part 4: pp. 196–197)

9. Clichés, awkward phrasing, wordiness (Part 4: pp. 201–204)

10. Punctuation (Part 5: pp. 218–219, 225–227, 232–239, 240–242, 246–248)
  Concluding punctuation (p. 218)
  Commas (pp. 225–227, 232–234, 239)
  Semicolons (pp. 218–219)
  Quotation marks (pp. 240–241)
  Underlining or italics (pp. 241–242)
  Capital letters (pp. 246–248)

FORMAT

1. Create a title for the paper

2. Address any assignment requirements
  Title page
  Correct placement of your name
  Minimum page and word count
  Line spacing
  Documentation style (if you've conducted research)

SAMPLE MULTI-PARAGRAGH PIECE

J. A. Student

Empty Night Skies

My brother, who has lived his whole life in Southern California, had seen the Milky Way only in photographs or via the Internet until he visited my farm in rural Saskatchewan. And he's not alone. In most of North America, environmental issues have restricted many people's ability to view the full splendour of the night skies. Especially in highly developed areas, heat haze, industrial pollution, and city lights dim the natural beauty of the stars above.

City dwellers have grown accustomed to the problems associated with heat haze. This issue is primarily the result of overly dense populations. Throughout North America's largest metropolitan areas, individuals live in warrens, one atop the other, creating heat columns. Despite town planners' attempts to provide adequate public transportation, when rush hour hits, the skies are alight with a shimmering glow as commuter traffic backs up and exhaust pipes belch. As well, towering office buildings give off tons of heat energy emissions from the thousands of bodies, computers, and hydroelectrical power generators they hold. Those same buildings, standing shoulder to shoulder, capture the daytime heat and offer no access to wind currents to remove its intensity.

Those who live in the more isolated areas less susceptible to heat haze must contend with a different challenge, industrial pollution. Taller smoke stacks simply ensure that the emissions make it into the jet stream where they can then travel for hundreds of kilometres before drifting back to earth. As a result, areas within the range of this airflow find their skies clouded by the discarded byproducts of chemical companies, coal-burning plants, and mineral refineries. Since many industries include midnight shifts, such emissions are continuous.

Besides the heat haze experienced in larger metropolitan areas and the industrial pollution affecting others, glowing city lights overwhelm the natural light from the stars. Cities of even moderate size can be seen from many kilometres away because they cast an eerie glow in the night sky. In residential areas, street after street is ablaze with halogen and fluorescent bulbs, separating the night sky from those who walk the streets below. Business districts maintain security through the heavy use of neon and other lighting. Highways are lit as bright as daylight. Stars cannot compete with such powerful light sources.

North Americans living in large cities have grown accustomed to the fact that their night skies appear empty of stars. *The reasons for the darkened skies, from heat haze to pollution to city lights, can be directly traced to environmental issues.* The sad result is that the constellations that people could easily pick out in the sky forty or fifty years ago are no longer visible to many North Americans except as pictures in books or illustrations on Internet sites.

Answers

PART 1 SPELLING

SPELLING PRE-TEST

1. laid
2. fiancée
3. too (proud)
4. allowed
5. whose
6. submitted
7. relied
8. dinghies
9. then
10. respectively

11. believe
12. vacuum
13. conscious
14. hanged
15. effect
16. led
17. You're
18. choose
19. a lot
20. ladies'

WORDS OFTEN CONFUSED, SET 1 (PP. 9–14)

EXERCISE 1

1. Here, a
2. advises
3. It's
4. conscious
5. do

6. already, know, it's, accept, desserts
7. Choose, have
8. affect, clothes
9. feel, fill, courses
10. complementing, an, effect

Exercise 2

1. It's

2. do

3. A, effect

4. a, affect

5. already, knew, effect

6. due

7. a, it's

8. Its

9. effect

10. advise, choose

Exercise 3

1. its, chose, an

2. an

3. Its, it's

4. conscious, a

5. effect, due

6. accept, clothes

7. fill

8. new, complement

9. course, cloths, coarse, it's

10. course, fill, our, clothes, cloths

Exercise 4

1. advise

2. a, complement, already

3. chose, advice

4. an, effect

5. have, chose

6. clothes, accept

7. do

8. conscious, hear

9. compliment, already

10. except

Exercise 5

1. our, an, are

2. It's, feel

3. clothes, know

4. due, do

5. conscious, an, effect, our

6. break, conscience

7. course, an, dessert, feel

8. advice, forth, conscious

9. it's

10. know, no, already, chose

Proofreading Exercise

I've always wanted to ~~no~~ *know* what makes a person want to set or ~~brake~~ *break* a Guinness world record. For example, if someone ~~all ready~~ *already* has a record for collecting more than 2,500 rubber ducks, does another person really need to beat that record? Also, the objects that people ~~chose~~ *choose* to collect ~~our~~ *are* often strange. There are records for collecting the highest number of erasers from all over the world, tags from designer ~~cloths~~ *clothes*, and labels from water bottles, to name just a few. Of ~~coarse~~ *course*, it's nice to receive ~~complements~~ *compliments* and recognition for ~~a~~ *an* impressive collection. Maybe I should ~~of~~ *have* kept all those takeout menus I just threw away and tried to set a new record myself.

WORDS OFTEN CONFUSED, SET 2 (PP. 19–24)

EXERCISE 1
1. through
2. women, than
3. whose, who's
4. past, their
5. whether, they're, their

6. woman, wear
7. quite, they're
8. principle, you're, then
9. personal, whether
10. There, lose, than, there

EXERCISE 2
1. your
2. You're, right, they're, quite
3. through, to, right
4. Their, wear, loose, there
5. to, quite, to, peace

6. than, their
7. who's, they're
8. piece
9. two
10. their, there

EXERCISE 3
1. through
2. You're
3. whose, too, to
4. past, there
5. peace, quiet, their

6. through, they're
7. there, lose, their, right, personal
8. where
9. Then, to, than
10. Whether, you're, quite

EXERCISE 4

1. where, your
2. two, piece
3. to
4. where
5. loose, than

6. two
7. quite, wear, your, piece
8. you're
9. their, peace, quiet
10. personal, you're

EXERCISE 5

1. through, their, principal
2. personnel, than, whose
3. peace, led, quiet
4. past, where
5. Then, loose

6. were, there, two
7. principal, there
8. you're, past
9. piece, quite
10. too, your

PROOFREADING EXERCISE

When I was in high school, the ~~principle~~ *principal* was always complaining about our homework record. The teachers had told him that about half the students didn't do ~~there~~ *their* homework on time, and some never did any at all. So one September he started the first-day assembly by saying, "This year ~~your~~ *you're* all going to do ~~you're~~ *your* homework every night for at least the first month of school. And if there is a school-wide perfect homework record during September, I will ~~where~~ *wear* a swimsuit to school on the first of October and dive off the high diving board into the school's outdoor pool in front of everyone no matter what the ~~whether~~ *weather* is like that day." We students were not about to ~~loose~~ *lose* a bet like that. September ~~past~~ *passed*, and on the first of October, the principal ~~lead~~ *led* us to the school pool; then he ~~through~~ *threw* off his heavy coat and climbed to the top of the diving board.

CONTRACTIONS (PP. 26–31)

EXERCISE 1

1. they're
2. they've
3. they're
4. I've
5. it's, that's

6. we're, I'm
7. he's
8. he's, it's
9. isn't, they're
10. there's

EXERCISE 2

1. don't, they've

2. You'll

3. can't, they've

4. They're, that's

5. can't, they're

6. it's, who's

7. there's, it's (even), that's

8. You'll

9. can't, they're

10. I'm, aren't

EXERCISE 3

1. I've, hasn't

2. they'd

3. it's (obvious), wouldn't

4. it's, they're

5. that's, there's

6. wouldn't

7. wasn't, it's

8. don't, wouldn't, that's

9. wouldn't

10. should've, wouldn't, that's

EXERCISE 4

1. should've

2. didn't, I'd

3. didn't, could've, didn't

4. wasn't, don't

5. It's, I've

6. I'm, it'd

7. wouldn't, they'd

8. who's, he'd

9. might've

10. there's

EXERCISE 5

1. isn't, he's

2. who's, there's

3. wasn't

4. He's

5. they'd

6. didn't, he'd

7. it's

8. He's

9. he'd

10. weren't

PROOFREADING EXERCISE

~~Iv'e~~ *I've* had trouble ~~excepting~~ *accepting* the fact that I ~~cant~~ *can't* learn to speak German. I have taken first- and second-year German, but ~~their~~ *there* ~~was'nt~~ *wasn't* much speaking in either of those ~~too~~ *two* classes. My mouth doesn't make the ~~write~~ *right* sounds when I try to say German words. I think that my teeth get in the way. I have decided to ask my teacher for ~~advise~~ *advice* but ~~cant~~ *can't* bring myself to go see her because I know that ~~shes~~ *she's* going to ask me to tell her about my problem—in German.

POSSESSIVES (PP. 34–36)

EXERCISE 4

1. Jagger's
2. couple's
3. Hall's
4. no possessives
5. Hall's

6. London's
7. characters'
8. theatres', actress's
9. role's, Hall's
10. judges', character's

EXERCISE 5

1. bat's, animal's
2. patient's
3. person's
4. condition's
5. bat's, victim's or victims'

6. no possessives
7. patients', bat's
8. enzyme's
9. DSPA's
10. bat's

PROOFREADING EXERCISE

The Labelles are a family that has lived next door to me for twenty years. I have grown up with the ~~Labelle's~~ *Labelles'* daughter, Nicole. My family is bigger than ~~her's~~ *hers*. When I go to her house, ~~Nicoles~~ *Nicole's* favourite pastime is doing jigsaw puzzles. We always start off by separating a ~~puzzles~~ *puzzle's* pieces into different categories. She makes piles of edge pieces, sky pieces, flower pieces, and so on. Then I start putting the edge ~~piece's~~ *pieces* together to form the border. The Labelles' son is named Marc, and he usually shows up just in time to put the last piece in the puzzle.

REVIEW OF CONTRACTIONS AND POSSESSIVES (PP. 37–38)

1. I've, *Seinfeld's*
2. show's, wasn't
3. I'm, television's, series'
4. wasn't, wouldn't, show's
5. no contractions or possessives needing apostrophes
6. no contractions or possessives needing apostrophes
7. show's, they'd
8. characters', witnesses'

9. jury's, they're

10. there's, it's

A Journal of My Own

~~Ive~~ *I've* been keeping a journal ever since I was in high school. I ~~dont~~ *don't* write it for my ~~teacher's~~ *teachers'* sake. I ~~wouldnt~~ *wouldn't* turn it in even if they asked me to. ~~Its~~ *It's* mine, and it helps me remember all of the changes ~~Ive~~ *I've* gone through so far in my life. The way I see it, a ~~diarys~~ *diary's* purpose ~~isnt~~ *isn't* just to record the facts; ~~its~~ *it's* to capture my true feelings.

When I record the ~~days~~ *day's* events in my journal, they ~~arent~~ *aren't* written in minute-by-minute details. Instead, if ~~Ive~~ *I've* been staying at a ~~friends~~ *friend's* house for the weekend, ~~Ill~~ *I'll* write something like this: "~~Sharons~~ *Sharon's* the only friend I have who listens to my whole sentence before starting hers. ~~Shes~~ *She's* never in a hurry to end a good conversation. Today we talked for an hour or so about the pets ~~wed~~ *we'd* had when we were kids. We agreed that ~~were~~ *we're* both 'dog people.' We ~~cant~~ *can't* imagine our lives without dogs. Her favourites are Pomeranians, and mine are golden retrievers." ~~Thats~~ *That's* the kind of an entry ~~Id~~ *I'd* make in my journal. It ~~doesnt~~ *doesn't* mean much to anyone but me, and ~~thats~~ *that's* the way it should be.

I know that another ~~persons~~ *person's* diary would be different from mine and that most people ~~dont~~ *don't* even keep one. ~~Im~~ *I'm* glad that writing comes easily to me. I ~~dont~~ *don't* think ~~Ill~~ *I'll* ever stop writing in my journal because it helps me believe in myself and value ~~other's~~ *others'* beliefs as well.

RULE FOR DOUBLING A FINAL LETTER (PP. 40–41)

EXERCISE 1

1. scanning	**6.** missing
2. trusting	**7.** reading
3. tripping	**8.** occurring
4. planning	**9.** skimming
5. benefiting	**10.** screaming

EXERCISE 2

1. shopping	**6.** omitting
2. rapping	**7.** honouring
3. wrapping	**8.** bragging
4. nailing	**9.** marking
5. knitting	**10.** hopping

EXERCISE 3

1. steaming
2. expelling
3. sipping
4. suffering
5. warring

6. setting
7. stressing
8. flopping
9. spinning
10. differing

EXERCISE 4

1. creeping
2. subtracting
3. abandoning
4. drooping
5. dropping

6. weeding
7. fogging
8. occurring
9. referring
10. submitting

EXERCISE 5

1. interpreting
2. preferring
3. betting
4. stooping
5. stopping

6. inferring
7. guessing
8. bugging
9. jogging
10. building

SPELLING PROGRESS TEST

1. A. complimented
2. B. where
3. A. could have
4. A. tutored
5. A. conscience

6. A. children's
7. B. already
8. B. effects
9. A. principle
10. A. You're

SPELLING POST-TEST

1. passed
2. counsellor (or counsellors)
3. flipped
4. quiet
5. threw
6. too (dangerous)
7. roommate
8. doesn't
9. ours
10. personnel

11. stationery
12. occurrence
13. witnesses'
14. brakes
15. it's
16. responsibilities
17. believe
18. lead
19. all right
20. know

PART 2 KNOWING SENTENCE ESSENTIALS

SENTENCE ESSENTIALS PRE-TEST

1. arrival, encourages
2. some, are planning
3. model, sells out
4. hiking, canoeing, remind
5. families, take, visit

6. days, bring
7. gardeners, start
8. others, turn
9. Does, game, need
10. one, prefers

IDENTIFYING SENTENCE PARTS (PP. 55–58)

EXERCISE 1

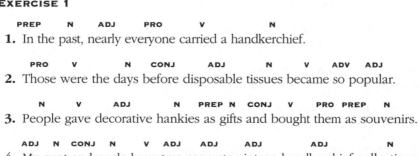

```
   PREP   N    ADJ      PRO      V          N
1. In the past, nearly everyone carried a handkerchief.
```

```
      PRO    V       N   CONJ      ADJ        N     V    ADV  ADJ
2. Those were the days before disposable tissues became so popular.
```

```
    N     V      ADJ        N   PREP N  CONJ   V    PRO PREP   N
3. People gave decorative hankies as gifts and bought them as souvenirs.
```

```
   ADJ   N  CONJ   N     V   ADJ   ADJ      ADJ          N
4. My aunt and uncle have two separate vintage handkerchief collections.
```

ADJ   N   V PRO PREP ADJ CONJ ADJ   N CONJ N PREP

5. Her collection includes ones with provincial and territorial flags or maps of

ADJ   N PREP PRO

famous cities on them.

PRO   V ADJ   N   ADJ   N CONJ ADJ   N PREP   N

6. Others have flower designs, geometric patterns, and clever sayings as decorations.

ADJ   ADJ   N   V   ADV ADJ CONJ ADJ PREP ADJ   N CONJ

7. Men's vintage handkerchiefs are usually white or grey with coloured lines or

N

monograms.

ADJ N ADV V   ADJ   N   PREP ADJ   N

8. My uncle still owns a few hankies from his childhood.

PRO   V   N   CONJ N PREP ADJ   N   CONJ ADJ N

9. They depict characters and animals from nursery rhymes and fairy tales.

ADJ ADJ   N   V ADV ADJ PREP ADJ N CONJ PREP PRO

10. These two collections are very valuable to my family and to me.

EXERCISE 2

PRO ADV V   N

1. I really love cookies.

PRO V ADJ ADJ   N

2. They are my favourite snack.

PRO V   PRO PREP ADJ   N CONJ N

3. I prefer the ones with chocolate chips or nuts.

N   V ADJ CONJ PRO V ADJ

4. Cookies taste best when they are fresh.

ADV   PRO V   N   CONJ N PREP   N

5. Sometimes, I have cookies and milk for breakfast.

ADV ADJ   ADJ   N   V   ADJ   N

6. Now some fast-food restaurants offer fresh-baked cookies.

ADJ   N V   ADJ   CONJ PRO V ADV ADJ

7. Oatmeal cookies are delicious when they are still warm.

N   V   ADJ N PREP ADJ   N

8. Companies release new versions of traditional cookies.

ADJ   N PREP N ADV V   ADJ   N

9. One variety of Oreos now has chocolate centres.

INTERJ V PRO ADJ

10. Wow, are they yummy!

EXERCISE 3

      ADJ ADJ   N   V   ADJ   PREP   ADJ   N PREP N

1. Tall office buildings are dangerous for migrating birds at night.

          ADJ   ADJ   N   V   N

2. The buildings' lighted windows confuse the birds.

       PRO V   PREP   ADJ   N   CONJ V ADJ   N

3. They fly toward the glowing windows and lose their way.

    ADJ   N   V   ADJ   N

4. Bird experts studied this phenomenon.

         N   V ADJ   N   PREP   N

5. McCormick Place is a tall building in Chicago.

        N   V   N   PREP ADJ   N   ADV PREP ADJ N

6. Scientists counted the number of bird deaths there for two years.

      N   PREP N   V PREP   ADJ   N

7. Hundreds of birds flew into the lighted windows.

   ADJ   N   PREP ADJ   N   V   ADJ   N

8. Only one-fifth of that number hit the dark windows.

      N   V   ADJ   N PREP ADJ   N   PREP   N   PREP N

9. Scientists suggest a lights-out policy for tall buildings from midnight to dawn

     PREP   ADJ   N

    during migration periods.

      N   V   PREP   N PREP N CONJ PREP   N   PREP   N

10. Birds migrate from March to May and from August to November.

EXERCISE 4

         N   ADV   V   ADJ   N PREP   N

1. Jan Demczur recently donated several objects to the Smithsonian Institution.

       N   V   ADJ   N   PREP   N

2. Demczur was a window washer at One World Trade Center.

    PRO V PREP   N   PREP   N   CONJ   N   V   N

3. He was in an elevator of the building when terrorists attacked the tower.

    PREP   N PREP ADJ ADJ   N   N   V   ADJ   ADJ   N

4. With the help of his squeegee handle, Demczur saved several people's lives.

      N   CONJ   PRO PREP   N   V   N   PREP N

5. Demczur and the others in the elevator used the handle as an axe.

PRO   V   N   PREP   ADJ   N   PREP   N

6. They cut an opening from the elevator shaft into the building.

N   CONJ ADJ ADJ   N   V ADV CONJ   N V

7. Demczur and his five elevator-mates escaped just before the tower fell.

ADJ   ADJ   N   V   N   N

8. Such survival stories give people hope.

N   V   ADJ   N PREP ADJ   N

9. The Smithsonian is the U.S.'s place for rare artifacts.

ADJ   ADJ   N CONJ ADJ ADJ   N V ADV PREP N   PREP

10. Demczur's squeegee handle and his dusty clothes are now on display at

N

the Smithsonian.

EXERCISE 5

N   V   N CONJ   N

1. Plants need water and sunlight.

ADV   N   V   ADV

2. Sometimes houseplants wither unexpectedly.

N   ADV V PRO ADV ADJ   N CONJ ADV ADJ   N

3. People often give them too much water or not enough water.

PRO V   N   PREP   ADJ   N   ADV

4. I saw an experiment on a television show once.

PRO   V   ADJ   N

5. It involved two plants.

ADJ   N   V   ADJ   N PREP   N CONJ   N

6. The same woman raised both plants with water and sunlight.

N   V PREP ADJ   ADJ   N

7. The plants grew in two different rooms.

PRO   V PREP ADJ N CONJ V   ADJ   N   PREP PRO

8. She yelled at one plant but said sweet things to the other.

ADV   ADJ   N   V   ADV   CONJ   ADJ PRO V

9. The verbally praised plant grew beautifully, but the other one died.

N   V   N   ADV

10. Plants have feelings too.

PROOFREADING EXERCISE

 ADJ   N   V   ADV   ADJ N   ADV   PRO   V   ADV CONJ PRO   V
Your eyelids blink regularly all day long. They stop only when you sleep.

  N   V   ADJ   ADJ   N   PREP   N   CONJ   PRO   V   PREP
Blinking protects your delicate eyes from injury. When something flies toward

PRO   ADV   ADJ   N   V   ADV   CONJ   V   ADJ   N
you, usually your lids shut quickly and protect your eyes.

     N   ADV   V   N   PREP ADJ   N PRO   V   ADJ   N   ADJ CONJ
Blinking also does a kind of washing job. It keeps your eyelids moist. If

   N   PREP N   V   PREP ADJ   N   ADJ   ADJ   N   V PRO ADV   ADJ   N
a speck of dirt gets past your lids, your moist eyeball traps it. Then your eyes

V   PREP   N   ADJ   N   V   CONJ   N   V   ADV PREP ADJ N
fill with water, your lids blink, and the speck washes out of your eye.

ADJECTIVES AND ADVERBS (PP. 62–65)

EXERCISE 1

1. adverb adding to the verb *attracts*

2. adjective adding to the noun *desk*

3. adjective adding to the noun *paperbacks*

4. adjective adding to the noun *topics*

5. adverb adding to the verb *discovered*

6. adverb adding to the adjective *simple*

7. adjective adding to the noun *subtitle*

8. adverb adding to the adjective *pink*

9. adverb adding to the verb *considered*

10. adverb adding to the verb *took*

EXERCISE 2

1. adjective adding to the noun *dollar*

2. adverb adding to the adjective *one*

3. adjective adding to the pronoun *I*

4. adverb adding to the verb *paints*

5. adjective adding to the noun *buildings*

6. adjective adding to the noun *shingles*

7. adjective adding to the noun *French*

8. adverb adding to the verb *speak*

9. adjective adding to the noun *child*

10. adjective adding to the pronoun *one*

EXERCISE 3

1. close

2. closely

3. close

4. badly

5. bad

6. bad

7. very happily

8. very happy

9. good

10. well

EXERCISE 4

1. largest

2. larger

3. large

4. ugly

5. ugly

6. ugliest

7. uglier

8. friendliest

9. friendly

10. friendlier

EXERCISE 5

           ADJ   ADJ
1. I took an optional but helpful class in the spring.

      ADJ   ADJ
2. A reference librarian taught us research skills.

        ADV ADJ   ADJ
3. We discovered very useful tools for Web research.

    ADV   ADV   ADJ
4. Then the librarian carefully explained the library's resources.

     ADV   ADJ ADJ   ADJ
5. She often presented our research assignments in the form of scavenger hunts.

       ADV   ADJ   ADJ
6. The topics were always interesting and fun.

               ADJ   **ADJ**   **ADV**

7. I see the benefits of these self-help classes now.

         ADV   **ADJ**   **ADJ**

8. I am more motivated in my studies as a result.

            ADV   **ADV** **ADJ**   **ADJ**

9. And I am definitely less afraid of the library's computer.

      ADJ   **ADJ**   **ADV**   **ADV**

10. Since that class, I write term papers easily and enjoy them completely.

PROOFREADING EXERCISE

   ADJ **ADJ**   **ADJ**   **ADJ**   **ADV** **ADJ**

My favourite movie of all time is *The Matrix*. This movie is ~~intenser~~ *more intense*

ADJ   **ADJ**   **ADJ**   **ADV** **ADJ**

than any other. The main character of Neo is smart and ~~more~~ *very* creative. He feels

    ADJ   **ADJ**

~~badly~~ *bad* in the beginning of the story. His job is dull, and he wants excitement.

      ADV   **ADJ**

~~Eventual~~ *Eventually*, he meets the team of real people from outside the Matrix. Neo

  ADJ   **ADV** **ADV**

joins their team and fights ~~real~~ *really* hard against the agents in the Matrix. *The Matrix*

        ADJ   **ADJ**   **ADJ**

is the first of a three-movie series. In my opinion, it is the best of the three.

FINDING SUBJECTS AND VERBS (PP. 68–70)

EXERCISE 1

1. Right after Thanksgiving, the <u>malls</u> <u>begin</u> to fill with Halloween shoppers.

2. There <u>are</u> many <u>reasons</u> for this.

3. Many <u>consumers</u> <u>spend</u> hundreds of dollars on this popular holiday.

4. Halloween <u>costumes</u> <u>are</u> the most popular items.

5. <u>Yards</u> and <u>homes</u> <u>fill</u> with exhibits of witches, ghosts, and black cats.

6. <u>Parents</u> and their <u>children</u> often <u>go</u> to Halloween house parties and then <u>cruise</u> their neighbourhoods for treats.

7. From the first knock on the door, <u>residents</u> <u>feel</u> the excitement.

8. There's [There is] nothing as alarming to most dogs as the sound of running feet pounding down the driveway.

9. In some neighbourhoods, the ages of trick-or-treaters range from newborns to teenagers.

10. Many seem to be in a contest to fill the most pillowcases with candies.

EXERCISE 2

1. Weather forecasts affect many people.

2. But they are not always correct.

3. Sometimes rain and wind arrive instead of sunny skies.

4. Travellers need accurate weather predictions.

5. There are many possible dangers in travelling.

6. A hurricane is never a welcome event on a vacation.

7. At times, the weather seems more enemy than friend.

8. Often the skies cooperate with people's travel plans.

9. At times like this, the sun shines as if by special request.

10. Then the weather is perfect and feels like a friend again.

EXERCISE 3

1. There is a long-standing tradition in aviation.

2. Passengers get peanuts and a drink as a mid-flight snack.

3. Any drink tastes better with peanuts.

4. And the tiny foil packages please people.

5. But peanuts are dangerous to passengers with peanut allergies.

6. Most people eat peanuts and feel fine.

7. A mildly allergic person gets watery eyes and hives.

8. In extreme cases, people with peanut allergies die.

9. So, many airlines propose peanut-free zones on airplanes.

10. Needless to say, peanut companies are not happy about the proposal.

EXERCISE 4

1. Plastic snow <u>globes</u> <u>are</u> popular souvenir items.

2. <u>They</u> <u>are</u> clear globes usually on white oval bases.

3. People <u>display</u> these water-filled objects or <u>use</u> them as paperweights.

4. Inside <u>are</u> tiny <u>replicas</u> of famous tourist attractions like the Eiffel Tower or Big Ben.

5. <u>Snow</u> or <u>glitter</u> <u>mixes</u> with the water for a snowstorm effect.

6. These <u>souvenirs</u> often <u>hold</u> startling combinations.

7. In a snow globe, even the <u>Bahamas</u> <u>has</u> blizzards.

8. There <u>is</u> also a <u>globe</u> with smog instead of snow.

9. Some <u>people</u> <u>consider</u> snow globes valuable collectables.

10. <u>Others</u> just <u>buy</u> them as inexpensive mementos.

PROOFREADING EXERCISE

My friend <u>Maria</u> <u>spends</u> every weekday afternoon in the school library. <u>She</u> <u>does</u> her homework, <u>finishes</u> her reading assignments, and <u>organizes</u> her notes and handouts. <u>I</u> <u>envy</u> her good study skills. <u>She</u> <u>is</u> always ready for the next day of class. <u>I</u>, however, <u>go</u> back to my apartment in the afternoon. There <u>are</u> so many <u>distractions</u> at home. The <u>television</u> <u>blares</u>, and my <u>roommates</u> <u>invite</u> their friends over. <u>I</u> <u>am</u> usually too tired to do schoolwork. Maybe the <u>library</u> <u>is</u> a better place for me too.

LOCATING PREPOSITIONAL PHRASES (PP. 72-77)

EXERCISE 1

1. <u>One</u> (of Canada's best-known virtues) <u>is</u> its health care system.

2. (Throughout the world), <u>governments</u> (of every type) <u>strive</u> to keep the costs (of health care) down (without sacrificing services).

3. <u>Nurses</u> (from Canada) <u>find</u> employment (at hospitals) (in almost any part) (of the world).

4. Their <u>training</u> (in Canadian postsecondary institutions) <u>places</u> them (at the top) (of the class).

5. <u>Physicians</u> (from Canada) often <u>move</u> (to the United States) to earn more money.

6. Several years ago, <u>one</u> (of Canada's former governors general, Roy Romanow), <u>chaired</u> a task force to study Canada's health care system.

7. <u>Members</u> (of the general public), health care <u>professionals</u>, and other interested <u>parties</u> <u>made</u> written submissions (before the Romanow Commission).

8. (In several Canadian communities), the <u>Commission</u> <u>listened</u> (to individual oral submissions) as well.

9. (Unlike reports) (from other commissions), the Romanow task force's final <u>document</u> <u>appeared</u> online (at a federal government website) and <u>drew</u> considerable attention.

10. Now, (after nearly ten years), <u>some</u> (of the Commission's recommendations), (including the concern) (about wait times), <u>are</u> the focus (of action) (at both the provincial and federal levels).

EXERCISE 2

1. <u>Most</u> (of us) <u>remember</u> playing (with Frisbees) (in our front yards) (in the early evenings) and (at parks or beaches) (on weekend afternoons).

2. <u>Fred Morrison</u> <u>invented</u> the original flat Frisbee (for the Wham-O toy company) (in the 1950s).

3. <u>Ed Headrick</u>, designer (of the professional Frisbee), <u>passed away</u> (at his home) (in California) (in August) (of 2002).

4. Working (at Wham-O) (in the 1960s), <u>Headrick</u> <u>improved</u> the performance (of the existing Frisbee) (with the addition) (of ridges) (in the surface) (of the disc).

5. Headrick's <u>improvements</u> <u>led</u> (to increased sales) (of his "professional model" Frisbee) and (to the popularity) (of Frisbee tournaments).

6. (After Headrick's redesign), <u>Wham-O</u> <u>sold</u> 100 million (of the flying discs).

7. <u>Headrick</u> also <u>invented</u> the game (of disc golf).

8. (Like regular golf) but (with discs), the <u>game</u> <u>requires</u> specially designed courses (like the first one) (at Oak Grove Park) (in California).

9. (Before his death), <u>Headrick</u> <u>asked</u> (for his ashes) to be formed (into memorial flying discs) (for select family and friends).

10. <u>Donations</u> (from sales) (of the remaining memorial discs) <u>went</u> (toward the establishment) (of a museum) (on the history) (of the Frisbee and disc golf).

EXERCISE 3

1. <u>*Romeo and Juliet*</u> <u>is</u> my favourite play (by William Shakespeare).

2. <u>It</u> <u>is</u> one (of the most famous love stories) (in the world).

3. Many <u>movies</u> <u>use</u> this story (as part) (of their plots).

4. One <u>thing</u> (about the story) <u>surprised</u> me.

5. Both <u>Romeo</u> and <u>Juliet</u> <u>have</u> other love interests (at some point) (in the play).

6. <u>Romeo</u> <u>has</u> his eyes (on another woman) (before Juliet).

7. And (after Tybalt's death), <u>Juliet</u> <u>promises</u> (against her will) to marry Paris.

8. But (before that), <u>Juliet</u> <u>marries</u> Romeo (in secret).

9. <u>Friar Lawrence</u> <u>helps</u> the newlyweds (with a plan) (for them) to escape (without anyone's notice).

10. However, the complicated <u>timing</u> (of the plan) <u>has</u> tragic results (in the lives) (of Romeo and Juliet).

EXERCISE 4

1. (For a change) (of pace), <u>I</u> <u>shopped</u> (for my Mother's Day gift) (at an antique show).

2. <u>I</u> <u>found</u> old jewellery (in every shade) (of yellow, red, blue, and green).

3. There <u>were</u> even <u>linens</u> (from all the way) (back to pre-Confederation).

4. One <u>booth</u> <u>sold</u> only drinking glasses (with advertising slogans and cartoon characters) (on them).

5. <u>Another</u> <u>stocked</u> old metal banks (with elaborate mechanisms) (for children's pennies).

6. (In the back corner) (of the show area), <u>I</u> <u>found</u> a light blue pitcher (with a dark blue design).

7. My <u>mother</u> <u>used</u> to have one (like it) (in the early days) (of my childhood).

8. My <u>sisters</u> and <u>I</u> <u>drank</u> punch (from it) (on hot days) (in the summer).

9. <u>I</u> <u>checked</u> the price (on the tag) (underneath the pitcher's handle).

10. But (at a moment) (like that), <u>money</u> was the least (of my concerns).

EXERCISE 5

1. (Over the weekend), <u>I</u> <u>watched</u> a hilarious old movie, *Genevieve*, (on late-night television).

2. The whole <u>story</u> <u>takes</u> place (in the countryside) (of England).

3. <u>It</u> <u>is</u> a black-and-white movie (from the 1930s or 1940s).

4. The <u>clothes</u> and <u>manners</u> (of the characters) (in *Genevieve*) <u>are</u> very proper and old-fashioned.

5. Two young <u>couples</u> <u>enter</u> their cars (in a road rally) (for fun).

6. <u>They</u> <u>participate</u> (in the race) strictly (for adventure).

7. <u>Genevieve</u> <u>is</u> the name (of the main couple's car).

8. (During the road rally), the two couples' polite <u>manners</u> <u>disappear</u> (in the rush) (for the finish line).

9. Predictably, <u>they</u> <u>begin</u> to fight (with each other) and <u>try</u> to sabotage each other's cars.

10. But (like all good comedies), *Genevieve* and its <u>ending</u> <u>hold</u> a surprise (for everyone).

PARAGRAPH EXERCISE

HEARSAY (ON Q-TIPS)

(In 1922), Leo Gerstenrang, an immigrant (from Warsaw, Poland), who had served (in the United States Army) (during World War I) and worked (with the fledgling Red Cross Organization), founded the Leo Gerstenrang Infant Novelty Co. (with his wife), selling accessories used (for baby care). (After the birth) (of the couple's daughter), Gerstenrang noticed that his wife would wrap a wad (of cotton) (around a toothpick) (for use) (during their baby's bath) and decided to manufacture a ready-to-use cotton swab. [Note: "To manufacture" and "to use" are verbals, not prepositional phrases.]

(After several years), Gerstenrang developed a machine that would wrap cotton uniformly (around each blunt end) (of a small stick) (of carefully selected and cured nonsplintering birch wood), package the swabs (in a sliding tray-type box), sterilize the box, and seal it (with an outer wrapping) (of glassine)—later changed (to cellophane). The phrase "untouched (by human hands)" became widely known (in the production) (of cotton swabs). The *Q* (in the name Q-Tips) stands (for *quality*), and the word *tips* describes the cotton swab (on the end) (of the stick).

IDENTIFYING VERB PHRASES (PP. 78–81)

EXERCISE 1

1. <u>Felix Hoffman</u>, a chemist trying to ease his own father's pain, <u>discovered</u> Aspirin (in 1897).

2. Each year, <u>people</u> (around the world) <u>give</u> themselves 50 billion doses (of the popular painkiller).

3. But <u>people</u> (in different countries) <u>take</u> this medication (in different ways).

4. The <u>British</u> <u>like</u> to dissolve aspirin powder (in water).

5. The <u>French</u> <u>have insisted</u> (on the benefits) (of slow-release methods).

6. <u>Italians</u> <u>prefer</u> aspirin drinks (with a little fizz).

7. And <u>North Americans</u> <u>have</u> always <u>chosen</u> to take their aspirin (in pill form).

8. <u>Aspirin</u> <u>continues</u> to surprise researchers (with benefits) (to human health).

9. <u>It</u> <u>has been found</u> to benefit people susceptible (to heart attack, colon cancer, and Alzheimer's disease).

10. Where <u>would</u> <u>we</u> <u>be</u> (without aspirin)?

EXERCISE 2

1. <u>I</u> <u>like</u> to walk (around the park) (with my two little poodles) (in the early evening).

2. The <u>three</u> (of us) <u>have enjoyed</u> this ritual (for several years) now.

3. (On Friday evening), a big <u>dog</u> (with no owner) <u>ran</u> over (to us) (near the duck pond).

4. <u>It</u> <u>was</u> obviously <u>looking</u> (for other dogs) to play with.

5. <u>Yip</u> and <u>Yap</u> <u>have</u> never <u>barked</u> so loudly before.

6. <u>I</u> <u>had</u> originally <u>named</u> them (for their distinct barking noises).

7. But lately <u>I</u> <u>had</u> not <u>heard</u> these short, ear-splitting sounds very often.

8. The big <u>dog</u> <u>was shocked</u> (by the fierceness) (of my little dogs' reply) and quickly <u>ran</u> to find other friends.

9. Even <u>I</u> <u>could</u> not <u>believe</u> it.

10. <u>I</u> <u>will</u> never <u>worry</u> (about their safety) (around big dogs) again.

EXERCISE 3

1. <u>Scientists</u> (of all kinds) <u>have been learning</u> a lot (about traffic safety lately).

2. (In their studies), <u>they</u> <u>have</u> recently <u>discovered</u> a puzzling truth.

3. Fewer traffic <u>signs</u> and traffic <u>lights</u> <u>affect</u> drivers (in a counter-intuitive way).

4. The <u>reason</u> (behind the "shared space" theory) <u>is</u> relatively easy to explain.

5. (Without signs and lights), <u>drivers</u> <u><u>will regulate</u></u> their speed and <u>pay</u> closer attention (to other vehicles).

6. Those traffic <u>lights</u> and <u>signals</u> apparently <u><u>give</u></u> drivers a false sense (of security).

7. (In locations) (without signs or signals) to provide guidance, <u>drivers</u> <u><u>must think</u></u>
more (about their own safety) and <u>drive</u> more cautiously.

8. Many <u>towns</u> (in Europe and North America) <u>have</u> already <u>taken</u> steps to test the
truth (of this theory) (through so-called "passive" road engineering).

9. (For example), (in some cases), all <u>lights</u>, <u>signs</u>, and <u>barriers</u> <u><u>have been</u></u>
<u><u>removed</u></u> (from the roadway).

10. (In such situations), all <u>drivers</u> and <u>pedestrians</u> <u><u>must negotiate</u></u> (with one
another) to proceed (through the town).

EXERCISE 4

1. <u>I</u> <u>have</u> just <u>discovered</u> "The Farnsworth Chronicles," an Internet site (about
Philo T. Farnsworth).

2. <u>You</u> <u><u>may</u></u> not <u>have heard</u> (of Farnsworth).

3. (In 1922), (at the age) (of 13), <u>he</u> <u>visualized</u> the concept (of transmitting television waves).

4. <u>Others</u> <u><u>were</u></u> already <u>working</u> (on the idea) (of sending images) (through the
air).

5. But young <u>Farnsworth</u> <u>solved</u> the problem (by looking) (at rows) (of ploughed
land).

6. (In his imaginative mind), <u>images</u> <u><u>could be broken</u></u> down (into rows).

7. Then each <u>row</u> <u><u>could be sent</u></u> (through the air) and (onto a screen).

8. Farnsworth's <u>idea</u> <u>made</u> television a reality.

9. Unfortunately, <u>he</u> <u><u>has</u></u> never <u><u>been recognized</u></u> (for this and several other
achievements).

10. (In 1957), <u>he</u> <u><u>was featured</u></u> (as a guest) (on *I've Got a Secret,* a television show)
(with mystery contestants).

EXERCISE 5

1. Most <u>people</u> <u><u>do</u></u> not <u>connect</u> bar codes and cockroaches (in their minds).

2. <u>We</u> <u><u>do expect</u></u> to see bar codes (on almost every product) (in shopping malls).

3. And <u>we</u> <u>might</u> not <u>be</u> surprised to see a cockroach (by a trash can) (outside one) (of those malls).

4. But <u>we</u> <u>would</u> definitely <u>look</u> twice (at a cockroach) (with a bar code) (on its back).

5. (In 1999), exterminator <u>Bruce Tennenbaum</u> <u>wanted</u> everyone to watch (for his roaches).

6. <u>He</u> <u>had attached</u> bar codes (to one hundred cockroaches) and <u>released</u> them (in Tucson, Arizona), (as a public-awareness campaign).

7. <u>People</u> capturing a bar-coded bug <u>could return</u> it (for a hundred-dollar prize).

8. <u>One</u> (of the roaches) <u>was</u> even <u>tagged</u> (with a unique bar code) and <u>was worth</u> fifty thousand dollars.

9. <u>Many</u> (of the tagged roaches) <u>were found</u>.

10. But the fifty-thousand-dollar <u>bug</u> <u>was</u> never <u>seen</u> again.

RECOGNIZING VERBAL PHRASES (PP. 83–87)

EXERCISE 1

1. Parents who <u>like</u> [to go clubbing] <u>can</u> now <u>take</u> their children along—well, sort of.

2. On weekend afternoons, nightclubs around the United States <u>childproof</u> their facilities [to allow children] [to dance the day away].

3. An organization [called Baby Loves Disco] <u>orchestrates</u> these events, [offering real drinks for the parents and juice boxes and healthy snacks for the kids].

4. The nightclubs <u>try</u> [to keep the club atmosphere realistic] for the families while [making sure] that the volume of the music <u>is</u> not too loud for the children's ears.

5. They <u>keep</u> the music real, too, [playing songs] by the best-[known] bands of the 1970s and '80s.

6. Kids up to eight years old <u>have</u> fun [dancing], [dressing in disco styles], [wearing fake tattoos], [jumping around], and [yelling with other kids and parents].

7. Baby Loves Disco <u>provides</u> special areas for parents [to change their children's diapers] or [to treat themselves to a massage].

8. Baby Loves Disco <u>has</u> its own website, [posting videos, news stories, and future events] [taking place in various cities].

9. [To attract parents who <u>don't</u> <u>like</u> disco music], the BLD home page <u>includes</u> links to a kids' version of hip hop—[called "Skip Hop"]—and jazz for kids.

10. Videos and testimonials on the site <u>show</u> that kids <u>love</u> [dancing at nightclubs] as much as adults do.

EXERCISE 2

1. I <u>have learned</u> how [to manage my leisure time].

2. I <u>like</u> [to go to the movies on Friday nights].

3. [Watching a good film] <u>takes</u> me away from the stress of my job.

4. I especially <u>enjoy</u> [eating buttery popcorn] and [drinking a cold pop].

5. It <u>is</u> the perfect way for me [to begin the weekend].

6. I <u>get</u> [to escape from deadlines and the pressure [to succeed]].

7. I <u>indulge</u> myself and <u>try</u> [to give myself a break].

8. All day Saturday I <u>enjoy</u> [lounging around the house in my weekend clothes].

9. I <u>do</u> a little [gardening] and <u>try</u> [to relax my mind].

10. By Sunday evening, after [resting for two days], I <u>am</u> ready [to start my busy week all over again].

EXERCISE 3

1. Many people <u>dislike</u> [speaking in front of strangers].

2. In fact, there <u>is</u> an almost universal fear of [giving speeches].

3. [Feeling insecure and [exposed]], people <u>get</u> dry mouths and sweaty hands.

4. Note cards <u>become</u> useless, [rearranging themselves in the worst possible order].

5. [To combat this problem], people <u>try</u> [to memorize a speech], only [to forget the whole thing].

6. Or the microphone <u>decides</u> [to quit at the punch line of their best joke].

7. [Embarrassed] and [humiliated], they <u>struggle</u> [to regain their composure].

8. Then the audience usually <u>begins</u> [to sympathize with and encourage the speaker].

9. Finally [used to the spotlight], the speaker <u>relaxes</u> and <u>finds</u> the courage [to finish].

10. No one <u>expects</u> [giving a speech] [to get any easier].

EXERCISE 4

1. Canadian astronaut Roberta Bondar <u>blasted</u> off into space [to gather data] on how [living] things <u>function</u> in space.

2. Bondar <u>was</u> aboard the space shuttle *Discovery* in January 1992, [setting a milestone as Canada's first woman in space].

3. After [graduating from high school], Bondar assertively <u>pursued</u> her career, [obtaining five university degrees in science and medicine].

4. She <u>applied</u> to the new Canadian Space Agency [to become a candidate for astronaut].

5. Bondar's wait [to go into space] <u>lasted</u> nine years.

6. [Leaving the launch pad on the *Discovery*], Bondar <u>thrust</u> her fists in the air, [shouting "Yes, yes, yes!"]

7. Bondar and her six colleagues <u>spent</u> eight days in space, [investigating the effects of weightlessness on the human body].

8. Today Bondar <u>does</u> research at the University of Western Ontario, [travelling around the country] [to encourage young people in the sciences].

9. Bondar <u>was appointed</u> chair of the Science Advisory Board, a board set up [to advise the federal health minister].

10. She <u>believes</u> that [protecting the environment] <u>is</u> one of the most important responsibilities we <u>have</u> today.

EXERCISE 5

1. E-mail <u>has begun</u> [to be the most popular form of [written] communication].

2. In the [beginning], people <u>searched</u> for a way [to show emotion].

3. It <u>was</u> time [to invent a new type of punctuation], now [known as "emoticons."]

4. Scott Fahlman <u>proposed</u> two of the first emoticons in the early 1980s [to show when something <u>was meant</u> [to be funny or not]].

5. [Called the "smiley" and the "frown,"] these combinations of colon, hyphen, and parentheses <u>look</u> like :-) and :-(

6. In an effort [to document computer history], Mike Jones, Jeff Baird, and others <u>worked</u> hard [to retrace the steps of the first uses of the smiley and the frown].

7. They <u>found</u> them [used by Scott Fahlman] in a [posting] to a computer bulletin board in 1982.

8. These and other emoticons <u>have continued</u> [to help people express themselves online].

9. So when you <u>finish</u> [typing your next joke in an e-mail], <u>don't forget</u> [to add a :-)]

10. [Frowning :-(] <u>is seen</u> by some as questionable net etiquette and <u>is</u> consequently not as common.

PROOFREADING EXERCISE

In the opinion of most westerners, "barkeeps <u>were</u> ... the hardest [worked] folks in camp.... " One of these burdens <u>was</u> [to act as a human fire alarm]. Western saloons never <u>closed</u>. Therefore, [to sound the alarm], the saloon owner <u>would dash</u> into the street, [running up and down] [hollering] and [emptying his six-shooter at the moon]. The commotion <u>would send</u> the volunteer firemen [pouring into the street in their long johns] [to put out the fire]. [Having done so], all and sundry naturally <u>assembled</u> in the saloon [to mull over the event] while [imbibing a tumbler of [gut-warming] red-eye].

SENTENCE WRITING

Your sentences may vary, but make sure that your verbals are not actually the main verbs of your clauses. You should be able to double underline your real verbs, as was done here.

1. I <u>enjoy</u> [speaking French].

2. [Typing on a small keyboard] <u>hurts</u> my wrists.

3. [Driving to Regina from here] <u>takes</u> about three hours.

4. I <u>spent</u> the day [reading the final chapters of my book].

5. I <u>love</u> [to eat breakfast outside in the summer].

6. We <u>were invited</u> [to go out to dinner].

7. I <u>would like</u> [to chat with you], but I am late for a meeting.

8. [To cook like a real gourmet] <u>takes</u> practice.

9. [Impressed by my grades], my parents <u>bought</u> me a new car.

10. [Taken in small doses], Aspirin <u>helps</u> prevent heart attacks.

USING STANDARD ENGLISH VERBS (PP. 89–93)

EXERCISE 1
1. walk, walked
2. is, was
3. have, had
4. do, did
5. needs, needed
6. am, was
7. has, had
8. are, were
9. does, did
10. works, worked

EXERCISE 2
1. is, was
2. do, did
3. have, had
4. asks, asked
5. have, had
6. learn, learned
7. are, were
8. does, did
9. plays, played
10. am, was

EXERCISE 3
1. started, like
2. offers
3. are, have
4. finished, needed
5. run, do
6. advise, comfort
7. enjoy, are
8. completed, expected
9. have
10. thank

EXERCISE 4
1. do, don't
2. am, is
3. need, explains
4. help, does
5. works, hope
6. did, dropped
7. was, do
8. work, check
9. learn, learns
10. expect, don't

EXERCISE 5
1. Last year all the students in our high school drama class *travelled* to London, England.

2. The sentence is correct.

3. We *were* all very excited about the trip.

4. Before the trip, we *learned* to read the London subway map.

5. We *discovered* that the people in London call the subway "the tube."

6. Once we *were* there, we understood why.

7. The underground walls *are* round just like a tube.

8. The sentence is correct.

9. We even *walked* right past the crown jewels.

10. The sentence is correct.

PROOFREADING EXERCISE

Every day as we drive through our neighbourhoods on the way to school or to work, we see things that *need* to be fixed. Many of them cause us only a little bit of trouble, so we forget them until we face them again. Every morning, I *have* to deal with a truck that someone *parks* right at the corner of my street. It *blocks* my view as I try to turn onto the main avenue. I need to move out past the truck into the oncoming lane of traffic just to make my left turn. One day last week, I *turned* too soon, and a car almost hit me. This truck *doesn't* need to be parked in such a dangerous place.

USING REGULAR AND IRREGULAR VERBS (PP. 98–101)

EXERCISE 1

1. looked

2. look

3. looking

4. look

5. looked

6. look

7. looked

8. looking

9. looks

10. look

EXERCISE 2

1. drive, driven

2. thinking, thought

3. take, takes

4. told, telling

5. wrote, written

6. knew, know

7. teach, taught

8. torn, tearing

9. ridden, ride

10. made, make

EXERCISE 3

1. were, heard

2. seen, begun

3. flown, eaten

4. got, did

5. take, eating

6. written, coming, lost

7. swore, felt

8. bought, paid

9. getting, thought

10. saw, told, lay

EXERCISE 4

1. use, puts
2. does, do
3. transfers, spend
4. is, like, choose
5. does, wants
6. trusts, is
7. imagine, made
8. talking, asked, worries
9. looked, said, lived, understand
10. wonder, is

EXERCISE 5

1. laid, lying, felt
2. know (or knew), been
3. broke, had
4. became, thought
5. was
6. read, frightened
7. kept, shook
8. worked, rose
9. left, find
10. lose, stung

SENTENCE ESSENTIALS PROGRESS TEST

1. types, are
2. Linda and one, agree
3. Homer, studies, works, plays
4. George and wife, spend
5. mother and niece, go, invite
6. Herman, has shared
7. Lydia, is finding, (is) sharing
8. Father, laughs, takes
9. He, told
10. we, learned

SENTENCE ESSENTIALS POST-TEST

1. children, have been born
2. Martha, welcomed
3. George, would have enjoyed
4. Kaitlyn Lori, arrived, went, sleeps
5. Marianne and Susanne, greeted, made
6. rest, have been
7. Martin, was born
8. sister, carried
9. names, are
10. three, sleep, play, recognize

PART 3 BUILDING EFFECTIVE SENTENCES

EFFECTIVE SENTENCES PRE-TEST

1. Monday; we (*or* Monday. We)

2. options so that

3. here but in

4. ago; regrettably (*or* ago. Regrettably)

5. OK

6. conditions; unionized (*or* conditions. Unionized)

7. strike although

8. middle when

9. side, in

10. union; these

IDENTIFYING CLAUSES (PP. 109–113)

EXERCISE 1

1. I am not a big talker in school.

2. Whenever a teacher asks me a question in class, I get nervous.

3. When I know the answer, I usually find the courage to speak.

4. If I don't know the answer, I look up at the ceiling as if I am thinking about it.

5. Usually, the teacher calls on someone else before I finish "thinking."

6. Obviously, when I take a public speaking class, I must talk sometimes.

7. In my last public speaking class, the assignment was to give a speech that demonstrated some sort of process.

8. The speech that I gave explained how crêpes suzettes are made.

9. Since I work at a French restaurant, I borrowed a crêpe pan to use in my demonstration.

10. The crêpes cooked quickly, and the teacher and students were so busy eating them that I didn't have to say much at all.

EXERCISE 2

1. Many of us remember when microwave ovens were first sold to the public.

2. People worried about whether they were safe or not.

3. Before we had the microwave oven, we cooked all of our food over direct heat.

4. At first, it was strange that only the food heated up in a microwave.

5. And microwave ovens cooked food so much faster than ordinary ovens did.

6. We had to get used to the possibilities that the microwave offered.

7. Since they are fast and don't heat up themselves, microwave ovens work well in offices, in restaurants, and on school campuses.

8. People who are on a budget can bring a lunch from home and heat it up at work.

9. Now that the microwave oven is here, we can even make popcorn without a pan.

10. As each new technology arrives, we wonder how we ever lived without it.

EXERCISE 3

1. When Canadians gather at sporting events, everyone sings "O Canada" while the Canadian flag proudly flies overhead.

2. "O Canada" is the song that Canada has chosen as its national anthem.

3. After Calixa Lavallée composed the music, the song was first performed at a banquet for skaters in Quebec City on June 24, 1880.

4. Adolphe-Basile Routhier wrote the French version, which he called "Chant national."

5. It was translated into English by Stanley Weir, who was a schoolteacher in Toronto.

6. Though French Canadians sang the anthem widely, English Canadians did not use it until the end of the 19th century.

7. When it gathered in 1967, the Parliament approved "O Canada" as the Canadian national anthem.

8. The words, which were altered somewhat after parliamentary debate, became official through the National Anthem Act, which was passed on June 27, 1980.

9. Canada's flag was hotly debated from Confederation to 1965, when the flag with the single red maple leaf became official.

10. Before that time, the Red Ensign was used for Canadian ceremonies, whether Canadian nationalists liked it or not.

EXERCISE 4

1. Many of us wouldn't mind shedding a few pounds from time to time.

2. There are a number of dieting problems that can leave you back at square one or worse.

3. For example, when you decide to lose weight, you need to be well prepared.

4. As part of your preparation, you should consider your long- and short-term goals before you commit to a specific action.

5. When some individuals begin a program, they pick the wrong course of action or have unrealistic expectations.

6. It's easy to become disappointed and frustrated if those expectations aren't met.

7. Skipping meals and not eating for long periods of time are common mistakes that you need to avoid.

8. When you go off your diet, the body's higher resting metabolic rate may drop.

9. Then your body will not be able to burn calories as quickly as it did before.

10. Since so many commercials, advertisements, and articles promise fast and easy ways to lose pounds, who knows which to believe?

EXERCISE 5

1. Tina, my twin sister, got a job that requires late-night hours.

2. The hours that I like the best are between six and eleven in the morning.

3. Now Tina sleeps until noon because she works all night.

4. When she comes home from work, our whole family is asleep.

5. Since Tina works all night and sleeps all day, I rarely see her.

6. Our dad thinks that Tina works too hard.

7. Our mom believes that Tina's new hours are a good challenge for her.

8. Yesterday, Tina's boss asked me if I wanted a job like Tina's.

9. I am not sure when I will find the right job for me.

10. Whenever I do find a good job, it will be during the day

PROOFREADING EXERCISE

We can think about an eclipse of the Sun in another way. Since sunlight cannot pass through the Moon, the Moon casts a shadow. The shadow is cone-shaped. It usually does not touch the Earth. But sometimes it moves across the Earth. When that happens, there is an eclipse. Inside the small place where the shadow touches, people can see a total eclipse. There is darkness. In places that are near the shadow, people can see only a partial eclipse. Farther away from the shadow, people can see no eclipse at all.

The Moon's shadow makes a circle when it touches the Earth. The circle moves as the Moon does. So an eclipse of the Sun can be seen in one place for only a few minutes.

CORRECTING PHRASE FRAGMENTS (PP. 115–117)

EXERCISE 1

Note: In each case below, the answer was created by merging the two word groups. If you added missing components to the phrase fragment, your answers will be different.

1. Deciding to further her education by attending college, Maiya discovered the process was a lengthy and confusing one.

2. Unlike many prospective students, she easily tackled the task of choosing a program without any help from her friends or family members.

3. Unfortunately, getting an adequate student loan wasn't nearly so easy because of the lack of youth employment opportunities during the summer.

4. As a result, her loan application form considerably overestimated the amount of the personal finances available to her at the beginning of the school year.

5. After speaking with the college's financial aid officer, Maiya decided to appeal the loan amount.

6. Arriving early on registration day without her birth certificate, her social insurance card, or any government-issued photo identification, she quickly became frustrated by long line-ups and huge delays.

7. After an exhausting day in several lengthy lines, including at the bank as well as at the college, Maiya finally clutched her official registration form and timetable.

8. Unfortunately, she had been too tired at the end of registration day to locate the classrooms displayed on her timetable.

9. On the first day of classes, after a desperate search down several corridors, Maiya was dismayed at her inability to find her first class's location.

10. Trying to stay calm and be rational, she finally returned to the financial aid office and asked its staff for directions.

EXERCISE 2

Answers may vary, but here are some possible revisions.

1. My car's compact disc player is difficult to use while driving.

2. The discs ~~reflecting~~ *reflect* the sunlight and ~~shining~~ *shine* in my eyes.

3. The old CD ejects from the slot with a hissing sound.

4. *There is* nowhere to put it while getting the new one.

5. Then *I try to insert* ~~inserting~~ the new CD without touching its underside.

6. Fumbling with those flat plastic cases can be really frustrating.

7. *There is* one case for the old one and one case for the new one.

8. Meanwhile I am driving along.

9. *I'm* not paying any attention to the road.

10. I hope I don't hit anything.

SENTENCE WRITING

The sentences below are examples of those that can be built from the original wording.

1. Playing video games all night instead of studying for my test *was a huge mistake.*

2. *At the time, it seemed more important* to reach the next level and beat my friend.

3. The weapons and coins needed *to move to a higher ranking were hard to find.*

4. *The video game market has gotten considerably more complicated* since Nintendo's original Mario Brothers game was released nearly twenty-five years ago.

5. *Now, most players find it* difficult to decide among all the gaming options.

6. Whether PS3, Xbox, iPhone, or the new Palm Pre, *every system offers options undreamed of even a decade ago.*

7. *Although some games seem to encourage violence, the primary objective of most is* to entertain gamers of every age.

8. Going online to play against others *perhaps halfway around the planet makes the world seem so much smaller.*

9. *For example, teenagers in British Columbia can test their skills against players* in other provinces and even other countries and continents.

10. Never winning, but sometimes coming close, *a teen in my neighbourhood has developed a real online addiction.*

CORRECTING DEPENDENT CLAUSE FRAGMENTS (PP. 118–121)

EXERCISE 1

1. My friends and I always go hiking in the fall although we risk running into cool, wet weather.

2. Crisp air and gloriously coloured maple leaves remind us to take advantage of the last decent weather before winter blusters in with its storms and frigid temperatures.

3. We sometimes need to bundle up with layers of clothing that we can shed if we generate too much heat during our hike.

4. Since we particularly enjoy wilderness hikes, we jump into our van and drive 45 minutes to our favourite spot.

5. This location features a lovely path that snakes beside a rushing river.

6. One of my classmates always packs a delicious picnic lunch because the hike increases our appetite.

7. As we are eating our lunch, we are often visited by three or four inquisitive squirrels.

8. Even though a chipmunk is an entirely different animal, some folks call these visitors "chipmunks."

9. For nearly ten years, we've been sharing our picnic lunches at the same location with an identical number of squirrels who might be members of the same family.

10. Each year the squirrels seem less and less nervous at our presence when we arrive at our traditional picnic site.

EXERCISE 2

Answers may vary, but here are some possible revisions.

1. Thrift stores, yard sales, and flea markets have become very popular places to shop because they sell items that are not available anywhere else as cheaply.

2. Most thrift stores benefit charities, which use the profits to help people in need.

3. Although the styles of clothing and furniture found in thrift stores are often outdated, many people prefer the old styles over the new.

4. Modern shelving units are made of particle board or plastic, but thrift store shoppers can find more substantial ones, which are made of solid wood or thick metal.

5. There are also famous stories of people becoming rich because they visited yard sales and flea markets.

6. One man bought a framed picture for a few dollars at a flea market. He liked the frame itself but not the picture.

7. When he returned home, he removed the picture from its frame and found the signature of a famous artist.

8. At a yard sale, a woman bought a small table. She later discovered that it was worth half a million dollars.

9. Of course, collectors always shop at these places. They hope to find treasures like rare cookie jars, pens, paintings, records, toys, and other objects of value.

10. In a way, shopping at thrift stores, yard sales, and flea markets is a kind of recycling that benefits everyone.

SENTENCE WRITING

The sentences below are examples of those that can be built from the original dependent clauses.

1. Whenever the first snowstorm hits, *drivers forget their winter driving habits.*

2. *Everyone seems surprised to find snow on the roads* although the weather reports give adequate notice.

3. *Some drivers get into trouble* unless their cars are equipped with ice tires.

4. While those cars without winter tires slide through intersections, *those with ice tires are capable of stopping in a relatively short distance.*

5. *Some provinces are considering the legalization of studded tires* because there are so many traffic accidents.

6. *Pieces of snow removal equipment are summoned* when the snow continues to fall.

7. *Some drivers continue at high speeds* until the lanes on the highway can no longer be seen.

8. *Following safe winter driving techniques is even more important* if drivers are unfamiliar with the roadway.

9. Until snowplows and other winter maintenance equipment clear the snow, *sometimes it's far wiser just to stop at a restaurant for a cup of coffee.*

10. *Newcomers to Canada learn quickly* how driving habits must change from season to season.

FRAGMENTS—COMBINED EXERCISES (PP. 121–123)

EXERCISE 1

1. OK (sentence)

2. OK (sentence)

3. Phrase fragment. Add to previous sentence: A forest of 345-million-year-old trees sticks out of a rock face outside Sussex, New Brunswick, about sixty-five kilometres from Saint John.

4. OK (sentence)

5. Dependent clause fragment. Add to previous sentence: A geology curator with the New Brunswick Museum found the fossilized forest while he was looking for roadside fish fossils six years ago.

6. OK (sentence)

7. OK (sentence)

8. Phrase fragment. Add to previous sentence: Then he saw it was a whole forest standing on end, sideways, and extending on and off the road for ten kilometres.

9. OK (sentence)

10. Dependent clause fragment. Add to previous sentence: Researchers have identified more than seven hundred trees, which were mostly mosslike plants that grew to twenty metres high.

EXERCISE 2

1. Phrase fragment. Add to first sentence: Kaitlyn's father recently purchased a used car after saving his money for over a year.

2. Phrase fragment. Add to first sentence: Now he is looking for a good mechanic because the car won't start, at least not in damp weather.

3. OK (sentence)

4. Dependent clause fragment. Add to previous sentence: The dealership doesn't offer extended warranties on used vehicles unless they have been regularly serviced by authorized service technicians.

5. Phrase fragment at end. Add to first sentence: Routine maintenance, including regular oil changes and other inspections, is critical to ensure a car's performance.

6. Dependent clause fragment. Add to first sentence: Kaitlyn is hoping to locate a good mechanic for her father because he has always tried to help her.

7. Dependent clause fragment. Add to first sentence: Generally, the hourly rate of independent licensed mechanics is over $65, which results in an expensive bill unless the problem is easy to identify and quick to repair.

8. Dependent clause fragment. Add to previous sentence: One of my neighbours is a student in the school's motive power program where cars are serviced as part of the students' hands-on learning activities.

9. Phrase fragment. Add to first sentence: I know the school is always looking for vehicles, especially those with complicated electrical problems.

10. Dependent clause fragment. Add to first sentence: I'll tell Kaitlyn about this program so that she can follow up on this possibility.

PROOFREADING EXERCISE

Here is one possible revision to eliminate the five fragments.

  Shark attacks have been on the rise. We've all heard the heartbreaking news stories of people on their honeymoons or children playing in only a few feet of water being attacked by sharks. Movies like *Jaws* and *Open Water* make us wary and scared when we watch them. But their effects fade over time, and we forget about the risks of entering the habitats of dangerous animals. Experts try to convince us that sharks and other powerful species are not targeting human beings on purpose. To a shark, a person is no different from a seal or a sea turtle. Facts such as these prompt many of us to think twice before we take a dip in the ocean.

CORRECTING RUN-ON SENTENCES (PP. 125–129)

EXERCISE 1

Your answers may differ depending on how you choose to separate the two clauses.

1. Nearly everyone yawns, but few understand the dynamics of yawning.

2. The sentence is correct.

3. The sentence is correct.

4. The sentence is correct.

5. Groups of people do similar things, for they are acting somewhat like herds of animals.

6. The sentence is correct.

7. The yawning helps the group act as one, so it minimizes conflict.

8. There are a few misconceptions about yawns. One of them has to do with oxygen levels.

9. The sentence is correct.

10. Surprisingly, studies show no changes in yawning patterns due to levels of oxygen; in fact, research subjects inhaling pure oxygen yawned the same number of times as those breathing normally.

EXERCISE 2

Your answers may differ depending on how you choose to separate the two clauses.

1. I am writing a research paper on Margaret Laurence; she was one of Canada's most celebrated novelists and a pioneer in the world of Canadian literature.

2. She was born in Neepawa, Manitoba. In her novels *The Stone Angel*, *A Jest of God*, *The Fire-Dwellers*, and *The Diviners*, the town was called "Manawaka."

3. Laurence was encouraged to write by Jack McClelland. He also published the works of other Canadian writers such as Mordecai Richler and Farley Mowat.

4. Margaret and her husband Jack briefly lived in England; then they moved to Africa.

5. She became very interested in European–African relations. As a result, her early books, *This Side Jordan* and *The Tomorrow-Tamer*, deal with this issue.

6. Her husband wanted her to be a traditional wife and mother, but Margaret wanted to be a full-time writer.

7. The sentence is correct.

8. The sentence is correct.

9. Twice her books were condemned or banned in schools, yet today they are taught as Canadian classics.

10. In 1986, she was diagnosed with inoperable and fatal lung cancer. Several months later she took her own life.

EXERCISE 3

Your answers may differ since various words can be used to begin dependent clauses.

1. On summer evenings, people around the world enjoy the sight of little lights that are flying around in the air.

2. Although most people know the glowing insects as fireflies, they are also called lightning bugs and glowworms.

3. Glowworms are unique since they don't fly.

4. The term *fireflies* is a little misleading because they are not technically flies.

5. Lightning bugs are beetles that have special substances in their bodies.

6. The substances that make them glow are luciferin and luciferase.

7. When the luciferin and luciferase combine with oxygen, they produce a greenish light.

8. The light can be so intense that people in some countries use caged fireflies as lamps.

9. The sentence is correct.

10. Incredibly, even though groups of fireflies blink out of order at first, they seem to coordinate their blinking within a few minutes.

Exercise 4

Your answers may differ since various words can be used to begin dependent clauses.

1. When Glenn Gould died, Canada lost a great musician.

2. While Gould was a sublime pianist, he was also a composer of international fame.

3. The sentence is correct.

4. Because he was a child prodigy, he was put on the stage at a very young age.

5. When he was fourteen years old, he became a soloist with the Toronto Symphony.

6. Though he began touring across Canada at age nineteen, in later years Gould stopped performing in public.

7. The sentence is correct.

8. Since he was an eccentric and a loner, few people knew much about his personal life.

9. The sentence is correct.

10. Gould's music continues to live on though he is no longer alive.

Exercise 5

Your answers may differ depending on how you choose to separate the two clauses.

1. There is a new way to find a date in Japan; singles use vending machines to sell information about themselves to others.

2. Men provide personal details in packets to be sold in the machines, but first the men swear they are not married.

3. If a woman chooses to purchase a packet for a couple of dollars, in it she will find a picture of the man, his age, and his employment status.

4. The packets also include the men's phone numbers so that the women can contact the men they like.

5. The system seems to be working, and many of the couples are dating more than once.

6. A lot of Japanese businesspeople use the machines since they do not have time to meet people in other ways.

7. Employees have little opportunity to socialize in Japan, where it is normal to stay at work until late into the evening.

8. Although a man might pay almost $50 to put many of his packets into the machines, that doesn't mean that women will call him.

9. Japan is famous for its vending machines, which are even used to sell meat and clothes.

10. Whereas other countries might find it unusual to sell personal information in vending machines, they seem to be working well as matchmakers in Japan.

REVIEW OF FRAGMENTS AND RUN-ON SENTENCES (PP. 130–136)

EXERCISE 1

1. Lydia's father graduated from high school in the mid-sixties when he was only sixteen years old.

2. Last September his class held its forty-fifth reunion, and he decided to travel more than one thousand kilometres to participate in the special events.

3. Although the football coach rarely called upon him to hit the field, his favourite part of high school was sports.

4. At the reunion, members of the varsity football team hosted a special party. He was amazed to find that he remembered almost every teammate's name.

5. "Dougie," the star quarterback, was a little guy who, at the time, stood up to the other players' armpits and weighed less than half as much as any player on the defensive team.

6. At the football team's special party, "Dougie" ran up to Lydia's father and gave him a giant bear hug.

7. To his delight, even some of the most popular girls remembered his name; apparently he had made a larger impact on classmates than he had thought.

8. The reunion's dinner/dance gave Lydia's father the chance to sit and chat with others he remembered more dimly; nonetheless, the conversations were animated and filled with warm laughter.

9. To reconnect with his friends from so long ago and so far away provided him with new memories to treasure for decades more.

10. Lydia says her dad acted like a teenager at the airport after his trip, and she doubts that any other trip could match this one for excitement.

EXERCISE 2

1. A famous Canadian coffee and doughnut chain conducts a special annual contest to give consumers added incentives to purchase the franchise's coffee.

2. Regular customers know the odds of winning; therefore they likely double their coffee intake during the contest period.

3. Customers can win prizes such as cars, computer equipment, cash, and the doughnut company's merchandise in a unique way by rolling up the rims of specially marked coffee cups.

4. Even when they have their coffee served in a china mug in the restaurant itself, purchasers get a cardboard contest cup in order to participate.

5. The effect on landfill sites must be notable because the cups are coated with a waxed substance and cannot be recycled.

6. Some in-store customers hesitate when offered the extra cardboard cup; after all, one of the reasons they choose to drink from china mugs is to minimize the negative environmental impact of the paper.

7. Although some geographical areas have more contest winners than others, this apparent advantage may be the result of easier store accessibility in some cities and provinces.

8. Some cities have five or more outlets of the same coffee and doughnut chain so that caffeine addicts can have a regular supply of their favourite beverage.

9. Eager contest participants once had to buy a cup of coffee from one of the brand's hundreds of outlets in Canada and the United States; however, modern technology now makes anyone with Internet access eligible to play.

10. Without purchasing a single cup of the beverage, anyone can register online and have a chance to claim a prize.

EXERCISE 3

1. Many scientists have blamed global warming for recent unusual weather patterns that include more severe storms throughout the world.

2. Hurricanes in North America and floods throughout Europe have made even the most skeptical person take notice.

3. To understand our planet's future, we need to study what climate changes have already taken place.

4. According to many climate studies, glaciers are melting at an unprecedented rate, sea levels are rising, and annual temperatures are climbing.

5. The Canadian government has recently recognized that the Northwest Passage may soon have open water year round.

6. Several other countries are beginning to take an interest in the Arctic's natural gas and mineral reserves that have traditionally been locked away under tonnes of ice.

7. As the ice shield melts, the sea levels rise, sometimes to alarming levels; around the world, many heavily populated cities sit at the current edge of oceans and seas.

8. The president of the Maldive Islands spoke at a recent session of the United Nations-sponsored climate summit; he predicted that his whole country would disappear below ocean water by the end of this century.

9. Canada is facing special global warming challenges like droughts in the Prairie provinces, rising sea levels along its three ocean borders, and reduced habitats for endangered species like the polar bear.

10. It took centuries for the world to get to its current state; some feel that extravagant styles of living and manufacturing demands in developing countries have taken the environment over its tipping point.

EXERCISE 4

1. Shortly after the collapse of the world's economies in October 2008, the Canadian government introduced a tax credit plan for taxpayers who chose to make permanent improvements to their primary places of residence.

2. As a result, many Canadians elected to renovate their homes and spent thousands of dollars to repaint rooms, refinish hardwood floors, and add decks.

3. As the Home Renovation Tax Credit program was rolled out, TV commercials showed enthusiastic homeowners making long-delayed improvements, but the devil was in the details.

4. Although the minority party in power had announced the program months earlier, the public relations campaign kicked into high gear before the House of Commons had approved the measure.

5. Only people in the habit of reading fine print saw the very small "Subject to Parliamentary approval" line appearing in each commercial as well as on all printed materials available at home building supply outlets.

6. It must have been a relief to the governing party when the opposition's threat to topple the government evaporated; after all, it would have been embarrassing to explain the situation in an election campaign.

7. When homeowners filed their 2009 income tax forms, they were able to claim a portion of their renovation expenses as a tax credit.

8. As it turned out, the timing of this tax credit hugely benefited building contractors who had been expecting low earnings as the result of the world's economic downturn.

9. Suddenly, roofers, painters, and other specialized tradespersons found themselves with more work than they could handle; whole neighbourhoods swarmed with pickup trucks belonging to contractors and their workers.

10. In fact, many residents couldn't locate a house painter to complete the necessary work within the program's time frame because all the painting contractors were too busy even to provide project estimates to homeowners.

EXERCISE 5

1. Hybrid cars have grown considerably in popularity since Toyota's Prius first arrived on the North American market in 2001.

2. The Prius has grown from a compact to a midsize car and now shares the market with hybrid SUVs and trucks.

3. Generally, consumers buy this car because it offers exceptional mileage and eco-friendly low emissions.

4. Toyota's development of the Prius took less than two years from concept to production.

5. Every little detail is assessed; for example, the weight of the engine and other components is minimized to reduce the power requirements.

6. In the newest version, even the sunroof serves multiple purposes; when the car is parked in the summer sun, its solar panel provides power to a small fan that keeps air circulating and provides a cooler interior.

7. Toyota developed the first hybrid technology, blending gasoline and battery power.

8. Although the Prius has competitors at several levels from both domestic and foreign automakers, the technology for electric hybrids varies.

9. Battery power alone will operate over only a short distance; an infrastructure of many battery recharging stations must be built to act as the electrical equivalent of gasoline stations.

10. A recharging station would allow a driver whose vehicle's battery is running low on charge to exchange it for a fully charged one and be on his or her way in moments; however, the establishment of these recharging stations isn't going to happen overnight.

PROOFREADING EXERCISE
Note: There are several other sentence-combining options other than those shown here. Check with your instructor to determine if your choices are correct.

The shiny black sports car zipped through the heavy rush hour traffic. Changing lanes without signalling, tailgating the car immediately in front of it, and acting as though he owned the <u>road were signs of an impatient driver</u>. When it approached the intersection with the red <u>light, the</u> car paused only long enough to allow the light to turn green. The driver quickly <u>accelerated; however</u>, another car was entering the intersection at the same time. The sports car slammed into it. Metal <u>screeched; glass</u> broke. Both cars were <u>immobilized, but</u> fortunately no one was hurt badly. Still, all the time that the driver had "saved" was lost <u>now. It</u> would be at least forty-five minutes before the police <u>arrived to</u> investigate the accident. If eyewitnesses stayed to give their <u>statements, likely</u> the sports car driver would get a <u>ticket; then</u> he would need to pay not only a large <u>fine but</u> also higher premiums for his auto insurance.

EXPLORING SENTENCE VARIETY (PP. 138–140)

EXERCISE 1

1. Complex (an independent clause followed by a dependent)

2. Simple (one independent clause)

3. Compound (two independent clauses linked by a *FANBOYS* word)

4. Simple (one independent clause)

5. Complex (an independent clause followed by a dependent)

6. Simple (one independent clause)

7. Complex (a dependent clause followed by an independent)

8. Compound-complex (an independent clause linked by a semicolon to an independent clause + dependent clause combination)

9. Simple (one independent clause)

10. Compound-complex (independent clause linked by a semicolon to a dependent clause + independent clause combination)

EXERCISE 2

1. Complex (an independent clause followed by a dependent)

2. Complex (an independent clause followed by a dependent)

3. Compound-complex (an independent clause + dependent clause combination linked by a *FANBOYS* word to a second independent clause)

4. Simple (one independent clause)

5. Compound-complex (an independent clause linked by a semicolon to an independent clause + dependent clause combination)

6. Complex (a dependent clause followed by an independent)

7. Compound-complex (an independent clause linked by a *FANBOYS* word to a dependent clause + independent clause combination)

8. Compound (two independent clauses linked by a semicolon)

9. Simple (one independent clause)

10. Complex (an independent clause followed by a dependent)

PROOFREADING EXERCISE

In this computer era most people have viewed many PowerPoint presentations[I]. While not all these presentations are ineffective[D], they seem to fall into one of three categories[I]. Poorly organized presentations are usually created by individuals[I] whose understanding of this method of presentation is weak or nonexistent[D]. At the other extreme, presentations by PowerPoint showoffs usually demonstrate more graphics skills than ideas[I]. Although most of us get really confused[D] when speakers clutter up their slides with too much material[D], the showoffs can't get enough action and content[I]. The good presentations lie somewhere in the middle[I]; the presenter limits each slide to just five bullets or one picture[I]. While these basic guidelines protect audiences from the other two extremes[D], most people soon get bored seeing slide after slide with the same pattern[I], and after a while all good PowerPoint presentations look alike[I].

SENTENCE ANALYSIS:

Simple, Complex, Complex, Simple, Complex, Compound, Compound-Complex

EFFECTIVE SENTENCES PROGRESS TEST

There are several other ways to correct the structure errors. Check with your instructor.

1. enclosed; an

2. ended, we

3. OK

4. force because

5. line. The

6. year, so

7. products; therefore

8. week although

9. plant, which

10. locations to

EFFECTIVE SENTENCES POST-TEST

1. options for voters

2. parties, many

3. country; as

4. Quebec because

5. issues, which

6. scope; specifically,

7. riding in the last election.

8. representative; however,

9. elected when

10. Canada although

PART 4 KEEPING THE MESSAGE CLEAR

CLARITY PRE-TEST

1. Committee, *the councillors* were confused

2. The plan for recommended ski hill changes *is* being debated …

3. Discussions at that meeting will involve city staff, *elected representatives,* and *interested citizens.*

4. Everyone in the sporting community *is wondering* …

5. *Does* either …

6. attention if *we* taxpayers supported …

7. … a bunny hill *and an intermediate hill, but it* needs a …

8. When the ski hill was first developed fifty years ago, it *had* only one …

9. *Ideally, taxpayers, politicians, and sport enthusiasts would cooperate* in developing plans for sports complexes like this hill.

10. Louis Mayer, the manager of Leisure Activities, *is unhappy that his brother* skis at a hill in another city now.

Or

Louis Mayer, the manager of Leisure Activities, *says his brother is unhappy* that he has to ski at a hill in another city now.

11. to be so complicated, expensive, and *controversial*.

12. Planning … thing; *making* … is another.

13. … positive about it as *she* (is).

14. … and voice *their* ideas.

15. … there *are* two kinds of people

16. … snowboarders, *and sledders* don't …

17. Please encourage everyone … but also to contact *his or her* councillor …

18. None of my other friends *is* a skier, …

19. hill; *he* and his wife will attend …

20. … hill as much as *they* (care).

MAINTAINING SUBJECT–VERB AGREEMENT (PP. 149–153)

EXERCISE 1

1. is

2. fly

3. knows, stand

4. are

5. is

6. seem, go

7. are

8. take

9. have

10. have

EXERCISE 2

1. is

2. was

3. cling

4. make

5. soften

6. are

7. is

8. radiate

9. overlooks

10. enjoy

EXERCISE 3

1. is, call
2. is, are, has
3. is, are, is
4. was, takes, connects
5. believes, are

6. happens
7. hypothesizes, control
8. gives
9. is
10. think, produces, activates

EXERCISE 4

1. has
2. have, have
3. love
4. makes
5. says

6. thinks
7. is, haven't
8. has
9. looks
10. knows

EXERCISE 5

1. are, require
2. is, exists
3. is, are
4. is, are
5. doubles, allows

6. request, make
7. are, maintains
8. is, are
9. fund, are
10. belongs, is

PROOFREADING EXERCISE

My courses for this academic year are really challenging. Each of the classes *is* difficult in a different way. Some of them *require* us to learn on our own in labs. And the others demand that students carefully *follow* the minute instructions of the professor. The assignments given by my geography instructor, for example, *are* harder than I expected. Everybody in the class *has* to prepare a scale model of a mountain range. All of the models so far have looked the same. But one of the models *was* a little out of scale, and the instructor failed it. The other students and I *have* decided to work together so none of us *make* the same mistake. I guess that all of this hard work *is* worthwhile. My instructors *say* it helps prepare us for our future careers.

CHOOSING THE RIGHT PRONOUN (PP. 155–159)

Exercise 1

1. My father and I went …

2. … time he and I have gone …

3. … between him and me.

4. … of this trip was he.

5. … so he and I use different …

6. [delete *Me*] I'm always …

7. … enabling us companions …

8. … more than I [did] every day.

9. … patient than he [is], but now …

10. … up to him and Mother Nature.

Exercise 2

1. … because her mother and she serve …

2. … artisans like them and us potters.

3. … much more noise than we [do].

4. … several of us potters …

5. … club members and I soon …

6. … as enthusiastic as she [was].

7. Since her mother and she work …

8. … day than we [had].

9. … one that we club members …

10. … told a friend and me that …

Exercise 3

1. … my sister and I heard …

2. … about energy than we [did].

3. … if only we energy consumers would …

4. … if you and I want to save …

5. … the audience and I were using …

6. … gas as I [did] throughout …

7. However, he and I had …

8. … Bill; he and his wife …

9. Just between you and me …

10. … winners will be we.

Exercise 4

1. … Rajih, Karyn, and I.

2. … likes the same music as we [like].

3. … Rajih and I wanted to see.

4. … to us older listeners than [to] her.

5. … judge of music as we [are].

6. … next time we friends decide …

7. … will be Rajih and I.

8. Although Rajih and I are …

9. … concert to him or me, we …

10. … when she and he were …

SENTENCE WRITING

The following are sample sentences using the pronoun phrases supplied (in italics).

1. I admire Mohammed because he knows more languages *than we* [know].

2. My best friend is pleased that I take the bus with *Sheila and her* every morning.

3. My mother likes my friend Amelia; *Bill and she* are Mom's favourites.

4. Everyone in my neighbourhood collected pledges for the Run for the Cure; *among us*, we raised over $5 000.

5. My sister is probably my best friend; *she and I* meet at least once a week for lunch.

MAKING PRONOUNS AGREE (PP. 160–164)

EXERCISE 1

1. Many Canadian cities now feature restaurants focusing on a wide variety of foods from around the world; <u>each</u> of these dining spots serves *its* host country's favourite dishes.

2. When my family first immigrated to Canada, we were surprised to find many Chinese <u>restaurants</u> that served *their* dishes in an all-you-can-eat buffet format.

3. *Canadians* living in large cities like Toronto, Montreal, or Vancouver can eat exotic meals from any continent <u>they</u> choose.

4. At the small East Indian restaurant down the street, *customers* ordering a hamburger *are* asked whether <u>they</u> want it served with hot or mild curry powder.

5. Still, a <u>restaurant</u> specializing in the cuisine of another country used to find *its* financial survival was dependent upon offering some Canadian standards, like poutine and chicken strips.

6. For example, traditional Mexican <u>restaurants</u> have sprung up and then disappeared, not because their food was too spicy but because *their* menus didn't include pizza or spaghetti.

7. However, the newest <u>restaurant</u> in town features shrimp and alligator on the menu, and *it seems* to be doing good business.

8. The <u>owners</u> seized upon the Acadian experience in New Brunswick; *they have* made eating Cajun food fashionable.

9. However, when it comes to volume of customers, ethnic eating <u>establishments</u> are often financially successful only if *they are* in small storefront *locations*.

10. To attract families, American chain restaurants or a small local dining <u>spot</u> has a natural advantage because *its* menu features food that children like.

EXERCISE 2

1. Either my partner or <u>his sisters</u> will soon need to make decisions about how best to care for *their* aging father Frank.

2. The three <u>siblings</u> are scattered across the world, but *all know* <u>their</u> dad won't be capable of living alone much longer.

3. Correct.

4. Because the other sister lives at the other end of the country, <u>she and her brother</u> call *their* father regularly to get up-to-date information about him.

5. *All members* of the family agree that <u>they</u> have taken this man's lifelong independence for granted.

6. Unfortunately, a recent <u>series</u> of mini-strokes has taken *its* toll on his well-being.

7. A recent fall from a ladder or the mini-strokes have caused <u>Frank</u> to worry about *his* independence.

8. The three <u>children</u> have hired a personal support worker to attend Frank's home three times a day because *they* lack confidence that <u>their</u> dad is safe on his own.

9. Frank has always provided help to *family members* who needed it; now <u>they</u> need to convince him that he needs *their* assistance.

10. *Parents* no longer able to live confidently on *their* own should discuss possible solutions with <u>their</u> children.

EXERCISE 3

1. *Individuals* should make a point of checking all medicine purchases with <u>their</u> *pharmacists*.

2. <u>Some</u> of the drugs on the market today carry labels that advise consumers not to use *them* with other specified medications.

3. When seeing a doctor, every patient should bring a list of all the medications he or she is currently taking.

4. This sentence has no pronouns and is correct.

5. Still, otherwise healthy *persons* may not be aware that an over-the-counter drug can be harmful in <u>their</u> specific situation.

6. As <u>individuals</u> age and suffer from more disorders, *they are* more likely to need several prescriptions.

7. <u>Each</u> of my mother's prescription drugs has *its* own side effects.

8. Adult family <u>members</u> need to pay close attention to all medications, prescribed or not, taken by *their* loved ones.

9. Some individuals' <u>parents</u> refuse to allow *their* children to be immunized against standard childhood diseases.

10. However, recent studies seem to have proven beyond any reasonable doubt that a <u>child</u> who receives inoculations will not suffer later in *his or her life* from a serious disorder like autism.

EXERCISE 4

1. *All* the patients in the chronic care wing of a retirement home have separate charts to indicate which treatments <u>they</u> are taking.

2. However, sometimes *charts* maintained by retirement home staff members *are*n't as up-to-date as <u>they</u> ought to be.

3. Chronic care <u>residents</u> often need specialized and timely care if *they* are to live meaningful *lives*.

4. For example, if a <u>resident</u> fails to take a prescribed medication as ordered by the doctor, *he or she* might develop even more severe health issues.

5. Many older <u>citizens</u> prefer to live *their* final days in their own private homes.

6. Without supervision, however, <u>issues</u> like drug interactions, poor nutrition, and inadequate exercise can go unnoticed unless *they cause* fainting.

7. Although several <u>individuals</u> die every year from drug interactions, the cause of *their deaths* might be difficult to determine without proper records.

8. *Deaths* resulting from drug interactions *are* unnecessary; <u>they</u> could have been avoided.

9. When a <u>relative</u> moves into a hospital setting with registered nurses providing constant care, *his or her* drug interactions are more closely monitored.

10. Still, the lack of alternative care beds in most <u>hospitals</u> restricts *their* ability to look after patients with the care and thoroughness necessary.

EXERCISE 5

1. When selecting *computers*, a consumer often finds the marketplace very confusing because <u>they</u> come with so many options. (Note the change to 'a consumer often finds')

2. A huge <u>company</u> like Microsoft has a huge portion of the market in *its* hands.

3. <u>Linda and her brother</u> have been contemplating *their* computer purchase for nearly six months; however, they really don't know much about computer basics.

4. The humorous Apple commercials appeal to *both* of them even though <u>they</u> know almost nothing about the differences between Apples and PCs.

5. Linda's boyfriend Amil is a real geek, but whenever he tries to explain computer terms like RAM and hard drive, *Linda's and her brother's* eyes glaze over.

6. They should listen carefully to him because no one *understands computer terminology* better than he does.

7. Nonetheless, Amil's understanding is useless when he speaks to <u>Linda or her brother</u> because *each needs* to acquire more basic information first.

8. Even the most confident computer <u>users</u> in class go to Amil when *they have* a question.

9. Amil is probably the most patient man I've ever met; when <u>one</u> of the computers in the lab crashed and lost all *its* files, he managed somehow to retrieve them.

10. Now, if *Linda and her brother* listen to Amil about how to choose a computer, <u>they</u> will make a sounder choice.

MAKING CLEAR PRONOUN REFERENCES (PP. 166–172)

EXERCISE 1

1. As is always the case with special events, this year's awards presentations weren't without their problems.

2. The awards programs didn't arrive on time from the printers and contained several misspelled names.

3. Although workers placed three hundred chairs in the hall late yesterday afternoon, the seats weren't clean at the time.

4. As the ceremony began, a serious accident outside the hall involved a truck and an ambulance; the truck's horn stuck and drowned out the introductions.

5. At last night's event, the award recipients were seated beside the sponsors, but the sponsors didn't have name tags.

6. Luanne was surprised when she won the President's Award.

7. The winners hardly spoke to the sponsors at their tables because the award recipients were too uncomfortable.

8. When she met Luanne's mother, the woman who organized the evening said, "Your dress is elegant."

9. Set for only eight people, the tables were too close together.

10. All the award winners enjoyed having their group photo taken after the ceremony.

EXERCISE 2

1. The set of patio furniture I ordered this summer for our new deck arrived the next day.

2. The set included a large glass-topped table, two mesh chairs, and two rockers, and the rockers are exceptionally comfortable.

3. The two types of chairs were listed with different prices before both went on sale at the end of the season.

4. I asked two salesclerks about the difference, although the prices seemed reasonable to me.

5. Once satisfied that the sale price was being applied, I needed to select the method of payment for this large purchase.

6. Now that my bank's credit card uses "chip technology," I didn't even have to sign the sales receipt.

7. Instead, I swiped my credit card, entered my PIN on the transaction machine, and returned the card to my wallet.

8. When I assembled the furniture set, one chair was clearly defective, so I had to return the chair to the retail store.

9. The clerk told his manager that a replacement chair was likely available from the warehouse.

10. The whole return process took only half an hour, but enjoying the new furniture on the deck was worth all the effort.

EXERCISE 3

1. Earlier this month, our neighbours the MacNeils bought some new trees, but the trees were too tall for them to handle.

2. With so many branches, the trees appeared to be several years old.

3. Planting mature trees requires specialized horticultural skills, which most homeowners don't have.

4. When Bill MacNeil asked a member of the local horticultural society how to plant such trees, the horticulturalist was confused.

5. The horticulturalist suggested that Bill get expert advice.

6. The root balls were beginning to dry out while the trees sat waiting for planting.

7. My mother smiled when the MacNeils finally asked my parents for help.

8. Sandra MacNeil told my mother, "You have a green thumb."

9. Sandra and Mom quickly rented several pieces of equipment necessary to move the trees.

10. The preparation work was finished within a week, and each tree was carefully planted; Mom says the prep work was a difficult job

EXERCISE 4

1. Lots of people who wear glasses can tell you horror stories about how eyeglasses affected their lives.

2. One sunny day at the beach, my brothers ran across my towel and smashed my glasses.

3. When the ophthalmologist took the lenses out of my glasses' frames, the frames broke.

4. Apparently the life expectancy of any set of eyeglasses is far shorter than advertised.

5. Some very expensive glasses are now sold with insurance policies to protect the owner against accidental breakage.

6. When they went on a trip together, my sister told our aunt, "You shouldn't sit on the bed."

7. The hotel bed's duvet had designs the same colour as my sister's glasses, so the glasses just disappeared into the fabric.

8. Although finding such a spot isn't always easy in unfamiliar places, I try to put my glasses in a safe place at night when I travel.

9. If people don't treat their glasses carefully, the glasses may need to be replaced.

10. Some people elect to wear flexible contact lenses, which can pose a different set of problems.

EXERCISE 5

1. Whenever Kareena puts gasoline into her mother's car, the smell of gas gives her a headache.

2. Strangely, one brand seems just as bad as another.

3. Kareena and her mother haven't owned cars very long because automobiles need too much attention.

4. Prior to moving to Canada, the budget-friendly bicycle once served as the family's primary source of transportation.

5. India's Tata Motors, a car and truck manufacturing company, has now introduced what is said to be the least expensive car in the world.

6. Still, neither Kareena nor her mother has much experience pumping gasoline into a vehicle, so this new task is unsettling.

7. The problem doesn't have anything to do with a low octane level, either, because the highest priced gasoline is just as smelly.

8. Possibly, other additives in the fuels cause the problem because petroleum companies now sometimes include ethanol for environmental reasons.

9. Some experts question ethanol's environmental benefits, which haven't been proven entirely.

10. Kareena is fortunate that her family's car is not fuelled by diesel; that fuel has a distinct smell.

PROOFREADING EXERCISE (CORRECTIONS ARE ITALICIZED.)

I told my cousin Miles a secret at our last family reunion, and as soon as I did, I knew *the secret* would get out. I forgot that Miles is six years younger than *I* when I told him that I was taking a job overseas. Right before I told him the secret, I said, "Now this is just between you and *me*, and you're not going to tell anyone, right?" He assured me that the only person he would talk to about it was *I*. I made the mistake of believing him. If I had *printed my secret* in a full-page ad in a newspaper that was then delivered to my family, *my secret* could not have been spread around faster. Miles and I are still cousins, but *he* and *I* are no longer friends.

MISPLACED MODIFIERS (PP. 174–178)

EXERCISE 1

1. My sister accidentally ran over a neighbour's cat.

2. We thought, from the volume of her weeping, that the neighbour mistook her pet for a child.

3. Perhaps hoping to make some financial gain from the unfortunate situation, the woman threatened my sister with a lawsuit for thousands of dollars.

4. My sister and I could only listen with disbelief as the angry woman complained bitterly about how much money she had spent to get the cat neutered.

5. Our whole family loves cats, but this one roamed the streets and, without any regrets, killed harmless little birds.

6. Because I knew my sister was incapable of intentionally hurting any animal, let alone a family pet, I quietly suggested to her that she replace the cat.

7. When she heard our offer to purchase a new cat, the neighbour suddenly stopped crying and smiled sweetly at my sister.

8. We adopted a fluffy-tailed cat for the neighbour.

9. Sadly, less than six weeks later, the new cat wandered away.

10. We were astonished that the neighbour just shrugged her shoulders at our offer to help find her missing pet.

EXERCISE 2

1. Most people, especially children, describe Robert Munsch as a master storyteller.

2. With his sparkling eyes, he makes his stories come alive.

3. On his storytelling tours, Munsch usually attracts children of all ages.

4. Janine's granddaughter is begging her grandmother to see Munsch at the Theatre Centre.

5. By entering a local radio station's contest, Janine hopes to win free tickets for the performance.

6. She's heard that these tickets for front-row seats will be awarded on the radio.

7. Munsch's performance will be the first time many in the audience will see the difference between a story reader and a storyteller.

8. Seated on chairs next to him on stage, children he has selected from the audience are transformed into the characters in the stories Munsch is telling.

9. Over several generations, Munsch has put smiles on listeners' faces and favourite stories on readers' lips.

10. Munsch smiles at the giggling children in the audience.

EXERCISE 3

1. Canada Day on July 1 is a time to celebrate in many Canadian cities and towns.

2. In the park, families with laughing children spread out blankets and eat picnic lunches.

3. Everyone has a smile; the summer season has begun for most individuals.

4. Groups line up along the streets downtown to watch the marching bands with their loud trumpets and drums.

5. Spectators run after candies designed with tiny Canadian flags distributed by some marchers and floats.

6. Face painters use red theatre makeup to decorate children's faces with maple leaves.

7. The added benefit of a warm day with blue skies puts everyone into a celebratory mood.

8. Teens and young adults wearing only lightweight clothes pack the parks for rock concerts later in the evening.

9. Keeping their eyes on the skies, onlookers are thrilled by the Canadian Forces' Snowbirds acrobatic team whenever it appears as part of the festivities.

10. As the sky darkens, fireworks with all colours and shapes produce ooh's and aah's from appreciative viewers.

EXERCISE 4

1. Citing the current worldwide economic situation, most employers are not offering job security.

2. One year after he became a manager, my brother was without any job at all when the company he worked for closed its doors.

3. Call centres are experiencing a particularly high turnover of staff members who see the fragile nature of their employment.

4. On the other hand, health care professionals with aging patients can count on bright futures.

5. Some disorders previously seldom encountered, like Alzheimer's, have become far more prevalent.

6. At family doctors' offices, after-hours clinics, and emergency rooms across the country, older patients also present with a wider range of symptoms and conditions.

7. The surging value of the Canadian dollar plays a significant role in slowing down the economy.

8. The prices of manufactured goods aren't always reflecting the higher value of the Canadian dollar compared to the U.S. dollar.

9. As the result of the near bankruptcy of Daimler-Chrysler and General Motors, North American taxpayers found their governments becoming significant shareholders in these companies.

10. Many mechanics, millwrights, and other skilled tradespersons found that their North American jobs were saved by the infusion of capital by governments that agreed to provide stimulus funding.

EXERCISE 5

1. When going through the pockets of her brother's pants while doing the laundry this weekend, Rani found a ten-dollar bill.

2. Smiling as she remembered her mother's rules for sorting clothes, Rani was delighted at the unexpected discovery.

3. At the age of six, she had been assigned the routine for preparing the family's laundry.

4. Not only did Rani learn to check pockets for their contents, but she also learned to verify the clothing's washing instructions tags to avoid mishaps.

5. Twenty years later and now a mother herself, Rani knew her mother would be proud to see that the lessons had been so well learned.

6. Rani couldn't remember ever finding anything except tissues and the occasional penny or nickel in anyone's pockets when she was a child.

7. Noting that the bill was carefully folded into quarters, she wondered why her brother didn't remember putting it into his pocket.

8. Rajit learned his sister had found money in his pants pocket in the laundry room.

9. When he whimpered quietly about plans to spend this money on their mother, Rani listened to Rajit without much sympathy.

10. Rajit was grateful that his sister had missed the twenty-dollar bill in his pants that somehow made it through the washing machine and dryer a week earlier.

DANGLING MODIFIERS (PP. 179–186)

EXERCISE 1

1. When purchasing a new car, a consumer needs to remember that the vehicle's appearance is only one factor to take into consideration.

2. Increasingly, due to their safety features, gasoline consumption, and technological options, cars make buying decisions trickier.

3. In the 1960s, when only a few automotive dealerships were available, "oak tree mechanics" filled the service gap to make cars reliable.

4. During trips, scenery was more important than a high-class sound system while families drove leisurely down a deserted country road.

5. Many small rural towns had small service stations to look after routine repairs and breakdowns.

6. Without being asked, attendants at these full-service stations cheerfully pumped gas, washed windshields, and checked oil levels on customers' cars.

7. When dealers sold well-equipped vehicles, owners were able to depend on full-sized spare tires along with jacks and other tools to change flat tires.

8. Offering many varieties of scenery, Canada delights automobile travellers with everything from flat, waving fields of grain on the Prairies to lofty, majestic pine forests in northwestern Ontario to invigorating salt water waves against the rocks of Newfoundland.

9. The splendid visual experiences in Canada during warmer periods of the year are completely eliminated by intimidating winter snow squalls and blizzards even when drivers use only major highways.

10. Especially while drivers are enjoying perfect weather and speeding along the Trans-Canada Highway to get from Point A to Point B in the shortest time possible, much of the beauty of the countryside is lost in a blur.

EXERCISE 2

1. Unless workers pay attention, industrial accidents can easily happen in virtually any workplace.

2. For example, roofing jobs can result in nasty tumbles from the tops of buildings when roofers aren't tied off securely.

3. Even when going down a residential street, a boom truck can snag on low overhead hydro lines, and the driver can be electrocuted.

4. Studies of workplace health and safety show new employees and those with many years of experience are the two categories of employees particularly susceptible to workplace accidents.

5. Young employees might not view on-the-job health and safety training as critically important.

6. However, some experts say that many employers fail to give appropriate instructions to individuals working for the first time.

7. The high pay associated with high-risk employment attracts students trying to quickly build healthy bank accounts to pay college or university expenses.

8. Routine safety rules can become boring and repetitive after workers have spent several years in the same workplace.

9. With a work history of scooping minerals from the earth for several years, miners may either forget or ignore safety procedures.

10. When a siren announces a mining accident, the production operations come to a stop in order to focus on rescuing those trapped.

EXERCISE 3

1. After I test-drove several cars, my first vehicle purchase was a Chevrolet Impala.

2. When I was twenty-one, the car seemed to include all my favourite features.

3. Worried at my lack of mechanical skills, I was relieved that the only technology onboard involved reading the owner's manual.

4. Fortunate that the used-car dealer had managed to provide one with the sale, I knew some of the manual would answer questions about the car's proper operation and troubleshooting procedures.

5. Although I am not a natural reader, the manual still offered several pleasant surprises.

6. The car was certainly clean and smooth running at the dealership when I was talking with the salesperson.

7. Not knowing, I was about to purchase a car that already had a leaky gas tank.

8. Seeing that the gas gauge read Full, I drove home from the dealer's lot.

9. After the car sat in my driveway all night, I couldn't drive to work the following morning.

10. Because the car was twelve years old, my boss said I shouldn't be surprised at the problem.

EXERCISE 4

1. Although Canadians were confused by media reports, H1N1 flu vaccination clinics were scheduled to open in early November 2009.

2. The vaccines available in Canada came in two forms after public health officials learned about the reactions of some patients.

3. Although this variant of the flu was called swine flu, consumers were quickly reassured that eating pork products carried no increased health risk.

4. Some children likely did not get the shot because their parents didn't want to inject vaccines unnecessarily.

5. However, while studying the disease's characteristics, researchers identified young children as a group that suffered the most severe symptoms and required the most intensive hospitalized care.

6. After determining risk levels through countrywide clinical trials, public health officials moved up the clinics by at least two weeks.

7. Visiting a doctor's office, after-hours clinic, or emergency room, concerned patients found waiting rooms completely filled regardless of the time of day.

8. Especially because of conflicting information, many citizens found advice about who should get the vaccine difficult to understand.

9. For youngsters under the age of five, experts originally recommended two doses of the vaccine.

10. Because viruses mutate each year, the virus in this year's H1N1 vaccination will likely become part of the seasonal flu vaccine in subsequent years.

EXERCISE 5

1. One day after I turned forty, my new car broke down in a hectic intersection during rush hour.

2. Because my stalled vehicle managed to bring all traffic to a complete stop, a nearby resident offered to call a tow truck for me.

3. As I became increasingly agitated, the traffic noises sounded louder and louder.

4. Although I turned on the hazard lights when my car refused to start, other drivers began honking their horns.

5. I watched in terror as vehicles zoomed past my stalled car and came very close to hitting it.

6. I groaned with relief when a tow truck with blinking lights finally appeared to take charge of the situation.

7. After the tow truck operator pushed my car to the side of the road, the other drivers could move more freely.

8. While thanking the helpful neighbour who called the tow truck, I was distracted by unhappy drivers.

9. I forgot his name, but he might read my thank you letter in tonight's newspaper.

10. I was able to get started on the road again after the car had cooled down for almost half an hour.

PROOFREADING EXERCISE

Corrections are italicized. Yours may differ slightly.

I love parades, so last year my family and I went to Toronto to see the Caribana parade. It turned out to be even more wonderful than I expected.

Although we arrived one day before the festivities, the city was already crowded with tourists. Early the next morning, people set up lawn chairs on Lakeshore Boulevard. We didn't want to miss one float in the parade, so we found our own spot and made ourselves at home. When the parade began, I had as much fun watching the spectators as *watching* the parade itself. I saw children *sitting on their parents' shoulders and* pointing at the breathtaking floats. I couldn't believe how beautiful the costumes were, with *their extravagant decorations of* feathers and sequins.

The crowd was overwhelmed by the sights and sounds of the parade. Everyone especially enjoyed hearing the steel drum bands, *marching and playing their instruments with perfect rhythm.* They must have practised the whole year to be that good.

My experience didn't end with the parade, however. After the last float had passed, I found a twenty-dollar bill *as I walked up Yonge Street. I framed it as a souvenir of my Caribana experience, and now it hangs on my wall at home.*

AVOIDING SHIFTS IN TIME AND PERSON (PP. 187–195)

SHIFTS IN TIME (PP. 187–190)

EXERCISE 1

1. Studying the history of words helps readers because many words *rely* on the same root.

2. For example, when looking at words that *contain* "graph," the linkage between "graphics," "telegraph," and even "photograph" becomes obvious.

3. Many vocabulary-building exercises build on how well the reader *understands* the meanings of words' prefixes, roots, and suffixes.

4. Prefixes like "hyper" and "hypo" appear in many health science textbooks; they *mean*, respectively, "over" and "under."

5. Knowing the history of a word also helps in its spelling; some winners of spelling contests *succeed* because they break words into several parts.

6. Using this method, such individuals are able to correctly spell a word they *have* never heard before.

7. On the other hand, some well-read individuals *find* it difficult to understand why some restaurants call a sandwich variety a "sub"; after all, "sub" as a prefix means "under."

8. To make matters worse, because "marine" means water, who wants a sandwich that *is* soaked under water?

9. Suffixes, additions to the ends of words, have special meanings and *need* to be memorized.

10. Some websites offer a new word every day; the site's manager often *provides* not only pronunciation keys but also a quote using the day's word.

EXERCISE 2

1. To open savings, chequing, or investment accounts, Canadians choose from a limited number of financial institutions while Americans get these services from a huge number of banks, some of which *have* only a single local branch.

2. The Canadian Deposit Insurance Corporation, a Crown corporation, insures the first $100,000 of deposits in registered Canadian financial institutions; however, deposits in credit unions *are* backed by separate provincial insurance plans.

3. CDIC insurance *extends* to guaranteed investment certificates (GICs) with terms under five years, but the CDIC protection doesn't cover any accounts using foreign currency, even if the accounts are deposited with a registered institution.

4. The verbs in this sentence shift correctly from a present tense to a past tense.

5. The verbs in this sentence shift correctly from a past tense to two present tense.

6. Besides banks, the Canadian financial industry includes credit unions, who *sell* shares to their clients.

7. As shareholders, credit union account holders attend annual meetings and *vote* for directors to oversee the business.

8. Perhaps because they *are* relatively small and customer-oriented, credit unions trace their history to rural and agricultural areas.

9. Since most Canadians have chequing and savings accounts at the major banks, homeowners usually also *keep* their residential mortgages at banks.

10. Although credit unions *offer* competitive interest rates, these institutions have still failed to capture any major slice of the financial investment pie.

EXERCISE 3

1. The shift from two past tense verbs to the present is correct.

2. There is no shift in this sentence.

3. Perhaps one of the most moving areas along the Pacific Ocean coastline is Border Field State Park, which, as its name suggests, *marks* the international border between Mexico and the United States.

4. Every weekend, farm labourers who came from Mexico to work the fields in California's lush valleys *met* with other family members still in Tijuana, Mexico, at a flimsy fence on the border.

5. It always delighted me to watch these families as they *shared* picnic lunches, *exchanged* notes, and *chatted* happily with one another while the sun beamed down on them and the ocean waves crashed onto the white beach nearby.

6. The shift from past tense to three present tense verbs is necessary.

7. The shift from present tense to past tense verb is necessary.

8. Formerly allowing crossings from Canada with minimal documentation, the U.S. government announced in 2007 that airline passengers *needed* passports.

9. Now, even travelling U.S. citizens on their way home are required to show a valid passport if they *hope* to cross the border without trouble.

10. Perhaps the world has become a dangerous place, but many on both sides of the border *don't* find it reasonable to make a grandmother remove her shoes for airport security.

PROOFREADING EXERCISE

1. I am taking an art history class right now. Every day, we *watch* slide shows of great pieces of art throughout history. We *memorize* each piece of art, its time period, and the artists who created it. I enjoy these slide shows, but I *have* trouble remembering the facts about them. I always get swept away by the beautiful paintings, drawings, and sculptures and *forget* to take notes that I could study from at home.

2. I enjoyed travelling by plane to Cuba. Even though I *had* to arrive three hours early at the airport, it didn't bother me. I *watched* all the people taking off their shoes for security. And once I *was* through to the boarding gates, I bought some food and *relaxed* until it was time to enter the plane. Before I *boarded* the plane, the passengers who were arriving walked off the ramp with all their carry-on luggage. They *looked* tired but happy and well tanned from their visit to the island. Both of my flights were comfortable, and the flight attendants *were* so nice and cheerful. I liked the way the Cubana flight crew *pumped* Calypso music through the cabin while we *waited* for takeoff. Before I even *touched* Cuban soil, these signs *convinced* me that this country offers a completely different lifestyle. No wonder the motto of Cuba's official airline translates to "Cuba's doorway to the world."

SHIFTS IN PERSON (PP. 191–195)

EXERCISE 1

1. Diabetes is looming as a larger health problem for <u>Canadians</u> than ever before, especially for *those* with a first-degree relative (a parent or sibling) already diagnosed with this disease.

2. *Individuals* from specific ethnic backgrounds *are* also at increased risk for diabetes.

3. In general, diabetes appears in one of two forms (Type 1 or Type 2), and the medication those with diabetes take is highly dependent upon which type *they have*.

4. *Diabetics* may also need to make some lifestyle changes in order to manage blood sugar levels in *their* blood.

5. *Diabetics are* often advised to watch <u>their</u> diets very carefully and to exercise whenever <u>they</u> can.

6. However, <u>people</u> who understand the risk factors know what symptoms *they* should monitor.

7. <u>Diabetics</u> understand that too much exercise, for example, can dramatically lower *their* blood sugar level, causing *them* to sweat profusely.

8. As well, *diabetics* need to have a clear understanding of the types of medical problems <u>they</u> might encounter.

9. <u>Individuals</u> with Type 1 diabetes have a good chance of developing medical problems related to *their* eyesight (glaucoma), liver, kidneys, and circulatory system.

10. Many <u>diabetics</u> find that they feel much healthier once they look after *themselves* more carefully.

EXERCISE 2

1. <u>Visitors</u> to the 2010 Winter Olympic Games in Vancouver, British Columbia, will face mounting challenges if *they* haven't already made arrangements for accommodations.

2. There is no shift in person in this sentence.

3. It's amusing that after <u>they</u> fought so hard to earn the right to host the Games, *some Vancouver residents* would choose to leave town during the competitions.

4. Part of *visitors'* decision-making needs to be based on which venues and events <u>they</u> hope to attend.

5. For example, the <u>thousands</u> of skating and hockey fans need to book their accommodations early so *they* can have easy access to the Richmond Olympic Oval or Canada Hockey Place venues.

6. On the other hand, *visitors* with *their hearts* set on seeing the ski jumpers or bobsledders will need to make a three-hour winter drive up mountainous highways to get to Whistler and the events planned for that venue.

7. Many <u>individuals</u> will finally decide that to save time and money, *they* will need to pick one type of Olympic sport and try to find locate lodging close by.

8. <u>Others</u> who enjoy surprises will probably elect to arrive in Vancouver and accept whatever accommodation *they* can find.

9. For *those* who don't feel comfortable taking chances, the only option is to make <u>their</u> reservations early.

10. Even *individuals* who *are* forced to sleep in <u>their</u> cars during the Games *are* sure to find the atmosphere thrilling.

EXERCISE 3

1. A <u>person</u> who is bit by an infected animal may not know a lot about rabies, but according to the World Health Organization (WHO), the disease is fatal once *a patient* develops its symptoms.

2. Many <u>humans</u> treated for rabies in North America are bitten by *their* own domestic pet after it has interacted with an infected wild animal like a fox.

3. Unfortunately, it's not at all unusual for a <u>child</u> to be bitten by *his or her* pet cat or dog who became infected when it took a hike through the woods.

4. A surprisingly large <u>number</u> of children in Canada suffer dog bites, but most people probably assume that the *children* somehow provoked the *dogs*.

5. However, when *this assumption is made, children may not get* the medical attention <u>they</u> need to prevent the onset of the rabies virus.

6. Another possible reason for people's general lack of alarm is the belief that all responsible pet <u>owners</u> routinely keep *their* pets' rabies vaccinations up-to-date.

7. <u>Parents</u>, particularly in rural areas, need to make sure that family pets get such vaccinations because a rabid wild animal like a fox could have infected the otherwise friendly dog that bites *their* three-year-old child.

8. Sometimes, *rabies outbreaks occur even in larger cities when vaccination procedures aren't enforced.*

9. To ensure that individuals are safe after being bitten or scratched, officials from Agriculture Canada can conduct tests to determine if *the involved animals are infected* with rabies.

10. These medical procedures need to be completed within twenty-four hours after people have been bitten because unless an autopsy can disprove the presence of rabies, health care providers will administer precautionary antiviral shots to *injured individuals.*

PROOFREADING EXERCISE

1. I love travelling by train. The rocking sensation makes *me* feel so calm, and the clackety-clack of the railroad ties as the train crosses them sounds like a heartbeat to me. I also enjoy walking down the aisles of all the cars and looking at the different passengers. Whole families sit together, with children facing their parents. I notice that the kids like to ride backward more than the adults. The food that *I* eat in the dining car is expensive, but it is always fancy and delicious to my taste buds. My favourite part of the train is the observation car. It is made of glass from the seats up so that *I can* see everything that *the train passes* along the way.

2. People, especially those who have money, are sometimes wasteful. *Wastefulness is exhibited* in different ways. Restaurants throw out a lot of food every day. Homeowners water *their* lawns for too long and let the excess run down *their* street. People cleaning out their garages discard their clothes and furniture when *they* could recycle these items by giving them to charities. *With a little thought,* individuals can reuse and recycle so much of what *they* consume. *It's* particularly alarming whenever people fail to think of second lives for items *they* plan to discard. *Instead of tossing* those items into the garbage, *consumers* can *store* them in large bags. Even *if they* pay more attention to the excess packaging on the products *they* purchase, consumers can go a long way to helping out others as well as the planet.

CORRECTING FOR PARALLEL STRUCTURE (PP. 197–201)

EXERCISE 1

1. The sentence is correct.

2. The article is written for adults, but *it is about young children.*

3. It explains that many kids have become frightened by information about global warming *and other environmental concerns.*

4. Children are watching the same scary news stories *and the same upsetting images* as adults.

5. The sentence is correct.

6. Some children suffer very strong reactions of fear *and helplessness* when they encounter such information.

7. Others ignore *or disregard* the same troubling pictures and stories.

8. The article makes an interesting point about the connection between today's children and their parents; as kids, some of today's parents were panicked by the idea of nuclear war, and now their children *are worried* about the *changing climate.*

9. The sentence is correct.

10. Adults can help children cope by pointing out the positive aspects of nature, limiting small children's exposure to frightening images or information, *and encouraging their children* to take positive action.

EXERCISE 2

1. Taking driving lessons was exciting but nerve-racking.

2. I was ready to learn how to start, how to manoeuvre, and hopefully how to stop.

3. Between lessons, I read driving manuals, watched driving videos, and even practised hand signals and turn indicators.

4. My instructors taught me, tested me, and encouraged me.

5. The sentence is correct.

6. Finally, my teachers decided that I had learned enough and that I was probably ready to take the test for my driver's licence.

7. I arrived at the testing location, waited in the lobby for a few minutes, and then heard someone call my name.

8. The sentence is correct.

9. The man who tested me said that I knew the rules and that I must have had good teachers.

10. The sentence is correct.

EXERCISE 3

1. I like coffee and sort of like tea.

2. I've heard that coffee is bad for you *but that tea is good* for you.

3. It must not be the caffeine that's bad because *both coffee and tea have caffeine.*

4. The sentence is correct.

5. All teas are supposed to be healthy, *but green tea is supposed to be the healthiest.*

6. The sentence is correct.

7. I love orange pekoe tea with tons of milk *and sugar.*

8. The sentence is correct.

9. I know that all coffee comes from coffee beans, but *I didn't know that all tea comes from Camellia sinensis* leaves.

10. The sentence is correct.

EXERCISE 4

1. The sentence is correct.

2. My *mother, father, and I* were all born on July 1.

3. My mother's *name is Sarah Louisa;* my cousin's *name is Louisa Sarah.*

4. The sentence is correct.

5. The sentence is correct.

6. When my father was in high school, he had three jobs: waiter, babysitter, and *newspaper carrier.*

7. To earn extra money, I often deliver newspapers, work in a restaurant, and *babysit for my neighbour.*

8. My cousin and I sometimes meet accidentally at the movies, *wearing the same shirts*

9. Is this just a coincidence *or do we* have something in common?

10. My cousin and I both hope to become veterinarians: I study science at school; she volunteers at an animal shelter.

EXERCISE 5

1. The sentence is correct.

2. First, I need to accept that my writing needs work *and that I can* make it better if I try.

3. Second, *I need to eliminate* wordiness.

4. Third, *I need to work* on my vocabulary.

5. The sentence is correct.

6. Fifth, *I need to vary* my sentence length.

7. Sixth, *I need to use* the active voice.

8. Seventh, *I need to budget* my time so that a first draft can sit for a while before I revise it.

9. Finally, *I need to look at* the overall structure of a paper when I revise, not just *at* the words and sentences.

10. The sentence is correct.

AVOIDING CLICHÉS, AWKWARD PHRASING, AND WORDINESS (PP. 204–209)

Your answers may differ from these possible revisions.

EXERCISE 1
1. I compare prices before I buy.

2. I often visit three or four stores.

3. I look for the lowest price.

4. I have saved $100 on one item this way.

5. Omit this sentence.

6. Prices may vary significantly on a single item.

7. But knowing when to buy is not easy.

8. Once I waited for a computer sale that never happened.

9. However, I am happy when I do find a bargain.

10. Looking for good prices is what I always try to do.

EXERCISE 2
1. I received a surprise in the mail today.

2. It was a small square brown box.

3. It came from Cape Dorset.

4. I wondered if I knew anyone in Cape Dorset.

5. Finally, I remembered that our former next-door neighbours had moved to Cape Dorset.

6. Their son Josh and I had been good friends, so I thought that it was from him.

7. As soon as I looked in the box, I knew Josh had sent it.

8. Josh had remembered that I collect snow globes as souvenirs.

9. Inside was a large snow globe with a polar bear and a man riding a dogsled; the nameplate said *Cape Dorset* in red letters.

10. When I shook the globe, it looked like a blizzard inside.

EXERCISE 3

1. Many supermarket shoppers want organic meats and vegetables.

2. They will buy fresh, canned, or packaged organic foods.

3. I've learned about shoppers' preferences by working at a busy supermarket.

4. Most shoppers prefer foods grown without pesticides and hormones.

5. (Sentence 5 was combined with the previous sentence.)

6. People care about what they eat and what their children eat.

7. I enjoy the taste of organic eggs.

8. I also feel good that the eggs come from happy, free-ranging chickens.

9. Price will always affect some people's choices.

10. These people will not buy organic foods if they cost more than traditionally grown foods.

EXERCISE 4

1. Old-fashioned places are hard to find these days.

2. Black Creek Pioneer Village is that kind of place; it's near Canada's Wonderland but the two parks are vastly different.

3. The original Pioneer Village was settled in the early nineteenth century, mainly by German farmers from Pennsylvania.

4. The village has been carefully restored and is shown as it was in the 1860s.

5. The village has more than thirty-five shops and homes.

6. Pioneer Village also has a blacksmith, a cabinet maker, and other tradespeople willing to discuss their crafts with visitors.

7. There are also a doctor's house, Roblin's Mill and water wheel, a local school-house, and other authentic homes and shops.

8. The village's costumed hosts lead guests through a part of Canadian history.

9. People can even take a ride on a horse-drawn wagon.

10. Special events include a pioneer festival in September and Christmas celebrations in December.

EXERCISE 5

1. The other day I stayed home from work because I was sick.

2. I told my boss I needed one day of rest, but I almost didn't get it.

3. I had forgotten that Thursdays were gardeners' days.

4. These gardeners use power leaf blowers and tree trimmers.

5. Due to the noise, I couldn't sleep.

6. I tried watching television.

7. The daytime shows were worse than the noise.

8. Once the gardeners finished in the afternoon, I fell asleep.

9. Omit this sentence.

10. After sixteen hours of sleep, I felt better and went happily back to work the next day.

PROOFREADING EXERCISES

1. As popular technologies advance, all my friends now have cell phones with cameras. Camera phones have become essential. For instance, when my friend was robbed, he took pictures of the robber and his truck as he was driving away. When the police arrived and saw the pictures, they sent out a description of the truck and its driver. The police arrested the criminal in just a few hours. Also, if my friend hadn't had his camera phone, he would not have been able to submit such strong evidence at trial.

2. My son has trouble finishing his first-grade homework every night. As his parent, I think that he is smart, but he doesn't always show his intelligence. He works for a few minutes on his homework and then runs off to play. I tell him how strict teachers were about homework when I was his age. Unfortunately, my son's teacher uses stickers to keep track of progress, and they just don't motivate him. I hope that my son will learn the value of keeping up in school.

CLARITY PROGRESS TEST

1. My father often asks my brother, "*Do you* understand …"

2. ... in the 1950s, when men and women *had* clearly defined ...

3. Today's moms and dads share the same responsibilities in the home.

4. Before the war, *the working man's expectation* of finding a good, hearty meal on the table at the end of a hard day *was reasonable*.

5. ... a wife and mother very seldom gave much thought to careers and schooling because *her* job was to look after ...

6. However, when comparing my mother and father, *I* can see that Mom saw the ...

7. ... baskets to complete high school, obtain technical training, *or find* employment ...

8. I doubt *if these women* thought ...

9. Soon, many women found themselves earning the family's food money and making major family decisions.

10. After the war ended, many women discovered that the husbands returning from the fields of battle expected *wives* to return to their pre-war roles.

11. *All my mother's friends* had worked outside the house during the war and were confused about how to use the skills they had acquired.

12. *Because some mothers* never did return to full-time homemaking, working mothers are no longer viewed as non-traditional.

13. ... male partners economically, politically, and *even sexually*.

14. Feminists faced a particularly bitter uphill battle in the workplace, where women's salaries *lagged* considerably behind their male counterparts'.

15. ... expectations of where they could work, how they could work, and even *what salary they could expect*.

16. ... one of my daughters, a mining technologist, *earns* only two-thirds ...

17. ... insist that the definition of traditional/non-traditional domestic roles *has* just moved into the workplace ...

18. *Those* with the same qualifications and job descriptions should feel that they are being fairly treated when it comes to calculating rates of pay.

19. ..., there *are* still many unaddressed issues.

20. *My daughters and I* now take ...

CLARITY POST-TEST

1. ... information about *their* community activities ...

2. *Many résumé consultants suggest including personal activities* because some employers appreciate getting this information right at the beginning.

3. *The human resource managers* at my husband's company admit …

4. … indicates that the applicant is *respected, influential, and positive*.

5. In other cases, applicants must exhibit the ability to *set and meet* deadlines consistently …

6. … one of the candidates *has* the type of personal skills …

7. … than *she* (has).

8. The skills she is referring to *were* acquired …

9. … he certainly is great at phoning clients, discussing their immediate and long-term requirements, and *listening to their concerns*.

10. Our daughter's career couldn't be more different because her supervisor, Mrs. Benton, thinks *my daughter* is better at keeping records than at speaking with clients.

11. … to hear that Mindy spends most of her leisure hours reading books, doing crossword puzzles, or *balancing her chequebook*.

12. Some activities in the community also *offer* the side benefit …

13. Then, when *these individuals* have a question or need advice, they can ask one of *these leaders*.

14. During my high school and university years, I read lots of books and newspapers, but I don't seem to *have time to read* much anymore.

15. My older sister, who dreamed of writing for a newspaper, lost interest after hearing our mother describe being a good wife and mother as the only important job in *a woman's* life.

16. Between you and *me* …

17. … they seem a lot happier than *I* (am).

18. … like volunteering at the hospital and *donating* their artwork to charity.

19. Neither of my sisters *has* a husband, children, or a full-time job.

20. But each of their résumés *is* packed with exciting …

PART 5 PUNCTUATING CORRECTLY

PUNCTUATION PRE-TEST

1. When the guest speaker *entered, the* room went quiet.

2. The speaker's topic was going to be an interesting and important *one; understanding it* would be necessary to pass the provincial exam.

3. Ms. *Saunders, the* dean of the School of *Trades, and* Mr. *Whitehorse, the* college *president, were* on the podium with the speaker.

4. When Ms. Saunders introduced Bill Lee, she *said that he had worked* in the skilled trades for over twenty *years.*

5. My friends and I wondered if Mr. Lee had to attend university or *college.*

6. In his introductory remarks, Mr. Lee explained his background, which included *attending—and being expelled from!—our* college.

7. He *was, he explained, the* type of student who assumed he would learn all the important skills once he finally landed an apprenticeship.

8. Unfortunately, in the 1980s, getting an apprenticeship was easier said than *done, and* although he personally visited one possible employer after another, he kept losing opportunities to those with certification from *a trades institute* or *college.*

9. Finally he decided to return to school with a new *focus and* a revised opinion of education's importance to his future success.

10. Lee's experience is typical of *many who* flooded into the skilled trades in the late 1980s.

11. The economic *recession, as* well as the relative youth of the trades' work force at the time, meant there were fewer employment opportunities.

12. Once he returned to his shop classes, *however,* he discovered that many other students didn't have the same motivation and understanding that he had.

13. Terrified of *computers, he* was puzzled and *irritated when* classmates surfed the Internet instead of listened to the instructor.

14. And were the students ever *loud!*

15. Could he have been like them when he first attended *college?*

16. He finally overcame his fear of computers by getting a *tutor, practising* keyboarding skills during his *spares, and* taking a course called Introduction to Keyboarding.

17. Once employed in *industry, he* discovered that virtually every job required some level of computer competency.

18. Later he became a computer-based training instructor with the *province* of Alberta's well-known *Apprenticeships Online program.*

19. "There were two courses I felt I would never use after college *graduation," Lee* admitted to the *audience. "They were English* and computers."

20. *Now, however, he* depends heavily on both to teach other tradespeople how to do their jobs.

PERIOD, QUESTION MARK, EXCLAMATION POINT, SEMICOLON, COLON, DASH (PP. 220–225)

EXERCISE 1

1. You've likely seen one of those inflatable jumping rooms at a community *festival;* sometimes, they can be found in a home's front yard during a child's birthday party.

2. These jumpers are popular for several *reasons:* children can have fun playing with their friends, adults can keep an eye on many children at once, and everyone gets lots of exercise.

3. Several years ago, a freak accident occurred on a *beach;* it involved an inflated castle-shaped bouncer, a few brave adults, and several lucky children.

4. As the kids bounced around and squealed with pleasure, a strong gust of wind—a whirlwind, according to many *accounts—lifted* the castle straight up into the air.

5. When the wind released its hold on the castle, the structure came crashing *down;* all but two of the children were knocked unconscious instantly.

6. The castle bounced on the sand once before flying into the sky and *landing—at* least fifty metres into the water.

7. As the castle flew into the air the second time, another child dropped out of *it;* luckily, he was unhurt.

8. Many *adults—both* lifeguards and *others—jumped* in to save the two-year-old girl who remained inside the castle.

9. One man was able to reach her in *time;* incredibly she was not seriously hurt.

10. A sunny day, laughing children, an inflatable *castle—everyone* on the scene agreed that a tragedy had been narrowly avoided.

EXERCISE 2

1. My friend Kristine and I arrived early for work yesterday; it was a very important *day.*

2. We had worked late the night before perfecting our presentation—wow, what a *job!*

3. The boss had given us an opportunity to train our colleagues in the use of a new computer *system.*

4. I wondered how the other workers would react when they heard that we had been chosen to teach *them.*

5. Would they be pleased or *annoyed?*

6. Kristine and I worked hard on the slide show of sample screens from the *program.*

7. Kristine thought that our workshop should end with a test—what a horrid *idea!*

8. I knew that our fellow employees—at least some of them—would not want us to test *them.*

9. By the time we ended our presentation, we both realized that I had been *right.*

10. Wouldn't you prefer that your coworkers see you as an expert, not a *know-it-all?*

EXERCISE 3

1. People have not stopped inventing *mousetraps;* in fact, there are more than four thousand different kinds.

2. Some are *simple;* however, some are complicated or weird.

3. The sentence is correct.

4. The most enduring mousetrap was designed by John *Mast;* it is the one most of us picture when we think of a *mousetrap:* a piece of wood with a spring-loaded bar that snaps down on the mouse just as it takes the cheese used as bait.

5. Mast created this version of the mousetrap over a century *ago;* since then, no other mousetrap has done a better job.

6. There is a long list of techniques that have been used to trap *mice:* electricity, sonar, lasers, super glues, *etc.*

7. One mousetrap was built in the shape of a multi-level house with several *stairways;* however, its elaborate design made it impractical and expensive.

8. In 1878, one person invented a mousetrap for *travellers,* it was a box that was supposed to hold men's removable collars and at night catch mice, but it was not a success.

9. Can you imagine putting an article of clothing back into a box used to trap a *mouse?* What an awful *idea!*

10. Would you guess that Toronto's longest running play for decades was *The Mousetrap,* which was based on a story of the same title by Agatha *Christie?*

EXERCISE 4

1. Who would have thought that educators were a nomadic *group?*

2. In 1899, Frontier College was founded by Alfred Fitzpatrick and a group of university *students;* their aim was to make education available to the labourers in the work camps of *Canada*.

3. Labourer–teachers were trained and sent to the *camps*; there they worked alongside the labourers during the *day* and taught reading and writing to them at *night*.

4. Frontier College was also involved in encouraging Canadians to take up *farming;* a woman by the name of Margaret Strang offered her tutorial and medical services for those who were interested at a model settlement at Edlund, *Ontario*.

5. The Department of National Defence made an agreement with Frontier College, which placed labourer–teachers in Depression relief camps to provide recreation and *tutoring*.

6. Some other projects that labourer–teachers were involved in were constructing the Alaska Highway, working in rail gangs after World War II, tutoring new Canadians, and working in long-term community development projects in northern *settlements*.

7. In the mid-1970s, Frontier College enlarged its focus to include urban *frontiers;* volunteers began working in prisons and with street youth, ex-offenders, and people with special *needs*.

8. More than a decade ago, Frontier College began doing work with children, teens, and families, while at the same time developing the workplace literacy program called Learning in the *Workplace*.

9. The original *idea—to* help out those isolated in work camps across *Canada— has* changed a great deal since Frontier College's founding in 1899, but it continues to be an important aspect in today's education *system*.

10. In 1999, Frontier College celebrated its *centenary—100* years of teaching and learning in *Canada*.

EXERCISE 5

1. Do you believe in *ghosts?*

2. On *Aug.* 14, 1999, the body of a young man was found on the Yukon and *B.C.* border by three teachers who went hunting for the *day*.

3. The *man—he* was named Kwaday Dan Sinchi by the Champagne and Aishihik First *Nations—was* found on a northern *B.C. glacier*.

4. Though the First Nations people of the area believed he was as old as ten thousand years, test results showed the remains to be about 550 years *old*.

5. Discovered along with the hunter were various *artifacts:* a hat, a robe made of animal skins, and spear *tools.*

6. Radiocarbon dating was done on two *samples:* the hat and the *cloak. The* results are considered to be ninety-five percent *accurate.*

7. The "ghost" is believed to be a hunter who is estimated to have lived between the years 1415 and 1445, about the time Henry V was king of England and the Black Plague ravaged *Europe.*

8. This means the hunter died more than three hundred years before the first known European contact on the northwest *coast;* however, it is still not known if he is an ancestor of the Champagne or Aishihik First *Nations.*

9. Scientists say that there are only two *certainties:* the "ghost" is a young male, and he was on a trading route between the coast and the *interior.*

10. The remains, which are now in the care of the Royal British Columbia Museum in Victoria, *B.C.,* will be studied for further historic *information.*

PROOFREADING EXERCISE

The ingredients you will need for a lemon meringue pie *are* lemon juice, eggs, sugar, cornstarch, flour, butter, water, and salt. First, you combine flour, salt, butter, and water for the crust and bake until lightly *brown;* then you mix and cook the lemon juice, egg yolks, sugar, cornstarch, butter, and water for the filling. Once the filling is poured into the cooked *crust,* you whip the meringue. Meringue is made of egg whites and *sugar.* Pile the meringue on top of the lemon *filling,* place the pie in the hot oven for a few minutes, and you'll have the best lemon meringue pie you've ever *tasted!*

COMMA RULES 1, 2, AND 3 (PP. 227–232)

EXERCISE 1

1. Whenever I ask my friend Nick a computer-related *question,* I end up regretting it.

2. Once he gets *started,* Nick is unable to stop talking about computers.

3. When I needed his help the last *time,* my printer wasn't working.

4. Instead of just solving the *problem,* Nick went on and on about print settings and font choices that I could be using.

5. When he gets like *this,* his face lights *up,* and I feel bad for not wanting to hear the latest news on software *upgrades,* e-mail *programs,* and hardware improvements.

6. I feel *guilty,* but I know that I am the normal one.

7. I even pointed his problem out to him by asking, "You can't control *yourself,* can you?"

8. The sentence is correct.

9. Nick always solves my *problem,* so I should be grateful.

10. When I ask for Nick's help in the *future,* I plan to listen and try to learn something.

EXERCISE 2

1. I've been reading Helen Keller's *autobiography,* and I have learned a lot more about her.

2. I originally thought that Keller was born deaf and *blind,* but I was wrong.

3. When she was just under two years *old,* Keller became ill with a terrible fever.

4. The sentence is correct.

5. Not long after the doctor shared his fears with her *family,* Keller recovered from her fever.

6. *Unfortunately,* this sudden illness left Keller without the ability to *see,* to *hear,* or to speak.

7. The only tools that Keller had left were her sense of *touch,* her active *mind,* and her own curiosity.

8. With her teacher Anne Sullivan's constant *assistance,* Keller eventually learned to *read,* to *write,* and to speak.

9. The sentence is correct.

10. In my *opinion,* Helen Keller was an amazing *person,* and her story inspires me to do my best.

EXERCISE 3

1. Over fifty years *ago,* weavers and spinners in Ontario met to form a provincial organization.

2. The Ontario Handweavers and Spinners (OHS) offers educational programs to fibre *artists,* fibre *hobbyists,* basket *makers,* recreational *spinners,* and weavers at every level of skill.

3. Weaving and spinning was once thought of as a task for older *women,* but today's fabric world has gone high-tech.

4. As they plan a *project,* modern weavers plot their designs with the assistance of a computer program.

5. My image of a weaver doesn't include her sitting in front of a computer *screen,* but times have obviously changed.

6. Several wonderful weaving websites are now available to the general *public,* for the art of weaving seems to be experiencing an unexpected renaissance.

7. Local weaving guilds sponsor wildly popular "sheep to shawl" competitions in which local shepherds shear a *sheep,* spinners *clean, card,* and spin the resulting *wool,* and weavers work feverishly to construct a shawl.

8. Even for those who don't *weave,* watching one of these competitions is very exciting.

9. All the steps of the shawl production process are carefully *choreographed,* so the final product is a true group effort.

10. Because many younger adults have never been taught to spin or *weave,* the OHS has an important role to play.

EXERCISE 4

1. When asked about what makes Canada *unique,* respondents have a wide variety of answers and sometimes amusing comments.

2. Some mention the Wawa goose or Niagara *Falls,* and others immediately think of the beaver or the maple leaf.

3. One constant Canadian icon is ice *hockey,* and almost everyone around the world acknowledges Canadian excellence in this sport.

4. As a *result,* it was interesting to hear that soccer has recently surpassed ice hockey as the sport played by more Canadians than any other.

5. When one considers the high cost of *hockey,* this shift is probably no big surprise.

6. Parents have been moaning for years about the price of hockey *equipment,* ice and travel *time,* and coaching clinics.

7. Teams in most junior leagues are heavily backed financially by team *sponsors,* for their monetary support keeps the leagues alive.

8. After the season is *over,* the shin and shoulder pads are stored away carefully beside the hockey helmets and sticks until next season's play.

9. *Unfortunately,* many youngsters grow so much during the intervening summer that they need larger-sized equipment by the opening whistle of the next season's first game.

10. Many parents and sponsors are facing external financial challenges this *year,* so players and teams can expect reduced financial support.

Exercise 5

1. Gold is *amazing,* isn't it?

2. Unlike metals that change their appearance after contact with *water, oil,* and other *substances,* gold maintains its shine and brilliant colour under almost any circumstances.

3. When a miner named James Marshall found gold in the dark soil of California in *1848,* the gold rush began.

4. Though few people are aware of *it,* the first gold in Canada was found in small deposits in central Nova Scotia and the Eastern Townships of Quebec.

5. Harry Oakes developed the deepest gold mine in North America at Kirkland *Lake,* Ontario.

6. Beginning with the Fraser River Gold Rush in *1858,* a series of gold discoveries in British Columbia transformed the colony's history.

7. During the famous Klondike Gold *Rush,* the huge influx of people searching for gold prompted the Canadian government to establish the Yukon Territory in 1898.

8. The sentence is correct.

9. Some people have become rich directly because of *gold,* and some have become rich indirectly because of gold.

10. For *example,* if it had not been for the gold *rush,* Levi Strauss would not have had any *customers,* and the world would not have blue jeans.

Proofreading Exercise

When Niels Rattenborg studied the brains of mallard *ducks,* he made an interesting discovery. Rattenborg wondered how ducks protected themselves as they slept. The ducks slept in *rows,* and these rows were the secret to their defence. To his *surprise,* Rattenborg found that the two ducks on the ends of the row did something special with the sides of their heads facing away from the row. *Instinctively,* the ducks on the edge kept one eye open and one half of their brains awake as they slept. The rest of the ducks slept with both eyes closed and both sides of their brains inactive. The two guard ducks were able to frame the ducks in the *middle,* watch for *danger,* and sleep almost as soundly as their neighbours.

Sentence Writing

Here are some possible combinations. Yours may differ.

I like to swim, but I have never taken lessons.

When the alarm rings, I get up and get ready for school.

Although he is currently an elementary school teacher, he was a math tutor in college, and he worked as a ski instructor.

Since Tricia and James are both practical, organized university graduates, they are equal partners in their business.

COMMA RULES 4, 5, AND 6 (PP. 234–239)

EXERCISE 1

1. The sentence is correct.

2. The sentence is correct.

3. Cats become confused when their owners react *angrily,* not *happily,* to these "presents."

4. Desmond *Morris,* renowned animal *expert,* explains this misunderstood behaviour in his book *Catwatching.*

5. The sentence is correct.

6. The sentence is correct.

7. In the absence of kittens, these cats treat their owners as the next best *thing,* kitten replacements.

8. The first step in the process of teaching "kittens" how to *hunt,* and the one cat owners hate *most,* is sharing the results of the hunt with them.

9. The owners' *reaction,* which usually involves yelling and *disappointment,* should include praise and lots of petting.

10. The sentence is correct.

EXERCISE 2

1. *Paula,* who left at *intermission,* missed the best part of the play.

2. The sentence is correct.

3. The sentence is correct.

4. Our teacher posted the results of the *midterm,* which we took last week.

5. The sentence is correct.

6. Mr. *Simon,* the math teacher, looks a lot like Mr. *Simon,* the English teacher.

7. My clothes *dryer,* which has an automatic shut-off *switch,* is safer than *yours,* which doesn't.

8. The sentence is correct.

9. The sentence is correct.

10. John and *Brenda,* who ask a lot of *questions,* usually do well on their exams.

EXERCISE 3

1. One of the weirdest competitions on *earth,* the Wife Carrying World *Championships,* takes place in Finland once a year.

2. These load-carrying *races,* which may have begun as training rituals for Finnish *soldiers,* have become popular all over the world.

3. Each pair of *participants,* made up of one man and one *wife,* has to make it through an obstacle course in the shortest time possible.

4. The sentence is correct.

5. She does not have to be married to the man who carries her; she *can, indeed,* be someone else's wife or even unmarried.

6. The wife-carrying course includes two *sections,* a part on land and a part in water.

7. The sentence is correct.

8. The wife-dropping *penalty,* which is fifteen seconds added to the pair's *time,* is enough to disqualify most couples.

9. Contest officials allow one piece of *equipment,* a belt that the man can wear so that the wife has something to hold on to during the race.

10. The winning couple wins a prize, but the coveted *title,* Wife Carrying World *Champion,* is reward enough for most.

EXERCISE 4

1. England's Prince Charles has two *sons,* William and Harry.

2. The sentence is correct.

3. *William,* whose full name is His Royal Highness Prince William Arthur Philip Louis of *Wales,* was named after William the Conqueror.

4. The princes' *grandmother,* Queen Elizabeth *II,* will pass the crown to her son *Charles,* who will then pass it on to William.

5. *William,* who was born in *1982,* stands over six feet tall and has become as popular as a movie star.

6. The sentence is correct.

7. William exchanged e-mails with Britney Spears *but,* as far as I *know,* never met her in person.

8. William is well read and intelligent; *however,* he is also athletic and fun-loving.

9. The sentence is correct.

10. It will probably be many years before William takes on his future *title,* which will be King William V.

EXERCISE 5

1. Guy *Laliberté,* the creator of the world renowned Cirque du *Soleil,* has never recognized limits in his lifetime.

2. Laliberté *is,* for *example,* one of only a handful of civilians who have flown into space.

3. He was already well known for his *creativity,* which appears to have no boundaries.

4. Pictures showing him boarding the International Space Station with his signature red clown nose beamed into houses *everywhere,* remember?

5. This citizen of the world hosted a show from space about the importance of clean *water,* a problem he has identified as a global issue.

6. The *program,* which was available in every time zone as the International Space Station passed over *it,* earned Laliberté even more respect.

7. *Laliberté,* who is a member of the Order of *Canada,* personally organized countless shows for activists on the ground.

8. This effort didn't come *cheaply, however,* as the cost to Laliberté for his flight to the International Space Station aboard a Russian Soyuz mission was over $35 million.

9. The sentence is correct.

10. To the Canadian who laughs and makes the rest of us chuckle along, all we can say is "*Thanks, Guy!*"

PROOFREADING EXERCISE

Two types of *punctuation,* internal punctuation and end *punctuation,* can be used in writing. Internal punctuation is used within the sentence, and end punctuation is used at the end of a sentence. *Commas,* the most important pieces of internal *punctuation,* are used to separate or enclose information within sentences. *Semicolons,* the next most *important,* also have two main functions. Their primary *function,* separating two independent *clauses,* is also the most widely known. A lesser-known need for *semicolons,* to separate items in a list already containing *commas,* occurs rarely in college writing. Colons and *dashes, likewise,* have special uses within sentences. And of the three pieces of end punctuation—periods, question marks, and exclamation points—the *period,* which signals the end of the majority of English *sentences,* is obviously the most common.

SENTENCE WRITING

Here are some possible combinations. Yours may differ.

I have seen *Shrek,* a very funny movie, several times.

I have seen the very funny movie *Shrek* several times.

I will, I believe, learn best in "hands-on" environments.

I believe [that] I will learn best in "hands-on" environments.

My friend, who has curly hair and sits in the back of the class, takes good lecture notes.

My curly-haired friend who sits in the back of the class takes good lecture notes.

REVIEW OF THE COMMA (PP. 239–240)

PROOFREADING EXERCISE

I am writing you this *note, Helen,* to ask you to do me a favour. [*4*] When you get home from work *tonight,* would you take the turkey out of the freezer? [*3*] I plan to get started on the *pies, the rolls,* and the sweet potatoes as soon as I walk in the door after work. [*2*] I will be so *busy, however,* that I might forget to thaw out the turkey. [*5*] It's the first time I've made the holiday meal by *myself,* and I want everything to be perfect. [*1*] My big enamel roasting *pan,* which is in the back of the cupboard under the *counter,* will be the best place to keep the turkey as it thaws. [*6*] Thanks for your help. Jim.

QUOTATION MARKS AND UNDERLINING/ITALICS (PP. 242–246)

EXERCISE 1

1. I am reading a book called *Don't: A Manual of Mistakes & Improprieties More or Less Prevalent in Conduct and Speech.*

2. The book's contents are divided into chapters with titles such as "At Table," "In Public," and "In General."

3. In the section about table don'ts, the book offers the following warning: "Don't bend over your plate, or drop your head to get each mouthful."

4. The table advice continues by adding, "Don't bite your bread. Break it off."

5. The sentence is correct.

6. For instance, it states, "Don't brush against people, or elbow people, or in any way show disregard for others."

7. When meeting others on the street, the book advises, "Don't be in a haste to introduce. Be sure that it is mutually desired before presenting one person to another."

8. In the section titled "In General," there are more tips about how to get along in society, such as "Don't underrate everything that others do or overstate your own doings."

9. *Don't* has this to say about books, whether borrowed or owned: "Read them, but treat them as friends that must not be abused."

10. And one can never take the following warning too much to heart: "Don't make yourself in any particular way a nuisance to your neighbours or your family."

EXERCISE 2

1. "Have you been to the bookstore yet?" Monica asked.

2. "No, why?" I answered.

3. "They've rearranged the books," she said, "and now I can't find anything."

4. "Are all of the books for one subject still together?" I asked.

5. "Yes, they are," Monica told me, "but there are no markers underneath the books to say which teacher's class they're used in, so it's really confusing."

6. "Why don't we just wait until the teachers show us the books and then buy them?" I replied.

7. "That will be too late!" Monica shouted.

8. "Calm down," I told her. "You are worrying for nothing."

9. "I guess so," she said once she took a deep breath.

10. "I sure hope I'm not wrong," I thought to myself, "or Monica will really be mad at me."

EXERCISE 3

1. *Women's Wit and Wisdom* is the title of a book I found in the library.

2. The sentence is correct.

3. England's Queen Elizabeth I noted in the sixteenth century, "A clear and innocent conscience fears nothing."

4. "Nothing is so good as it seems beforehand," observed George Eliot, a female author whose real name was Mary Ann Evans.

5. Some of the women's quotations are funny; Alice Roosevelt Longworth, for instance, said, "If you don't have anything good to say about anyone, come and sit by me."

6. "If life is a bowl of cherries," asked Erma Bombeck, "what am I doing in the pits?"

7. Some of the quotations are serious, such as Gloria Steinem's statement, "The future depends on what each of us does every day."

8. Maya Lin, the woman who designed Washington D.C.'s Vietnam Veterans Memorial, reminded us, "War is not just a victory or a loss.... People die."

9. Emily Dickinson had this to say about truth: "Truth is such a rare thing, it is delightful to tell it."

10. Finally, columnist Ann Landers advised one of her readers, "The naked truth is always better than the best-dressed lie."

EXERCISE 4

1. Kurt Vonnegut, in his novel *Slapstick*, describes New York City as "Skyscraper National Park."

2. "The past is still, for us, a place that is not safely settled," wrote Michael Ondaatje.

3. In her book *The Mysterious Affair at Styles*, Agatha Christie wrote, "Every murderer is probably somebody's old friend."

4. "Swear not by the moon," says Juliet to Romeo.

5. Pierre Trudeau told a U.S. audience, "Living next to you is like sleeping next to an elephant."

6. Norman Bethune stated, "The function of the artist is to disturb."

7. "Writers are always selling somebody out," Joan Didion observed.

8. The expression "All animals are equal, but some animals are more equal than others" can be found in George Orwell's novel *Animal Farm*.

9. A Swahili proverb warns, "To the person who seizes two things, one always slips from his grasp!"

10. Groucho Marx once remarked, "I wouldn't want to belong to any club that would accept me as a member."

EXERCISE 5

1. The sentence is correct.

2. "We know what a person thinks not when he tells us what he thinks," said Isaac Bashevis Singer, "but by his actions."

3. The Spanish proverb "El pez muere por la boca" translated means "The fish dies because it opens its mouth."

4. "Ask yourself whether you are happy, and you cease to be so," John Stuart Mill wrote.

5. A Russian proverb states, "Without a shepherd, sheep are not a flock."

6. Stephen Leacock felt, "The essence of humour is human kindliness."

7. St. Jerome had the following insight: "The friendship that can cease has never been real."

8. Oscar Wilde found, "In this world there are only two tragedies. One is not getting what one wants, and the other is getting it."

9. "Self-respect," observed Joe Clark, "permeates every aspect of your life."

10. "Choose a job you love," Confucius suggested, "and you will never have to work a day in your life."

PROOFREADING EXERCISE

It may be decided, sometime off in the future, that the sum of Douglas Coupland's literary contribution equals the two words he used for the title of his 1991 debut as a novelist. In *Generation X*, Coupland pointed and clicked onto the generation born in the late 1950s and the 1960s as it stared into the future and tried to figure out what was going to fulfill it there. If the book didn't attract universally favourable reviews, it was a resounding commercial success and made Coupland an instant spokesperson for his generation. It didn't matter so much that he didn't want the job—"I speak for myself," he's said, repeatedly, "not for a generation." No, he'd been deemed a sociological seer and, like it or not, each of his subsequent novels—books like *Microserfs* (1995) and *Girlfriend in a Coma* (1998)—found itself judged less as fiction than as the words of an oracle between hard covers.

CAPITAL LETTERS (PP. 248–252)

EXERCISE 1

1. *Mom* and *I* have both decided to take classes next fall.

2. *Fortunately*, in *Toronto* we live near several colleges and universities.

3. *Classes* at the community colleges usually begin in late *August* or early *September*.

4. *We* could easily drive to *York University*, the *University* of *Toronto*, *Ryerson University*, *Humber College*, *George Brown College*, or *Sheridan College*.

5. *I* want to take credit classes, and my mom wants to sign up for community education classes.

6. *For* instance, *I* will enroll in the academic courses necessary to transfer to a university.

7. *These* include *English*, math, science, and history classes.

8. *My* mother, on the other hand, wants to take non-credit classes with titles like "*Learn* to *Play Keyboards*," "*Web Pages Made Easy*," and "*Be Your Own Real Estate Agent*."

9. *Mom* already has a great job, so she can take classes just for fun.

10. *I* know that if *I* want to go to one of the colleges at the *University* of *Toronto*, I will have to be serious from the start.

EXERCISE 2

1. Newfoundland and *Labrador*, the youngest province in *Canada*, joined *Confederation* at midnight on *March* 31, 1949, little more than half a century ago.

2. Sixty years later, many *Newfoundlanders* feel strongly that the real date was *April* 1, *April Fool's Day*.

3. The province is actually composed of the island of *Newfoundland* and a section of land on the *North American* continent between *Quebec* and the *Atlantic Ocean* coastline.

4. Along this easternmost coast, *Europeans* caught their first view of the *North American* continent.

5. In the tenth century, *Viking* explorers from *Iceland* and *Greenland* settled briefly in the north of the island of *Newfoundland*.

6. Nearly five hundred years later, a *Venetian* navigator, *John Cabot*, sailed on a voyage of discovery for *Henry VII* of *England* and discovered new lands, including a "new isle," in 1497.

7. *Canada's* tenth province's economic, political, and cultural history has been checkered, especially since *World War II*.

8. The nearby provinces of *Nova Scotia*, *New Brunswick*, and *Prince Edward Island* combined have a smaller land mass, but due to rugged terrain and climate, less than 0.01% of *Newfoundland* and *Labrador's* vast land area is farmed.

9. Postsecondary educational opportunities are limited; the *Memorial University* of *Newfoundland* in *St. John's* was founded in 1925 as *Memorial University College* and made the province's only university by a special act of the *House* of *Assembly* in 1949.

10. The economic outlook turned exceptionally bleak when the cod fishery was banned by the federal government's *Department* of *Fisheries*, but more recently, the province found riches under the sea in the *Hibernia* oil fields and in substantial reserves of nickel in *Voisey's Bay*.

EXERCISE 3

1. Imagine an ocean on the *Prairies* and mountains higher than the *Himalayas* in *Ontario*.

2. That's part of the picture unveiled by *Lithoprobe*, the name of a 20-year examination of *Canada's* ancient geological history.

3. Since 1984, more than 800 university, government, and industry scientists, led by *Dr. Ron Clowes*, have been examining the movements of ancient continents, oceans, and islands.

4. "*Underneath* the surface of *Alberta*, we found a subsurface mountain range," reported *Dr. Clowes*, a professor of earth and ocean sciences at the *University of British Columbia*.

5. Even more spectacular was the evidence that there was once an ocean the size of the *Pacific* under modern day *Saskatchewan* and *Manitoba*.

6. The results of the *Lithoprobe* study provide a map of *Canada's* origins.

7. From the *Maritimes* through the *Prairies* to the *West Coast* and from the *Great Lakes* to the *Arctic Ocean*, the study maps a view of the country eighty kilometres deep and six thousand kilometres wide.

8. The sentence is correct.

9. The sentence is correct.

10. The study is providing data on the process that might lead the volcano in *Mount St. Helens, Washington*, to erupt again.

EXERCISE 4

1. *I* grew up watching *The Wizard of Oz* once a year on *TV* before video stores like *Blockbuster* even rented movies to watch at home.

2. *I* especially remember enjoying it with my brother and sisters when we lived on *Maple Drive*.

3. *Mom* would remind us early in the day to get all of our homework done.

4. "*If* your homework isn't finished," she'd say, "you can't see the *Munchkins!*"

5. *My* favourite part has always been *Dorothy's* house dropping on one of the wicked witches and her feet shrivelling up under the house.

6. *The Wicked Witch* of the *West* wants revenge after that, but *Dorothy* and *Toto* get help from *Glinda*, the *Good Witch* of the *North*.

7. *Glinda* tells *Dorothy* about the *Emerald City* and the *Wizard* of *Oz*.

8. *On* their way, *Toto* and *Dorothy* meet the *Scarecrow*, the *Tin Man*, and the *Cowardly Lion*.

9. *Together* they conquer the witch and meet *Professor Marvel*, the real man who has been pretending to be a wizard.

10. *The* ruby slippers give *Dorothy* the power to get back to *Kansas* and to *Auntie Em* and *Uncle Henry*.

EXERCISE 5

1. In spring 2004 viewers of the *CBC TV* series *The Greatest Canadian* nominated ten individuals for the title: *Frederick Banting, Alexander Graham Bell, Don Cherry, Tommy Douglas, Terry Fox, Wayne Gretzky, Sir John A. Macdonald, Lester B. Pearson, David Suzuki*, and *Pierre Trudeau*.

2. Macdonald, the first prime minister, united the *French* and the *English* and facilitated the construction of the *Canadian Pacific Railway*.

3. Under *Pearson's* leadership in the 1960s, the *Canada Pension Plan*, a national healthcare system, the *Bilingualism* and *Biculturalism Commission*, a national labour code, and the *Maple Leaf* flag were introduced.

4. Pierre *Trudeau*, the most contemporary prime minister to make the list, worked to promote bilingualism, stamp out *Quebec* separatism, and patriate the *Canadian Constitution* and *Charter* of *Rights*.

5. The winner of the title *Greatest Canadian* was the late *Tommy Douglas*, five-term *Saskatchewan* premier, who is credited as being the "*Father* of *Medicare*."

6. After *Bell* patented the invention and staged a demonstration of the telephone at the *Centennial Exhibition* in *Philadelphia, Pennsylvania*, in 1876, he went on to form the *Bell Telephone Company* in 1877.

7. A contemporary ambassador of science, *David Suzuki* taught at the *University* of *Alberta* and *University* of *British Columbia* before moving his teaching out of the classroom and into the media as host of "*Suzuki on Science*," "*Quirks and Quarks*," and, most recently, *The "Nature* of *Things*."

8. Known as the man who discovered insulin, *Frederick Banting* brought new hope to diabetics the world over, earned a knighthood in the *British* crown, and was awarded *Canada's* first-ever *Nobel Prize* in *Medicine*.

9. Another medical hero was *Terry Fox*, whose *Marathon* of *Hope* to collect funds for cancer research is reenacted every year across the country.

10. Don *Cherry*, the outspoken host of *CBC's Hockey Night in Canada*, and *Wayne Gretzky*, the greatest scorer in *NHL* history and winner of four *Stanley Cups*, represented the sports world on the list of nominees.

PUNCTUATION PROGRESS TEST

1. … *challenges facing* many newcomers …

2. … learn a word's *spelling, they* have …

3. … the person *can spell,* pronounce, define, and use …

4. … friend, who is from *Sri Lanka, tells* me …

5. … find Canadian English so *difficult.*

6. Unless he stops to think about *it, my* neighbour from Britain still …

7. The sentence is correct.

8. … the importance of *words; she* told us that …

9. … *Cutter*—I think that was her *name—clearly* explained …

10. … vocabulary building *fun, so* I remember taping …

11. … essential *information: correct* spelling, …

12. … cluttering the *house, I* learned another …

13. … at a *time; then* mastering …

14. … flash *cards like* the ones she …

15. … had studying *together!*

16. … difficulty in *spelling words* could be traced …

17. … introduced many new *words; at* the same time, they …

18. … between "*pronunciation*" *and* its verb …

19. Even though they appeared on my cards for *months, I* still have …

20. Perhaps the most important *lesson was* how many …

PUNCTUATION POST-TEST

1. ... system, a creation of government that has become a cultural *icon, is* ...

2. ... paramedic *care, this* country ...

3. ... accessibility for *granted and* expect their ...

4. ... *individuals*—my brother is one of *them—require* ...

5. ... system is *perfect, especially* a health care web ...

6. ... health care *professionals; others,* Canadians ...

7. ... *Hospital* for *Sick Children* ...

8. ... twelve years *old, but* she still needs ...

9. ... *concerned because* so many ...

10. ... the *thousands and* can't spend ...

11. When my *niece* gave birth last *spring* to ...

12. ... death, retirement, or *relocation, that* physician's patients ...

13. ... that *mistakes—some* of them *tragic!—can* occur.

14. ... horror story or two to *tell about* a relative or friend who ...

15. ... to find out that the *surgeon* had removed the wrong *part?*

16. *Nurses and* pharmacists are increasingly ...

17. As well as *these, front-line* health care professions now ...

18. Regrettably, many of the *services offered* by these *individuals are* not covered ...

19. ... only those *Canadians who* have extended health care plans through their *employment are* likely to take advantage ...

20. ... without the same level of service—what a *shame!*

PART 6 WRITING WELL

EXERCISE: TOPIC SENTENCES (PP. 261–262)

1. Everyone loves the excitement of shopping for a new automobile.

2. The writer's responsibility for clear writing can't be taken lightly.

3. There is no topic sentence in paragraph 3.

EXERCISE: MAIN IDEAS AND SUPPORTIVE DETAILS (P. 262)

(Topic)   Lovable Pets

    I.   Devoted Dogs
        A. Pampered Poodles
        B. Huggable Hounds

    II. Curious Cats
        A. Sassy Siamese
        B. Talkative Tabbies

EXERCISE: TRANSITIONS (P. 264)

Finding a family doctor in Northern Ontario is not an easy task. In the <u>first</u> place, most family physicians already have huge <u>practices.</u> <u>To illustrate this problem,</u> statistics from the Sudbury District Health Unit indicate that the average Sudbury doctor maintains a <u>practice</u> with between four thousand and five thousand patients. A <u>second</u> problem is the <u>age</u> of those currently practising family medicine. With an average <u>age</u> of fifty-two, many family doctors are <u>burning out</u> under the strain of the work they are facing. <u>Such burnout</u> has several results: a reluctance to take on any new patients, a desire to take time off or retire prematurely, the decision to withdraw from hospital privileges, and sometimes a willingness to move to another area where the workload is less onerous. <u>Finally,</u> Sudbury's family doctors often find themselves without specialists to whom patients with unique needs can be referred for more detailed diagnoses. <u>For all these reasons,</u> a newcomer to Sudbury is sure to face challenges in locating a family physician willing to take the person on as a new patient.

EXERCISE: THESIS STATEMENTS (PP. 267–268)

1. FACT

2. THESIS

3. THESIS

4. THESIS

5. THESIS

6. FACT

7. FACT

8. THESIS

9. THESIS

10. FACT

Index